Endorsements for *The God I Don't Understand* by Christopher J. H. Wright

Chris Wright boldly explores four of the most difficult subjects Christians will generally face: the problem of evil, the genocide of Joshua, how modern culture can make sense of the cross, and prophecies about the end of the world. In each case, Wright uses his long experience as a theologian/teacher to skillfully and winsomely bring us through the dead-end solutions we often hear and lead us in fruitful and promising directions. This is not a book filled with the usual piety or apologetic drivel so often found in such treatments: it is a tough-minded and courageous wrestling match with profound issues of faith reminiscent of John Stott. Few of us would take on such a task. Wright has not only done it well—but supremely well.

—Gary M. Burge, professor of New Testament at Wheaton College and Graduate School, author of *The Anointed Community: The Holy Spirit in the Johannine Tradition*

It's refreshing to read a book that begins by admitting there is much about God we don't and can't understand, yet doesn't back away from wrestling. Christopher Wright shepherds the reader into topics about God that perplex and disturb us all and demonstrates how our tough questions are actually pathways to a deeper faith in God.

—Carolyn Custis James, author of *The Gospel of Ruth*

This hopeful and challenging book begins with some of our hardest questions about God and ends with some of God's greatest promises to us. It is a gift to all of us who care enough about our faith to question it.

—Andy Crouch, author of *Culture Making*

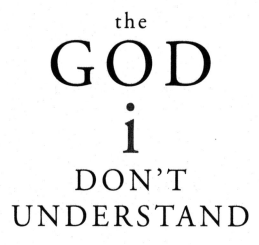

the
GOD
i
DON'T
UNDERSTAND

the
GOD
i
DON'T
UNDERSTAND

reflections on TOUGH QUESTIONS *of faith*

CHRISTOPHER J. H.
WRIGHT

ZONDERVAN®

ZONDERVAN.com/
AUTHORTRACKER
follow your favorite authors

We want to hear from you. Please send your comments about this book to us in care of zreview@zondervan.com. Thank you.

ZONDERVAN®

The God I Don't Understand
Copyright © 2008 by Christopher J. H. Wright

This title is also available as a Zondervan ebook.
Visit www.zondervan.com/ebooks.

Requests for information should be addressed to:

Zondervan, *Grand Rapids, Michigan 49530*

Library of Congress Cataloging-in-Publication Data

Wright, Christopher J. H.
    The God I don't understand : reflections on tough questions of faith /
Christopher J. H. Wright.
       p. cm.
    Includes bibliographical references.
    ISBN 978-0-310-27546-6 (hardcover, jacketed)
    1. Suffering — Religious aspects — Christianity. 2. Good and evil. 3. Theodicy. 4. Faith
I. Title.
BT732.7.W75 2008
231'.8 — dc22   2008037333

All Scripture quotations, unless otherwise indicated, are taken from the *Holy Bible, Today's New International Version*™. TNIV®. Copyright © 2001, 2005 by International Bible Society. Used by permission of Zondervan. All rights reserved.

Internet addresses (websites, blogs, etc.) and telephone numbers printed in this book are offered as a resource to you. These are not intended in any way to be or imply an endorsement on the part of Zondervan, nor do we vouch for the content of these sites and numbers for the life of this book.

Interior design by Ben Fetterley

Printed in the United States of America

---

08 09 10 11 12 13 14 • 20 19 18 17 16 15 14 13 12 11 10 9 8 7 6 5 4 3 2 1

For
Gordon and Ann

CONTENTS

What about the End of the World?

FOREWORD

The first time I met and heard Chris Wright was at a Christian Ethics Conference. He had been given a somewhat controversial topic and he handled it with courage and balance. I went up to him afterwards and thanked him for it.

Since then I have read much of what he has written and listened to a number of his lectures and sermons; on each occasion I have been struck by the same characteristics of courage and balance. He is thoroughly committed to the supreme authority of Scripture. At the same time he faces with integrity the problems of biblical interpretation.

However strongly we believe in divine revelation, we must acknowledge both that God has not revealed everything and that much of what he has revealed is not plain. It is because Dr Wright confronts biblical problems with a combination of honesty and humility that I warmly commend this book.

—John Stott, August 2008

PREFACE

Some of my friends raised their eyebrows when I told them I was writing a book entitled *The God I Don't Understand*. This may have had something to do with the fact that they know I have written three books with titles beginning *Knowing God*.[1] Was this a sudden collapse into apostasy or backsliding? I told them it was a sign of healthy balance.

As I hope will be evident all through this book, I live daily with the grateful joy of knowing and trusting God. But knowing and trusting does not necessarily add up to understanding. Even knowing somebody very well is not the same as understanding them fully, as the most happily married couples will readily testify. And in everyday life we often have to trust people without ever quite understanding how they operate, as I am obliged to do every year in my tax return to the Inland Revenue. Similarly, to know God, to love and trust him with all one's heart and soul and strength, is not the same as to understand God in all his ways. For as God himself reminds us,

> "... my thoughts are not your thoughts,
>   neither are your ways my ways,"
>   declares the Lord.
> "As the heavens are higher than the earth,
>   so are my ways higher than your ways
>   and my thoughts than your thoughts.

—Isaiah 55:8–9

This is a more personal kind of book than most I have written, since my own struggles are apparent at times. I was going to say that this is not a book of theology, but that would be wrong. It is not a book of systematic theological construction. But it is a book that tries to bring biblical teaching, personal faith, pressing questions, and life experience together – and that ought to be what theology does. My hope is that it does so with a healthy balance of honesty (where I don't understand) and clarity (where I think there are things we can and should understand), of biblical truth and Christian humility. That at least has been my prayer.

Many people participate in the writing of a book. I would like to thank Stan Gundry of Zondervan along with Pieter Kwant, Director of Langham Literature and my literary agent, for the initial conversation that encouraged me to put together into a single book several of the topics that were at that time in an unsorted jumble in my head. Katya Covrett has been among the most encouraging and attentive editors I have ever worked with and I thank her warmly. I am grateful also that Hugh Palmer, Rector of All Souls Church, Langham Place, London, allowed me to preach a series of sermons in September 2007 under the same title as this book, to give preliminary airing to some of my reflections. My wife and family know the daily gratitude I express to God for the blessing they are, as the living personal evidence of the grace of God that goes beyond my understanding.

The book is dedicated to Gordon and Ann McBain, whose family and ours are linked by many years of enriching friendship, in appreciation for the conversations with Gordon that set in motion the train of thought that has now reached its destination in this small volume.

Notes

1. *Knowing Jesus through the Old Testament*, *Knowing the Holy Spirit through the Old Testament*, and *Knowing God the Father through the Old Testament* (all published in the UK by Monarch Press, and in the USA by InterVarsity Press).

INTRODUCTION

This book began around our dining room table. I was drinking coffee with my wife and Gordon, an old friend of ours. We were talking about other friends and members of our wider families. Some of them were coping with really stressful circumstances or family tragedies of one kind or another. These were fine Christian folk, and so we fell to wondering about the strangeness of the ways of God and about why he allows some of his children to suffer greatly and others to have lives that seem virtually pain-free.

I mused that people are often quick to say, "That's not fair", when they or people close to them go through suffering that seems utterly undeserved, whereas I sometimes feel it is just as unfair that I have suffered so *little* in my own life while in my family I have siblings who have faced all kinds of stresses, illness, bereavement, and other agonies in theirs. There seems to be no rhyme or reason to explain such unevenness of experience, when all of us are believers. None of us is any better as a saint. None of us is any worse as a sinner. Yet God has permitted great suffering for some and spared it for others.

"I just don't understand why God does that," I said.

Gordon's reaction was a mixture of surprise and relief.

"I thought that you, being a Bible scholar and theologian and all that, had all these things sorted out," he said. "It's somehow comforting to think that you have problems just like the rest of us."

"Far from having them all sorted out," I answered, "it seems to me that the older I get the less I think I really understand God. Which is not to say that I don't love and trust him. On the contrary, as life goes on, my love and trust grow deeper, but my struggle with what God does or allows grows deeper too."

This train of thought began, then, with the problem of suffering – which, of course, has been a much-pondered problem for sensitive believers since biblical times down through the ages. But that conversation led me to reflect that there are several other ways in which, if I'm honest, I don't understand God. None of these causes me to doubt God's existence or to fall into unbelief or rebellion. None of them threatens the deep, lifelong love for the Lord and his Word that has shaped my life since childhood. But I am aware that for many people, these problem areas can be a real stumbling block. They can raise so many questions and uncertainties that faith itself becomes a struggle, and the very person and character of God is called into question or worse.

It's not that these are even remotely new problems or that I've only recently become aware of them. I well remember having arguments with friends at school and university more than forty years ago about some of the issues in the chapters of this book. But I think when you are young, you put these questions on a mental shelf marked "To be sorted out later". You half hope that there must be an answer to them, with a bit more reading and study, or by listening to more senior and learned Christian leaders. Surely somebody somewhere must have cracked these problems. But as life goes on, you find that nobody seems to have done so convincingly. Does anybody *really* have an answer to these things? Perhaps not. Perhaps we are not meant to.

Moreover, as life goes on, the problems themselves become even more pressing as issues like suffering and mortality begin to invade one's life and circle of family and friends. Thus, as I put it above, while my love for the Lord and my gratitude and faith are daily strengthened through his rich blessings, the questions remain and the lack of understanding assumes sharper contours. "Why, Lord?" and "How long, Lord?" seem to float more frequently to the surface of one's daily conversation with God.

Since Gordon (like many others, no doubt) thought that theologians and biblical scholars were supposed to understand all these things, I think it is good for those of us whom God has called and gifted in that particular ministry to be the *first* to affirm that this is far from the case. Now, of course, biblical and theological study does lead to greater understanding of God, his words and his ways, in all kinds of rich dimensions. I am grateful for the modest share in that great heritage that God has allowed me. It is a joy and an immense privilege to have been granted time and opportunity over many years to study and teach God's Word to others and to find deep personal fulfilment in being enabled to explain what can be explained and so to help others to greater understanding. But there are areas of mystery in our Christian faith that lie beyond the keenest scholarship or even the most profound spiritual exercises.

One biblical writer who had tried harder than most to probe the mysteries of life and of God and who seems to have been a teacher by profession came up with the following conclusion,

> When I applied my mind to know wisdom and to observe the labor that is done on earth – people getting no sleep day or night – then I saw all that God has done. No one can comprehend what goes on under the sun. People toil to search it out, but no one can discover its meaning. *Even if the wise claim they know, they cannot really comprehend it.*
>
> —Ecclesiastes 8:16 – 17 (my emphasis)

Even those who claim to have final answers to the deep problems of life on the earth God created are living in some degree of delusion. They don't really know what they claim to know. My hope is that this book will share some of the honesty and realism of Ecclesiastes while being able to affirm wider dimensions of God's action and revelation that were not available to the author in his day.

So then, I am not at all embarrassed to say that there are many things I don't understand about God.

Different Kinds of Not Understanding

But my "non-understanding" takes different forms and produces different inner reactions.

There are things I don't understand about God that leave me *angry or grieved*, because they were, or still are, horrible and inexplicable. All of us struggle to make sense of the presence of evil in the midst of God's good creation (though perhaps we are not meant to, and never can, "make sense" of evil; the very essence of evil is the negation of all goodness – and "sense" is a good thing. In the end, evil does not and cannot "make sense").

The philosophical and theological problem of evil is one thing, however; the wrenching reality of actual suffering is another, and the more we see of it, the harder it gets to understand God in connection with it. How are we supposed to respond to the baffling and appalling scale of suffering that goes on in this world? One response that we find in the Bible itself is lament. A more modern word for the same thing is protest. What does it mean to lament and protest before God in the face of things we cannot understand? And why do we seem to think it is somehow wrong to do so?

There are things I don't understand about God that leave me *morally disturbed*. Some of these are things that happen in the Bible itself, and especially in the Old Testament. There is a great deal of violence—violent acts, violent words, violent metaphors. The outstanding example that everybody thinks of is the destruction of the Canaanites when the Old Testament Israelites took control of the land God had promised to them. Is there any way we can interpret such things that is consistent with what the rest of the Bible tells us about the character of God?

There are things I don't understand about God because they are so *puzzling*. Why did God say and do things in the Bible that have then been so misunderstood in later generations? Maybe this is more a problem I have in understanding the way many Christians seem to go wild in the way they interpret the Bible than a problem with God himself. But still, I sometimes wonder if God himself scratches his head over what we have done with a few verses about a mysterious thousand years, or how we fantasize and fictionalize over a rapture and its aftermath, or how we get obsessed with "end of the world" timetables in breathtaking defiance of Jesus' warnings not to do so.

There are things I don't understand about God, but they flood me with *gratitude* because I couldn't live without the reality of their truth, accepted by faith. The supreme example is, of course, the cross itself. Who is bold enough to say they *understand* exactly *how* the cross has dealt with our deepest needs? And yet we cling to the fact that, by God's grace and on the authority of God's Word, it has. It has been wisely pointed out that when Jesus set out to explain the atonement to his disciples, he did not give them a theory but a meal. That, of course, has not stopped people theorizing, beginning indeed with those early disciples and the one soon to join their number, the apostle Paul. And still controversy rages around the meaning of the cross. Without claiming to understand it totally, can we at least dispel some of the worst misunderstandings?

There are things I don't understand about God, but they fill me with *hope* in the midst of the depressing destruction of the earth and its inhabitants. The Bible faces up to all the darkest truths about life on earth in the present, including those issues mentioned above. But it does so with a slow crescendo of expectation of a better world ahead. In both Old and New Testament we are enthralled by a vision of God's new creation. Here again, I find myself rapidly out of my depth in terms of being able to explain what it will be like or how it will be accomplished. But what I do find is that the truly biblical portrait of the new creation outshines so many of the popular myths and caricatures of "heaven" and seems to me to be far more worth looking forward to.

I am content to look forward to God's new creation without full understanding (believing with Paul that the time for that will come), but not without joyful confidence.

These, then, are some of the things that I found I did not really understand about God—not all of the same kind, not all of the same emotional or spiritual burdensomeness. And yet as we wrestle with these problems, with the help of our Bibles, it seems that we can at least clear away some wrong, inadequate, or misleading answers to them. So wherever that is possible in this book, I try to show why some kinds of answers that are given to the troubling questions are not really helpful at all.

Nevertheless, there are some perspectives on these things that *are* helpful and instructive—even if not finally satisfying all our questions. So wherever there are such considerations, I want to share them for whatever light they can shed on the difficult issues under discussion. So, through exploring both sides of what can be said, I hope to show that it is possible to be as clear as we can be on things that we *do* understand, or *should* understand, because God has made them clear in the Bible, while accepting our lack of understanding (even our confusion and pain) about many other things that God has not chosen to explain to us—and to do so with humility and even gratitude and relief. We can be perfectly honest about the things we don't understand without threatening our core faith in the truth of the things we can and should understand.

In Good Company

Then, as I went on thinking about the contours of my own lack of understanding in some of these areas, I found myself in reassuringly good company.

The Bible provides us with many examples of people who stood before God in confusion, grief, anxiety, or fear and addressed their questions to him. It would be well worth doing a comprehensive survey of all the questions we find in the Bible. Many are rhetorical, of course—merely a way of making a strong affirmation. But many of the questions in the Bible seem to arise out of a profound longing to understand the ways of God when he speaks or acts or when he declares his intention to do so, in ways that transcend our comprehension.

Abraham is bold enough to become the first person in the Bible to initiate a conversation with God by asking him questions, questions about the justice of his intentions regarding Sodom and Gomorrah. "Will not the Judge of all the earth do right?" he asks (Gen. 18:25).

Sarah's question, locked in the reality of barrenness and muttered in bitter laughter, was addressed indirectly to God, even though ironically she did not know he was on the other side of the tent door, listening (Gen. 18:12).

Hagar may or may not have been talking to the God of the family that had just expelled her when she turned away in despair, "I cannot watch the boy die" (Gen. 21:16), but it was that God who intervened to help her, as he had done before when Hagar became the first person in the Bible to give God a name—and a remarkably perceptive and comforting one at that (Gen. 16:13).

Moses, more than once, questions God, sometimes about his intentions regarding the Israelites and sometimes about his own exclusion from the promised land–something that Moses seems never to have understood, nor have those who have reflected on that divine decision in all the centuries since (Deut. 3:23–28).

Naomi, in the bitter grief of having buried her husband and two childless sons (a kind of triple widowhood), is a boiling conflict of emotions, as she trusts God and prays to him, yet accuses him of treating her like an enemy (Ruth 1:13b); she lays full responsibility for all the bitterness, emptiness, and affliction in her life on the Lord himself (1:20–21).

David cannot fathom the generosity of God in relation to himself and his household and can only ask, "Who am I?" (2 Sam. 7:18).

Elijah cannot understand how God could save life only later to destroy it, and he protests (successfully) against such inconsistency (1 Kings 17:20–21). Later he laments something similar in his own case (1 Kings 19:4, 10).

Job's whole book is a question hurled at God in the wake of his loss and suffering. God answers *Job*, but does he answer the *question*?

Jeremiah struggles to understand what God is saying through him when the words of other prophets and the external circumstances all point in the opposite direction. His anguish often takes the form of grieving and sometimes angry questions (Jer. 12:1–3; 15:15–18; 20:7–18).

Habakkuk cannot understand the sovereign justice of God in international affairs (Hab. 1:12–17). It does not stop him trusting God with teeth-gritting joy (Hab. 3:16–19).

The book of Psalms is full of anguished questions: "Why?" "When?" "How long?" It would probably be possible to tackle most of the questions in this book through careful and creative exegesis of the book of Psalms alone. Here, above all, is the book of faith, trust, love, joy, praise, and hope–coexisting with a pervasive and painful deficit of understanding.

This is why it is a word from the Psalms that formed the most profound question at the most crucial moment in history–the cry of abandonment on the lips of Jesus as he entered into the depths of his suffering on the cross: "My God, my God, why have you forsaken me?" (Ps. 22:1; see Matt. 27:46). We must hear Jesus' question, and discern the answer, in the light of the whole of the rest of the psalm, as undoubtedly Jesus did. But it still remains a question that points us to the heart of the mystery of the atonement itself. To me it is a profoundly moving thought that the word that introduces our most tormenting questions – "Why . . . ?" – was uttered by Jesus on the very cross that was God's answer to the question that the whole creation poses.

Then, another thing began to impinge on my consciousness. Have you noticed how many Christian hymns and songs express the most profound aspects of our faith through asking questions (where we can never give an adequate answer), or through openly affirming that there are things we cannot understand but nevertheless receive with joy and thanks?

> *And can it be, that I should gain*
> *An interest in the Saviour's blood?*
> *Died he for me, who caused His pain—*
> *For me, who Him to death pursued?*
> *Amazing love! How can it be*
> *That Thou, my God, shouldst die for me?*
>
> —Charles Wesley

> *'Tis mystery all! The Immortal dies:*
> *Who can explore His strange design?*
> *In vain the first-born seraph tries*
> *To sound the depths of love divine.*
>
> —Charles Wesley

> ***Why should I*** *gain from his reward?*
> *I cannot give an answer;*
> ***But this I know*** *with all my heart*
> *His wounds have paid my ransom.[1]*
>
> —Stuart Townend, my emphasis

> ***I cannot tell*** *why he whom angels worship*
> *Should set his love upon the sons of men,*
> *Or why as shepherd he should seek the wanderers,*
> *To bring them back, they know not how or when.*
> ***But this I know,*** *that he was born of Mary*
> *When Bethlehem's manger was his only home,*

And that he lived at Nazareth and laboured;
And so the Saviour, Saviour of the world, has come.

— William Fullerton, my emphasis

I know not why *God's wondrous grace to me he hath made known,*
Nor why, with mercy, Christ in love redeemed me for his own.
But I know whom *I have believed, and am persuaded that he is able*
To keep that which I've committed unto him against that day.

— Daniel W. Whittle, my emphasis

Perhaps this is the special feature and gift of poetry, but it is also a profound recognition that faith *seeks* understanding, and faith *builds* on understanding where it is granted, but faith does not finally *depend* on understanding. This is not to say, of course, that faith is intrinsically irrational (quite the contrary), but that faith takes us into realms where explanation fails us – for the present.

Lack of Understanding Anchored in Worshiping Faith

One final thought before plunging into our list of questions.

Psalm 73 provides a powerful biblical precedent for what I hope to do in this book. It is a psalm that begins by affirming the essential faith of Israel: "Surely God is good. . . ." But it goes on to express profound anguish over the apparent moral and spiritual inversion that the author (like us) can see all around him – namely, the constant triumph of evil over good, the success of the wicked, and the apparent futility of striving to live a godly and upright life (vv. 1 – 14). Here is someone speaking about the God he doesn't understand, insofar as God seems to leave the situation unchallenged and unredressed.

In the middle of the psalm he does two things. First, in verse 15, he cautions himself not to go too far down the road of broadcasting his own struggles on these matters, for fear of betraying God's people. That is, he knows that the children of God have enough problems of their own without being dangerously unsettled by their worship leader flaunting his doubts and questions. There is a proper pastoral *limit* to the voicing of protest – as God reminded Jeremiah on one occasion (Jer. 15:19) and as Isaiah warned his listeners (Isa. 45:9 – 13). I have prayed constantly in working on this book that I may not transgress that limit. I want to explore questions that the Bible itself wrestles with, but I want to build up God's people, not betray their faith.

And secondly, in Psalm 73:16–17, the psalmist goes to worship in the house of God with God's people. There, in the context of worship, his perspective is changed and he sees things in the light of God's ultimate will and moral government. This does not change the realities of the present. But it injects into them a transforming expectation from the future that is both sobering and comforting. Crucially, however, having reached the place of trust and contentment by the end of the psalm ("as for me, it is good to be near God"), the author does *not* go back and erase all that he has written in the first half. He lets us hear *both* his struggling lack of understanding *and* his restored, worshiping faith.

I pray that this book will follow the example of the writer of Psalm 73 in all these respects. In seeking to be honest and realistic, I do not want to upset further the faith of those already disturbed. Rather, I want us to face up to the limitations of our understanding and to acknowledge the pain and grief this can often cause. But at the same time, I want us to be able to say, with this psalmist (73:28), "But that's all right. God is ultimately in charge and I can trust him to put things right. Meanwhile, I will stay near to God, make him my refuge, and go on telling of his deeds."

Note

1. This is from Stuart Townend's hymn, "How Deep the Father's Love for Us"; used by permission.

PART ONE

WHAT ABOUT EVIL AND SUFFERING?

In practical terms, everybody has a problem with evil and suffering. All human beings experience the realities of life in this world, with its pain, cruelty, illness, violence, accidents, bereavement, torture, emotional and physical suffering, and death. These things are problems of just living in the world. They bombard us at every turn in daily life. We suffer the pain of experiencing some of them ourselves, and we suffer the pain of witnessing others suffer them, often far worse than our own. So, yes, suffering and evil are *practical* problems for everybody.

But in *theoretical* terms, evil and suffering constitute a uniquely Christian problem. Christians struggle *mentally* with the problem of evil in a way that others do not. I don't mean that non-Christians do not suffer mentally or wrestle mentally with the terrible enigmas of suffering and evil. Of course they do. Some of the greatest human art, literature, and music have emerged out of that mental and emotional wrestling with the reality of suffering and evil. What I mean is that the *existence of evil in itself* is not quite the fearsomely contradictory challenge to other worldviews that it certainly is for the Christian worldview. When you think of what we Christians believe about God and the world, the existence of evil really is a problem.

How can we possibly explain it?

Why does it exist?

Where did it come from?

Evil is not a problem (theoretically) for *polytheistic* worldviews and religions (those that believe in the existence of many gods). The many gods are themselves a mixture of good and evil—in motives, relationships, and actions. So, since life in the human and physical world is closely bound up with what is going on in the world of the gods, evil and suffering are "normal". That is, they are just what you would expect if you believe that the divine world itself has dimensions of evil. If the gods, or some of them, are like men behaving badly, why should the world of human behaviour be any different, if it is governed by such malevolent influences? Polytheism, indeed, can be understood as a plausible way of solving the problem of evil. You simply locate the origin of the problem in the world of the gods. Why does evil exist in the world? Because some of the gods are evil all the time and most of the gods are evil some of the time. What else can you expect to be the case also in the world they influence?

Evil is not a problem for *monistic* worldviews and religions. Monism is the view that ultimately all reality is one and indivisible. Spiritual or transcendental monism, as found, for example, in some forms of Eastern religion, such as Hinduism and Buddhism, affirms that everything is part of the one utterly transcendent Being (Brahman), and that all the distinctions we see in the world – including the way we *appear* to be distinct individuals – are illusory. There is ultimately no difference between you and me, between me and "it", between the seen and the unseen world, between physical or spiritual – all is one. There is no distinction (as there definitely is in the biblical worldview) between the creator and the created.

That too is purely an illusion or a myth to explain how things seem to be (for Hinduism does have such myths to satisfy lesser minds). The ultimate goal of enlightenment is to realize the utter oneness of everything, without differentiation. Eventually, this transcendent blending includes all moral distinctions too. In the great "beyond" there is no difference between good and evil. The idea that there *is* a difference between good and evil is in itself a persistent illusion that we have to overcome on the path to enlightenment. All is one. So again, there is no real 'problem' with evil. Evil is ultimately illusory, like everything else in the material world of our unenlightened state.

Materialistic monism also takes the view that there is only one reality – the physical, material reality of the universe. "Stuff is all there is", as it has been summarized. The more common form of this is usually simply called *atheism*. There is no transcendent realm at all. Reality is nothing more than the sum total of the mass and energy of the universe, and for us as human beings, reality is nothing more than the end product of our long evolutionary history of gene mutation.

Evil is not a *theoretical* problem for the atheist. It is simply a dimension of the way the world is at its current state of evolution within the universe.

It could not have been different, so why complain? Indeed, the reality of *goodness* is far more of a theoretical problem for atheism (i.e., much harder to explain). It is not at all easy or obvious to provide an explanation for altruism, goodness, love, and other unselfish human attitudes and actions in purely evolutionary terms.

But for Christians, evil really is a problem at every level.

This is because of our commitment to biblical theism. On the basis of what the Bible teaches – unequivocally and repeatedly – we Christians believe that there is one living God, the creator of the whole universe, who is personal, good, loving, omnipotent, and sovereign over all that happens.

Now once you are convinced of those great biblical truths about the living God, you cannot help but have a massive problem with the existence of evil. To put it the other way around, as many people do when they want to condemn and reject Christian belief, how can you believe in the existence of a God who is both loving *and* omnipotent in a world filled with evil and suffering? Are the two things not mutually incompatible and exclusive? The accusation against Christian belief at this point often takes the form of a well-worn dilemma: either God is omnipotent so he *could* prevent all evil and suffering, but since he obviously doesn't, *he cannot be loving*; or, God is loving and *longs* to prevent all evil and suffering if only he could, but he can't, in which case *he cannot be omnipotent*.

Are we really impaled on one of the horns of this dilemma? Do we have to say: either God is all-powerful but doesn't love us enough to deal with evil; or, God loves us but doesn't have the power to deal with evil? I hope that, even if we have to confess that there is something in all of this that we can never finally understand, we will nevertheless find by the end of this part of the book that we are not reduced to such dire alternatives.

So we turn to our Bible.

Unquestionably, the Bible affirms that God is all-loving *and* all-powerful, and yet the Bible also describes the terrible reality of evil. What help does the Bible give us in holding these jarring contradictions together in our minds in such a way that, even if it does not give us an answer we can fully understand, it does give us a hope that we can fully trust?

Or to put it another way: Whereas we often ask "Why?" people in the Bible more often asked "How long?" Their tendency was not to demand that God give an explanation for the *origin* of evil but rather to plead with God to do something to bring about an *end* to evil. And that, we shall see, is exactly what God has promised to do.

1

THE MYSTERY OF EVIL

It's all very well to say, "Turn to the Bible", but you can read the Bible from cover to cover, again and again, looking for a simple, clear answer to the question of the ultimate origin of evil, and you won't find an answer. I am not talking here about the entry of evil into human life and experience in Genesis 3, which we will think about in a moment, but about how the evil force that tempted human beings into sin and rebellion came to be there in the first place. That ultimate origin is not explained.

This has not stopped many people from trying to come up with an answer for themselves and dragging in whatever bits of the Bible they think will support their theory. But it seems to me that when we read the Bible asking God, "Where did evil come from? How did it originally get started?" God seems to reply, "That is not something I intend to tell you." In other words, the Bible compels us to accept the mystery of evil. Notice I did not say, "compels us to accept evil". The Bible never does that or asks us to do so. We are emphatically told to reject and resist evil. Rather, I mean that the Bible leads us to accept that evil is a mystery (especially in terms of its origin), a mystery that we human beings cannot finally understand or explain. And we will see in a moment that there is a good reason why that is so.

Moral Evil

However, in one sense, there is no mystery at all about the origin (in the sense of the actual effective *cause*) of a great deal of suffering and evil in our world. A vast quantity – and I believe we could say the vast majority – of suffering is the result of human sin and wickedness. There is a moral dimension to the problem. Human beings suffer in broad terms and circumstances because human beings are sinful.

It is helpful, I think, even if it is oversimplified, to make some distinction between what we might call "moral" evil and "natural" evil. This is not necessarily the best kind of language, and there are all kinds of overlaps and connections. But I think it does at least articulate a distinction that we recognize as a matter of common sense and observation.

By "moral" evil is meant the suffering and pain that we find in the world standing in some relation to the wickedness of human beings, directly or indirectly. This is evil that is seen in things that are said and done, things that are perpetrated, caused, or exploited, by human action (or inaction) in the realm of human life and history. To this we need to link spiritual evil and explore what the Bible has to say about "the evil one" – the reality of satanic, spiritual evil forces that invade, exploit, and amplify human wickedness.

By "natural" evil is meant suffering that appears to be part of life on earth for all of nature, including animal suffering caused by predation and the suffering caused to human beings by events in the natural world that seem (in general anyway) to be unrelated to any human moral cause – things like earthquakes, volcanoes, tsunamis, tornadoes and hurricanes, floods, etc., that is, so-called natural disasters.

In the case of moral evil, sometimes there is a *direct* link between sin and suffering. For example, some people directly cause other people to suffer through violence, abuse, cruelty, or just sheer callousness and neglect. Or sometimes people suffer directly the effects of their own wrong actions. Someone who drives too fast or drinks too much and ends up killing themselves in a road accident suffers the direct impact of their own sin or folly. Or we may suffer the punishment of the laws of our society for wrongdoing. Being put in prison is a form of suffering and in that respect it is an evil thing. And yet we recognize that some form of punishment for wrongdoing is a necessary evil. More than that, we have a strong instinct that when people are *not* punished when they are guilty of wrongdoing, that is another and even greater evil. Punishment, when deserved as a part of a consensual process of justice, is a good thing too.

But there is also a vast amount of suffering caused *indirectly* by human wickedness. The drunken driver may survive, but kill or injure other innocent people. Wars cause so-called collateral damage. Stray bullets from a gang fight or bank robbery kill innocent bystanders. A railway maintenance crew goes home early and fails to complete inspection of the track; a train is derailed and people are killed and injured. Whole populations suffer for generations after negligent industrial contamination. We can multiply examples from almost every news bulletin we see or hear. These are all forms of *moral* evil. They cause untold suffering, and they all go back in some form or another to culpable actions or failures of human beings.

Somehow, we manage to live with such facts, simply because they are so common and universal that we have "normalized" them, even if we regret or resent them and even if we grudgingly admit that humanity itself is largely to blame. But whenever something terrible on a huge scale happens, like the 2004 tsunami, or the cylone in Myanmar in 2008, or the earthquakes in Pakistan, Peru, and China, the cry goes up, "How can *God* allow such a thing? How can *God* allow such suffering?" My own heart echoes that cry and I join in the protest at the gates of heaven. Such appalling suffering, on such a scale, in such a short time, inflicted on people without warning and for no reason, offends all our emotions and assumptions that God is supposed to care. We who believe in God, who know and love and trust God, find ourselves torn apart by the emotional and spiritual assault of such events.

"How can God allow such things?" we cry, with the built-in accusation that if he were any kind of good and loving God, he would *not* allow them. Our gut reaction is to *accuse* God of callousness or carelessness and to *demand* that he do something to stop such things.

But when I hear people voicing such accusations—especially those who don't believe in God but like to accuse the God they don't believe in of his failure to do things he ought to do if he did exist—then I think I hear a voice from heaven saying:

"Well, excuse me, but if we're talking here about who allows what, let me point out that thousands of children are dying every minute in your world of *preventable* diseases that you have the means (but obviously not the will) to stop. How can *you* allow that?

"There are millions in your world who are slowly dying of starvation while some of you are killing yourselves with gluttony. How can *you* allow such suffering to go on?

"You seem comfortable enough knowing that millions of you have less per day to live on than others spend on a cup of coffee, while a few of you have more individual wealth than whole countries. How can *you* allow such obscene evil and call it an economic system?

"There are more people in slavery now than in the worst days of the pre-abolition slave trade. How can *you* allow that?

"There are millions upon millions of people living as refugees, on the knife-edge of human existence, because of interminable wars that you indulge in out of selfishness, greed, ambition, and lying hypocrisy. And you not only *allow* this, but collude in it, fuel it, and profit from it (including many of you who claim most loudly that you believe in me).

"Didn't one of your own singers put it like this, 'Before you accuse me, take a look at yourself.' "[1]

So it seems to me that there is no doubt at all, even if one could not put a percentage point on the matter, that the vast bulk of all the suffering and pain in our world is the result, direct or indirect, of human wickedness. Even where it is not caused directly by human sin, suffering can be greatly increased by it. What Hurricane Katrina did to New Orleans was bad enough, but how much additional suffering was caused by everything from looters to bureaucratic incompetence? HIV-AIDS is bad enough, but how many millions suffer preventable illness and premature death because corporate and political greed and callousness put medicines that are affordable and available in the West totally out of their reach? What the cyclone did to Myanmar was horrendous, but its effects were multiplied by the characteristically brutal refusal of the government to allow international aid organizations into the country until weeks later. Human callousness undoubtedly precipitated the death of thousands and prolonged the misery of the survivors.

The Bible's Diagnosis

In a sense, then, there is no mystery. We suffer because we sin. This is not to say, I immediately hasten to add, that every person suffers directly or proportionately because of their own sin (the Bible denies that). It is simply to say that the suffering of the human race as a whole is to a large extent attributable to the sin of the human race as a whole.

The Bible makes this clear up front. Genesis 3 describes in a profoundly simple story the entry of sin into human life and experience. It came about because of our wilful rejection of God's authority, distrust of God's goodness, and disobedience of God's commands. And the effect was brokenness in every relationship that God had created with such powerful goodness.

The world portrayed in Genesis 1 and 2 is like a huge triangle of God, the earth, and humanity.

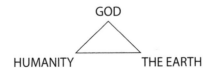

Every relationship portrayed was spoiled by the invasion of sin and evil: the relationship between us and God, the relationship between us and the earth, and the relationship between the earth and God.

Genesis 3 itself shows the escalation of sin. Even in this simple story, we can see sin moving from the heart (with its desire), to the head (with its rationalization), to the hand (with its forbidden action), to relationship (with the shared complicity of Adam and Eve). Then, from Genesis 4–11, the portrayal moves from the marriage relationship to envy and violence between brothers, to brutal vengeance within families, to corruption and violence in wider society and the permeation of the whole of human culture, infecting generation after generation with ever-increasing virulence.

The Bible's diagnosis is radical and comprehensive.

- Sin has invaded every human person (everyone is a sinner).
- Sin distorts every dimension of the human personality (spiritual, physical, mental, emotional, social).
- Sin pervades the structures and conventions of human societies and cultures.
- Sin escalates from generation to generation within human history.
- Sin affects even creation itself.

We read a chapter like Job 24, and we know it speaks the truth about the appalling morass of human exploitation, poverty, oppression, brutality and cruelty. And, like Job, we wonder why God *seems* to do nothing, to hold nobody to account, and to bring nobody to instant justice.

> Why does the Almighty not set times for judgment?
> > Why must those who know him look in vain for such days?
> There are those who move boundary stones;
> > they pasture flocks they have stolen.
> They drive away the orphan's donkey
> > and take the widow's ox in pledge.
> They thrust the needy from the path
> > and force all the poor of the land into hiding.
> Like wild donkeys in the desert,
> > the poor go about their labor of foraging food;
> > the wasteland provides food for their children.
> They gather fodder in the fields
> > and glean in the vineyards of the wicked.
> Lacking clothes, they spend the night naked;
> > they have nothing to cover themselves in the cold.
> They are drenched by mountain rains
> > and hug the rocks for lack of shelter.

The fatherless child is snatched from the breast;
　　the infant of the poor is seized for a debt.
Lacking clothes, they go about naked;
　　they carry the sheaves, but still go hungry.
They crush olives among the terraces;
　　they tread the winepresses, yet suffer thirst.
The groans of the dying rise from the city,
　　and the souls of the wounded cry out for help.
　　But God charges no one with wrongdoing.

—Job 24:1 – 12 (my emphasis)

And then we shudder because we know that if God were to do that right now and deal out instant justice, none of us would escape. For whatever grades and levels of evil there are among people in general, we know that it is something that lurks in our own heart. The evil we so much wish God would prevent or punish in others is right there inside ourselves. None of us needs to be scratched very deep to uncover the darker depths of our worst desires and the evil action any of us is capable of, if pushed. As we try to stand in judgment on God, we don't really have a leg to stand on ourselves.

If you, LORD, kept a record of sins,
　　Lord, who could stand?

—Psalm 130:3

Answer: Not a single solitary one of us.

And even apart from such latent or overt evil within ourselves, there is also the fact that it is practically impossible to live in this world without some complicity in its evil or some benefit from evils done elsewhere. We have to get on with living, and as we do so, our lives touch hundreds of other human lives – all over the planet – for good or ill. We are connected to the vast net of human experience worldwide. We may not be directly to blame for the sufferings of others, but we cannot ignore the connections.

The shirt on my back was made in an Asian country. I have no way of knowing if the hands that stitched it belong to a child who hardly ever sees the light of day, never has a square meal, or knows what it is to be loved and to play, and who may by now be deformed or even dead by such cruelty. But it is likely too that such wickedness is woven into the fabric of more than my shirt. In the week I write this, several major international companies in the UK are under investigation for profiting from virtual slave labour (a few pence an hour) in the majority world. Doubtless I have bought goods from some of them. Injustice and suffering plagues the global food industry, such that it is probable that some of what I eat or drink today is likely to have reached my table tinged with exploitation and oppression somewhere in the chain. The hands that have contributed to my daily bread undoubtedly include hands stained by the blood of cruelty, injustice, and oppression – whether inflicted or suffered.

Evil has its tentacles through multi-layered systems that are part of global-ized reality. We can, of course, (and we should) take steps to live as ethically as possible, to buy fair-traded food and clothes, and to avoid companies and products with shameful records in this area. But I doubt if we can escape complicity in the webs of evil, oppression, and suffering in the world entirely. I say that not to turn all our enjoyment of life into guilty depression. Rather, as we enjoy the good gifts of God's creation, we must at the same time accept the Bible's diagnosis of how radical, pervasive, and deeply ingrained sin has become in all human life and relationships.

Only God in his omniscience can unravel such inter-weavings of evil, but the point the Bible makes is that it puts the blame for suffering and evil where most of it *primarily* belongs, namely, on ourselves, the human race. The Bible makes it equally clear that we cannot just draw simple equations between what one person suffers and their own personal sinfulness. Often it is terribly wrong to do so (and makes the suffering even worse, as Job discovered). But in overall, collective human reality, the vast bulk of human suffering is the result of the overwhelming quantity and complexity of human sinning. There is no mystery, it seems to me, in this biblical diagnosis, which is so empirically verified in our own experience and observation.

Where Did Evil Come From?

It is when we ask this question that our problems begin.

It is important to see that Genesis 3 does not tell us about the *origin* of evil as such. Rather, it describes the *entry* of evil into human life and experience. Evil seems to explode into the Bible narrative, unannounced, already formed, without explanation or rationale. We are never told, for example, how or why "the serpent was more crafty than any of the wild animals the LORD God had made" (Gen. 3:1). We are not told why it spoke as it did, though the very fact that it did should raise our suspicion that something is not right in God's good creation. But why such "not-right-ness" was there, or where it had come from – these questions are not answered in the text.

What then can we say about this mysterious source of temptation that led Eve and Adam to choose to disobey? *It was not God* – evil is not part of the being of God. *It was not another human being*—evil is not an intrinsic part of what it means to be human either. We were human once without sin, so we can be so again. *It was something from within creation*—and yet it was not a "regular" animal, since it "talked". And how could such evil thoughts and words come from within a creation that has seven times been declared "good" in chapters 1 – 2? Whatever the serpent in the narrative is, then, or whatever it represents, it is out of place, an intruder, unwelcome, incoherent, contrary to the story so far.

If evil, then, comes from within creation in some sense (according to the symbolism of the story in Genesis 3), but not from the human creation, the only other created beings capable of such thought and speech are angels.[2] So, although the connection is not made in Genesis 3 itself, the serpent is elsewhere in the Bible symbolically linked to the evil one, the devil (e.g., Rev. 12:9; 20:2). And the devil is portrayed elsewhere as an angel, along with other hosts of angels who rebelled against God along with him (2 Peter 2:4; Jude 6; Rev. 12:7 – 9).

What, then, is the devil or Satan?

First of all, he (or it) is *not God*. Nor even just some other god. The Bible makes it very clear that we are not to fall into any kind of dualism—a good god (who made the world all nice and friendly), and an evil god (who messed it all up). Some kinds of popular folk Christianity do slide in that direction and give to Satan far more assumed power and far more obsessive attention than is warranted by the Bible. And such dualism is the meat and drink of a large amount of quasi-religious fiction, which sadly many Christians read with more frequency and more faith than their Bibles.

But Satan is *not* God, never has been and never will be. That means that, although the Bible clearly portrays Satan as powerful indeed, he is *not omnipotent*. Likewise, although Satan is said in the Bible to command hosts of other fallen angels (demons) who do his dirty work, he is *not omnipresent*. Satan cannot be everywhere at once (as only God can be and is). And although the Bible shows Satan to be very clever, subtle, and deceitful, he is *not omniscient*. He does not know everything and does not have sovereign knowledge of the future in the way God has in carrying forward his plans for creation and history.

As an angel among other fallen angels, even as their prince, the devil is a created being. That means that he is subject to God's authority and ultimate control. Like everything else in creation, Satan is limited, dependent, contingent—and ultimately destructible. We should take Satan seriously, but we should not dignify him with greater reality and power than is proper for a creature.

But is the devil *personal?* Is Satan a person like us? Is he a person like God?

We must be careful in answering this question. It seems to me that there are dangers in either a simple yes or no. On the one hand, the Bible clearly speaks about the devil in many ways that we normally associate with persons. He is an active agent, with powers of intelligence, intentionality, and communication. That is, the Bible portrays the devil as acting, thinking, and speaking in ways that are just like the way we do such things and are certainly greater than any ordinary animal does. When the devil is around in the Bible, it is clear that the Bible is talking about more than just some abstract evil atmosphere or tendency or a merely metaphorical personification of evil desires within ourselves – individually or collectively. The Bible warns us that, in the devil, we confront an objective intelligent reality with relentless evil intent. And the Gospels reinforce this assessment in their description of the battle Jesus had with the devil throughout his ministry. The devil, says the Bible, is very real, very powerful, and acts in many ways just like the persons we know ourselves to be.

But on the other hand, there is one thing that the Bible says about us as human persons that it never says about the devil, or about angels in general, at all. *God made us human beings in God's own image.* Indeed, this is what constitutes our personhood. What makes human beings uniquely to be persons, in distinction from the rest of the nonhuman animal world, is not the possession of a soul,[3] but that human beings are created in the image of God. The human species is the only species of which this is true. We were created to be like God, to reflect God and his character, and to exercise God's authority within creation.

Even as sinners, human beings are still created in God's image. Though it is spoiled and defaced, it cannot be eradicated altogether, for to be human is to be the image of God. So even among unregenerate sinners there are God-like qualities, such as loving relationships, appreciation of goodness and beauty, fundamental awareness of justice, respect for life, and feelings of compassion and gentleness. All these are dimensions of human personhood, for all of them reflect the transcendent person of God.

Now we are not told in the Bible that God created angels *in his own image.* Angels are created spirits. They are described as servants of God who simply do his bidding. They worship God and carry out God's errands. The common words for them (*mal'ak* in the Old Testament and *angelos* in the New Testament) simply mean "messenger" in everyday language. Don't misunderstand: this is not meant in anyway to diminish the exalted status and function that angels have in the Bible. It is simply to note that they are distinguished from human persons. And ultimately it is the human, in and through the man Christ Jesus, who will take the supreme place in the redeemed created order (Heb. 2). *Personal* qualities are the unique possession of human beings because, as God's image, we are the only beings in creation who were uniquely created to reflect God's own divine personhood.

So, among the fallen angels, especially the devil himself, there is no trace of that image of God which is still evident even in sinful human beings. And this is most easily explained if we assume it was never there in the first place. In Satan there is no residual loving relationship, no appreciation of goodness or beauty, no mercy, no honour, no "better side", no "redeeming features". And most of all, whereas no human person, however evil and degraded, is ever in this life beyond our loving compassion and our prayers that they might repent and be saved, there is no hint whatsoever in the Bible that Satan is a *person* to be loved, pitied, prayed for, or redeemed. On the contrary, Satan is portrayed as totally malevolent, relentlessly hostile to all that God is and does, a liar and a murderer through and through, implacably violent, mercilessly cruel, perpetually deceptive, distorting, destructive, deadly – and doomed.

"So, Do You Believe in the Devil?"

Faced with this question I feel the need to make a qualified "yes and no" answer. Yes, I believe in the existence of the devil as an objective, intelligent and "quasi-personal" power, utterly opposed to God, creation, ourselves, and life itself. But no, I do not "believe *in* the devil" in any way that would concede to him power and authority beyond the limits God has set. The Bible calls us not so much to believe in the devil as to *believe against the devil*. We are to put all our faith in God through Christ and to exercise that faith *against* all that the devil is and does – whatever he may be. Nigel Wright makes this point very well:

> To believe in somebody or something implies that we believe in their existence. But it also carries overtones of an investment of faith or trust.... To believe in Jesus means, or should mean, more than believing in his existence. It involves personal trust and faith by virtue of which the power of Christ is magnified in the life of the believer. The access of Christ to an individual's life, his power or influence within them, is in proportion to their faith. The same use of language applies in the wider world. To believe in a political leader implies more than believing in their existence; it implies faith in the system of values for which they stand and confidence in their ability to carry it through.

The reply to the question should Christians believe in the devil must therefore be a resounding 'No!' When we believe in something we have a positive relationship to that in which we believe but for the Christian a positive relationship to the devil and demons is not possible. We believe in God and on the basis of this faith we disbelieve in the devil ... Satan is not the object of Christian belief but of Christian disbelief. *We believe against the devil*. We resolutely refuse the devil place.

... The power of darkness against which we believe has its own reality. Even though it has a reality it lacks a validity – it ought not to exist because it is the contradiction of all existence. Its existence is unthinkable even as it is undeniable. It exists, but for the Christian it exists as something to be rejected and denied.[4]

That is why Paul urges us to "put on the full armor of God so that you can *take your stand against* the devil's schemes" (Eph. 6:11, my emphasis). That is why Peter, as soon as he has warned his readers about the devil's predatory prowling, urges them to *resist* him – not pay him the compliment of any form of "believing": "Your enemy the devil prowls around like a roaring lion looking for someone to devour. Resist him, standing firm in the faith" (1 Peter 5:8 – 9).

That is why one of the most ancient formulas of the church, in the baptism liturgy, calls upon Christians undergoing baptism to "*renounce* the devil and all his works". That is probably also why, when a popular series of books on Christian doctrines, the "I Believe" series of Hodder and Stoughton, came to the doctrine of Satan, it did not follow the simple formula of other volumes (e.g. *I Believe in the Historical Jesus; I Believe in the Resurrection*). There is no book in the series with the title, *I Believe in Satan*, but rather and quite rightly, *I Believe in Satan's Downfall*.

The Fall of Angels?

So the Bible tells us that the devil and his hosts are rebel angels. But what does the Bible teach us about this so-called fall of the angels? Well, actually, it doesn't really "teach" anything clearly or systematically, though we do get a number of hints that point in that direction.

Isaiah 14:4 – 21 and Ezekiel 28:1 – 17 are poems that "celebrate" the fall of the kings of Babylon and Tyre respectively. They are typical of the taunting songs of lament that were used when great imperial tyrants were brought low and the world breathed a sigh of relief. Some Christians see in these two songs a kind of symbolic portrayal of the fall of Satan. However, we do need to remind ourselves that they were written originally to describe the defeat and death of historical human kings, and so it is a dubious exercise to try to build detailed doctrinal statements about the devil or the "underworld" upon them. Nevertheless, we may discern the fingerprints of Satan in what is described in these poems, since it is clear that these arrogant human beings were brought low because of their blasphemous pride and boasting against God. Indeed, they are portrayed as wanting to usurp God's throne. In the poem, such claims are probably metaphorical for the human kings' *hybris*, but they have a spiritual counterpart that is recognizably satanic.

Jude, 2 Peter, and Revelation give us some clearer affirmations of the fall of Satan and his rebel angels:

> And the angels who did not keep their positions of authority but abandoned their proper dwelling – these he has kept in darkness, bound with everlasting chains for judgment on the great Day.

> —Jude 6

> God did not spare angels when they sinned, but sent them to hell, putting them into chains of darkness to be held for judgment.

> —2 Peter 2:4

> And there was war in heaven. Michael and his angels fought against the dragon, and the dragon and his angels fought back. But he was not strong enough, and they lost their place in heaven. The great dragon was hurled down – that ancient serpent called the devil, or Satan, who leads the whole world astray. He was hurled to the earth, and his angels with him.

> —Revelation 12:7–9

That seems to be it, as far as direct Bible references to this matter are concerned. In our curiosity, we ask for more information, such as:

- When did this happen?
- Why did created angels turn to become rebellious?
- Were the angels themselves tempted by something evil, as the serpent tempted Eve?
- If so, how did such evil come into existence?
- Where did the evil come from that led created angels to fall, who then led humans to fall?

But for such questions, we get no answer from the Bible. We are simply never told. Silence confronts all our questions. The mystery remains unrevealed.

Now God has revealed to us vast amounts of truth in the Bible – about God himself, about creation, about ourselves, our sin, God's plan of salvation, the gospel of our Lord Jesus Christ, the future destiny of the world, and so on. Thus, in light of all this abundant revelation, the Bible's silence at this point on the ultimate origin of evil seems all the more significant, and not merely accidental. It's not as if God were now saying, "Oops, I forgot to mention that point, but never mind, they can figure it out for themselves." No, the truth is that God has *chosen* in his wisdom *not* to give us an answer to our questions about the ultimate origin of evil within creation. It is simply not for us to know – and that is God's sovereign decision, the prerogative of the one who is the source of all truth and revelation in the universe.

Now I think there is a good reason for this, but before we turn to that, let us briefly summarize what we've seen so far, so that we can keep track of our reflection.

We have argued that a vast amount of the suffering and evil in the world can be explained in relation to human wickedness, directly or indirectly. Evil has a fundamentally moral core, related to our moral rebellion against God.

But we also know from the Bible that at the point where this entered into human experience and history (the fall as portrayed in Genesis 3), it involved our human collusion with some preexisting reality of evil, a sinister presence that injected itself into human consciousness, invited us to stand over against God in distrust and disobedience, and then invaded every aspect of human personhood – spiritual, mental, physical, and relational – and every aspect of human life on earth – social, cultural, and historical.

But if we ask, "Where did *that* preexisting evil presence come from?" – we are simply not told. God has given us the Bible, but the Bible doesn't tell us.

So then, to return to the title of this chapter, the Bible compels us to accept the mystery of evil. But here's the key point: we can recognize this negative fact. We know what we don't know. *We do understand that we cannot understand.* And that in itself is a *positive* thing.

Why is that?

Evil Makes "No Sense"

It is a fundamental human drive to understand things. The creation narrative shows that we have been put into our created environment to master and subdue it, which implies gaining understanding of it. To be human is to be charged with ruling creation, and that demands ever-growing breadth and depth of understanding the created reality that surrounds us. The simple picture in Genesis 2 of the primal human naming the rest of the animals is an indication of this exercise of rational recognition and classification. Our rationality is in itself a dimension of being made in the image of God. We were created to think! We just *have* to investigate, understand, explain; it is a quintessentially human trait that manifests itself from our earliest months of life.

So then, to understand things means to integrate them into their proper place in the universe, to provide a justified, legitimate, and truthful place within creation for everything we encounter. We instinctively seek to establish order, to make sense, to find reasons and purposes, to validate things and thus explain them. As human beings made in God's image for this very purpose, we have an innate drive, an insatiable desire, and an almost infinite ability to organize and order the world in the process of understanding it.

Thus, true to form, when we encounter this phenomenon of evil, we struggle to apply to it all the rational skill – philosophical, practical, and problem-solving – that we so profusely and successfully deploy on everything else. We are driven to try to understand and explain evil. But it doesn't work. Why not?

God with his infinite perspective, and for reasons known only to himself, knows that we finite human beings cannot, indeed *must not*, "make sense" of evil. For the final truth is that *evil does **not** make sense.* "Sense" is part of our rationality that in itself is part of God's good creation and God's image in us. So evil can have no sense, since sense itself is a good thing.

Evil has no proper place within creation. It has no validity, no truth, no integrity. It does not intrinsically belong to the creation as God originally made it nor will it belong to creation as God will ultimately redeem it. It cannot and must not be integrated into the universe as a rational, legitimated, justified part of reality. Evil is not there to be understood, but to be resisted and ultimately expelled. Evil was and remains an intruder, an alien presence that has made itself almost (but not finally) inextricably "at home". Evil is beyond our understanding because it is not part of the ultimate reality that God in his perfect wisdom and utter truthfulness intends us to understand. So God has withheld its secrets from his own revelation and our research.

Personally, I have come to accept this as a providentially good thing. Indeed, as I have wrestled with this thought about evil, it brings a certain degree of relief. And I think it carries the implication that whenever we are confronted with something utterly and dreadfully evil, appallingly wicked, or just plain tragic, we should resist the temptation that is wrapped up in the cry, "Where's the *sense* in that?" It's not that we get *no* answer. We get silence. And that silence *is* the answer to our question. There *is* no sense. And that is a good thing too.

Can I understand that?

No.

Do I want to understand that?

Probably not, if God has decided it is better that I don't.

So I am willing to live with the understanding that the God I don't understand has chosen not to explain the origin of evil, but rather wants to concentrate my attention on what he has done to defeat and destroy it.

Now this may seem a lame response to evil. Are we merely to gag our desperate questions, accept that it's a mystery, and shut up? Surely we do far more than that? Yes indeed.

We grieve.

We weep.

We lament.

We protest.

We scream in pain and anger.

We cry out, "How long must this kind of thing go on?"

And that brings us to our second major biblical response. For when we do such things, the Bible says to us, "That's OK. Go right ahead. And here are some words that you may like to use when you feel that way." But for that, we must turn to our next chapter.

Notes

1. Eric Clapton, "Before You Accuse Me", from the album *Eric Clapton Unplugged.*
2. It is interesting that the only other time an animal is said to speak in biblical narrative is Balaam's donkey, and on that occasion an angel is also involved. See Numbers 22.
3. Genesis 2:7 is sometimes said to be the moment when God breathed a soul into Adam. But this is exegetically impossible. The "breath of life" means the breath shared by all animals that live by breathing (as in Gen. 1:30 and 6:17), and "living being" is the same term used for all "living creatures" (e.g., in Gen. 1:24, 28). The verse speaks of special intimacy in the relationship between God and his human creation, but not of a "soul" as distinct from animals. The distinguishing mark of the human is being made in the image of God.
4. Nigel G. Wright, *A Theology of the Dark Side: Putting the Power of Evil in Its Place* (Carlisle: Paternoster; 2003), 24–25 (my emphasis).

The Offence of Evil

Accepting the mystery of evil, as we argued in chapter 1, is one thing. But this is far from all the Bible has to say about our response to evil. There is something within us that reacts to evil in the way the body reacts to a "foreign body"—with rejection and protest. We want to expel the offending object. All our bodily systems protest and fight back, sometimes with convulsive regurgitation. So it is with evil. We struggle against it with lament, grief, anger, disgust, and protest. And the point of this chapter is to say that we are absolutely right to do so, and the Bible not only gives us permission but even gives us the words to do so.

In the previous chapter we said that even if we cannot explain the ultimate origin of evil per se, there is something about moral and spiritual evil that *can* be explained—namely, that so much of it is related in some way (directly or indirectly, as we emphasized) to human wickedness and wrongdoing. But that recognition still falls far short of a satisfactory answer when we face other aspects of evil. We are often most baffled and troubled by so-called natural evil, precisely because it doesn't seem to have any such moral or rational explanation.

Natural Disasters

For no reason that we seem able to explain, great human suffering is often caused by natural phenomena such as earthquakes, volcanoes, hurricanes, tsunamis, floods, and the like. Now I know that we are being told that some freak weather events that cause devastating floods, for example, may be the result of climate change – global warming that has been brought on, or aggravated, by human action. I do not dispute this possibility. However, I am thinking here of events in the natural world that, as far as we can tell, are quite unconnected to any human action or inaction, and yet often hundreds and thousands of people are killed and whole communities devastated, sometimes for generations.

The tectonic plates of the earth's crust shift under the Indian Ocean floor and heave its surface over the shores for a few terrifying minutes, leaving thousands dead around the rim. The Himalayan and Andean mountain ranges groan and creak, and thousands again are left dead or homeless in Pakistan and Peru. Another earthquake wrecks a whole province of China. Hurricane Katrina drowns New Orleans. Excessive monsoon rain floods swathes of India and Bangladesh. A devastating cyclone rips into southern Myanmar and obliterates whole villages in the Irrawaddy delta and leaves millions uprooted. Such things fill us with awe and dread. They wreak suffering on such a mammoth scale that we find it hard even to contemplate them.

Or we might include that uniquely terrible pandemic of HIV-AIDS. We know that there are elements of human responsibility in the suffering of many, but there are vast numbers of people – from babies in the womb to youngsters sacrificially caring for dying relatives – who are infected or affected through no fault of their own. The scale of human suffering caused by HIV-AIDS seems to dwarf almost all the others put together. Africa suffers roughly the equivalent of the 2004 tsunami every month through HIV-AIDS related deaths.

One question surges up every time we confront evil on this scale: *Why?* How can such things happen in a world where God is supposed to be in charge? Once again, in our grief and pain, or our anger and bewilderment, we struggle to make sense of things that numb our senses, to find some explanation behind the inexplicable.

Curse or Judgment?

Some "explanations" that are offered are so old that they go back to the Bible, where they are questioned or denied, but that doesn't stop them being trotted out again. At least two ways of "explaining" such things as the tsunami were heard in the wake of that terrible day in December 2004. Both have some element of truth (that is to say, they refer to things that are biblically affirmed), but both seem to me dangerously misleading when pressed into service as full explanations.

"It's the Curse of God"

There are those who believe that natural disasters like the tsunami are all part of God's curse on the earth as a result of the fall. This view has the effect of removing the category of "natural evil" altogether, since it puts all such things back into the box of "moral evil". That is to say, if these things happen because of God's curse, then that curse came about in response to human sin and rebellion, according to Genesis 3. So in some mysterious sense, even something as utterly beyond human causation or control as the tsunami ends up being our own fault, if you push back far enough. If that were so, only some unfortunate people suffer the effects in our fallen world because they happen to live in the "wrong" place, but all of us collectively as a human race bear the blame. We brought God's curse on the earth by our sin, and this is part of the result.

I personally find this improbable, though I know it is a view held by many. Genesis 3:17 says that God cursed the *ground* because of human sin. The word ʾ*adamah* most often refers to the ground or soil, or the earth in the sense of the place of human habitation, rather than the created planet (for which ʾ*eres* is more normally used – though this distinction is not absolute). So God's words seem most naturally to describe the struggle that humans will have to wrench their bread from the earth in toil and sweat, and with constant frustration and opposition from "thorns and thistles". Probably this does not mean that such plants had never existed before the fall, but that they now come to symbolize the tension and struggle of human existence. Whereas before, humans were commissioned to subdue the earth, now they will toil and sweat just to survive on soil that seems to fight back.

So I am inclined to view the curse on the earth as *functional*. That is, it consists in the breakdown in the relationship between humanity and the soil, in our lives as workers. Human life on earth stands under God's curse in all that affects our engagement with the earth itself. This is a state of affairs from which early humans longed to be liberated (Gen. 5:29), which Paul described as creation being subjected to frustration until we humans are liberated from our bondage to sin (Rom. 8:20 – 21), and which will come to an end only in the new creation, when God will again dwell with us in the new earth and there will no longer be any curse (Rev. 21:1 – 4; 22:3).

I do not think that the curse on the ground refers to an *intrinsic* (or *onto-logical*, if you like such words) curse on the whole natural order, which, at a particular moment in human history (the fall), changed the way the planet actually "behaves". Those who take such a view have to say that earthquakes and other such phenomena in creation that are dangerous or destructive (or even just apparently nasty from our point of view—like animals eating each other), *only came into existence* as a result of the fall. Before the historical fall of human beings, then, there would have been no such thing as earthquakes.

But there is no evidence that our planet has ever been geologically different from the way it is now, or that animals were ever nonpredatory, or that tectonic plates in the earth's crust were somehow perfectly stationary before the human species emerged and sinned. On the contrary, the available evidence suggests that the early history of the planet included even more catastrophic events long before the emergence of human life. As Tom Wright said, "A tectonic plate's got to do what a tectonic plate's got to do."[1]

Of course, if one takes the view adopted within some forms of "young earth creationism", that the whole universe had only been in existence for five literal earth days before Adam and Eve arrived, then there would not have been much time for earthquakes or tsunamis before the fall. But I am not persuaded by that position.

Rather, it would seem that the earth being the way it is, as a living, moving, incredibly complex planet, is an essential part of the very possibility of our living on it. God made the universe with a view to human creatures living on this small planet in one particular galaxy, at this stage of its natural history, when the conditions are such that biological life can be sustained at all. I don't pretend to understand *why* the earth has to be like this, such that moving slabs of the earth's crust can heave the ocean temporarily over the shore. I might like to wish that it could be otherwise. But I don't think I can be presumptuous enough to tell the Creator, "You should have thought of some other way of making a home for us."

So I find it unconvincing to put down all things in nature that are unpleasant at the best of times and cataclysmically disastrous at the worst of times as nothing other than the outworking of God's curse in response to human sin.

"It's the Judgment of God"

Another view that regularly surfaces among Christians when some natural disaster strikes is that such things are the judgment of God.

Now again, just as when we were thinking above about God's curse on the earth, we have to affirm that there is a general sense in which there is a biblical truth operative in this perspective. The Bible leaves us no option but to accept the reality of God's judgment. God acts within human history and through the created order. And the Bible likewise warns us that if human beings and whole societies ignore the basic moral structures that God has built into our life on earth—including our proper care for the earth itself—then the natural world suffers the effects of our wilful disregard. And sometimes it fights back. There may well be a sense in which some of the effects of global warming and the resultant climate change, to the extent that they are connected to human destructive greed and pollution, may be construed theologically as incorporating elements of God's judgment, mediated within the natural order.

However, what we cannot and must not go on to assume or affirm is that the actual people who suffer the effects of natural events like earthquakes, tsunamis, volcanoes, hurricanes, floods, and so on (whether connected or totally unconnected with human activity) are *worse sinners*, and therefore stand more under God's judgment, than those who are fortunate enough to live somewhere else than where the disaster struck. It is one thing to say that there may be elements of God's judgment at work in the natural order as a result of prolonged human wickedness. It is another thing altogether to say that the people whose lives are snuffed out or devastated by a natural disaster are the ones deserving that judgment directly.

Yet, in the wake of the tsunami in December 2004, that is exactly what some people actually did say, leaving me wondering whether I was more shocked and angry with God or with the appalling things some Christians jumped up to say. Certainly I was profoundly sad when a grieving pastor from Sri Lanka, where whole churches were washed away, emailed me to *ask* if it might be interpreted as God's judgment on the Christians of Sri Lanka. Why should he even begin to think that it was, or that they were any more deserving of such judgment than Christians in India, or Britain, or America?

What words are there for the website of a church in America that asserted that it was a matter of *thanksgiving* that 1,900 Swedish people had been killed, as God's judgment on the wickedness of Sweden's sexually licentious culture and laws? How does that kind of callous nonsense differ from the Muslim cleric in Britain who said that it was Allah's judgment on the sex tourists in Thailand (who were the ones most *unlikely* to be among those enjoying a day with their families at the beach when the waves struck, one imagines). The sheer crass arrogance of such responses staggers the imagination.

But the Bible itself teaches us otherwise. The trouble is, we so easily take some aspects of what the Bible teaches, then invert the logic, and apply it quite wrongly. What do I mean?

The Bible and "Natural" Disaster

The Bible does include examples of God's using nature, or natural forces, as agents of his judgment or salvation (e.g., the flood; the parting and return of the sea at the exodus; the flooding of a river in Judges 4–5; hailstones destroying an enemy). But these narratives are given with clear and authoritative interpretation in the text that this is how those events were to be understood–at the time and by later readers. So the Bible does tell us that God used *some* (though actually not many) natural disasters as acts of divine judgment.

But we cannot invert the logic and assume that *any or every* natural disaster is therefore an act of divine judgment on somebody. And we certainly lack an authoritative scriptural interpretation that gives us the dogmatic right to explain contemporary events in that way. On the contrary, the Bible actually *discourages* us from jumping to the assumption that people who suffer some disaster are the victims of God's judgment on their particular sins.

Jesus gives us the clearest examples of rejecting such perverted "logic". In John 9:1–3 Jesus was asked if a man who had been born blind was the victim of God's judgment on his own sin or his parents' sin, and Jesus replied that neither was correct. The man's blindness was not a matter of God's judgment on sin at all.

In Luke 13:1–5, Jesus responded to two local incidents. One was a case of moral evil–an act of savagery by the Roman governor that had claimed the lives of some Galileans; the other was a case of natural or accidental evil–the collapse of a tower, possibly on a construction site, which killed eighteen people in Jerusalem. Jesus asked (or he may have been asked) if these events proved that those who were killed were greater sinners than others–that is, that their deaths were God's specific judgment on them. Again, *in both cases, Jesus says emphatically No.* Jesus rejected jumping to the easy explanation that when disaster happens it must be the judgment of God on somebody's sin.

The book of Job had already argued that point in great depth. Job's friends insisted that the disasters that had come on him were God's judgment on his wickedness. But God and the readers know that the friends were wrong. And Job, though he did not know what the readers know, refused to believe that the friends were right about *him*, no matter how right their theology was. His suffering was a testing, but it was definitely not judgment. The friends came up with a lot of true general theological affirmations about sin and judgment, but then made a false specific application to Job's particular suffering. Job's three friends were orthodox and scriptural in their theology, but totally mistaken in their diagnosis and disastrously callous in their pastoral application. Sadly many Christians follow their example, whether responding to disaster on a grand scale or to illness and suffering of individuals.

Now Jesus did say that the man's blindness created an opportunity for the glory of God to be displayed (when Jesus healed him). And Jesus also used the two local disaster events as a warning that people need to repent. But again we must be careful not to invert what Jesus said about the *results* of these cases into a principle of *causation*. Jesus was not saying that God *caused* Pilate to slaughter people or *caused* the tower to collapse and kill people, with the purpose of issuing a warning to everybody else. He simply used the events, quite legitimately, as a pointer to the shortness of life, the possible suddenness of death, and the necessity therefore of repentance here and now.

In the same way, we can certainly agree that the tsunami gave us a most appalling reminder that all our lives are constantly vulnerable in this world and can be snuffed out in an instant—even in the most idyllic situations and unexpected moments. If that led some people to reflect on life and death and to come to Christ in repentance and faith, we can be thankful for that. But it would be horrendous to suggest that "God did it for that reason". That 250,000 people were swept to their death in a few hours was an awful demonstration of the fragility of human life. That God somehow did it "on purpose", just to give a warning to the rest of us, is grotesque.

So if these are the wrong explanations, what is the right one?

There just is not, as far as I can see or find in Scripture, any "right" explanation as to why such things happen. Science can tell us their natural causes, and they are awesome enough. That is the achievement, but also the limit, of scientific explanation of "what really happened". But *neither science nor faith* can give a deeper or meaningful reason or a purpose for a disaster. Thus we are left with the agony of baffled grief and protest. "God, how can you allow such things? Why don't you stop them?" I don't think it is wrong to cry out such things, even if we know that no answer is going to come in a voice from heaven.

When we run out of explanations or reject the ones we try, what are we to do? We lament and protest. We shout that it simply isn't fair. We cry out to God in anger. We tell him we cannot understand and demand to know why he did not prevent it. Is it wrong to do this? Is it something that real believers shouldn't do, just like "real men don't cry"? Is it sinful to be angry with God? Again I turn to my Bible and find that the answer simply has to be No. Or at least, I find that God allows a great deal of anger to be expressed even if, at times, he corrects it where it threatens to lead a person into sin or rebellion (as in the case of Jeremiah, 15:19–21).

The Bible's Voice of Lament and Protest

In the Bible, which we believe is God's Word, such that what we find in it is what God wished to be there, there is plenty of lament, protest, anger, and baffled questions. The point we should notice (possibly to our surprise) is that it is all hurled at God, not by his enemies but *by those who loved and trusted him most*. It seems, indeed, that it is precisely those who have the closest relationship with God who feel most at liberty to pour out their pain and protest to God—without fear of reproach. Lament is not only allowed in the Bible; it is modeled for us in abundance. God seems to want to give us as many words with which to fill in our complaint forms as to write our thank-you notes. Perhaps this is because whatever amount of lament the world causes us to express is a drop in the ocean compared to the grief in the heart of God himself at the totality of suffering that only God can comprehend.

Job gives us a book full of such protest, and at the end, God declares that Job is more in the right than his friends, who so dogmatically gave their "explanation" (and solution) to his suffering. Job himself is outrageously bold in his complaints to God and about God:

> … *God* has wronged me
>   and drawn his net around me.
> Though I cry, "Violence!" I get no response;
>   though I call for help, there is no justice.
> *He* has blocked my way so I cannot pass;
>   *he* has shrouded my paths in darkness.
>
> —Job 19:6–8 (my emphasis)

Jeremiah (like Job) wishes he'd never been born, accuses God of cheating him, and pours out his pain to God (read especially Jer. 15:10–21; 17:14–18; 20:7–18).

> Why is my pain unending
>   and my wound grievous and incurable?
> You [God] are to me like a deceptive brook,
>   like a spring that fails.
>
> —Jeremiah 15:18

There is even a whole book in the Bible called Lamentations! Mind you, it is written in the wake of calamity that is acknowledged to be the direct judgment of God, but even then the writer feels at liberty to pour out a mixture of protest and pleading to God. It is a powerfully pain-filled book constantly crying out to God against the terrible calamity that had befallen Jerusalem.

> My eyes fail from weeping,
>   I am in torment within;
> my heart is poured out on the ground
>   because my people are destroyed,

because children and infants faint
in the streets of the city.
They say to their mothers,
"Where is bread and wine?"
as they faint like the wounded
in the streets of the city,
as their lives ebb away
in their mothers' arms.

—Lamentations 2:11–12

Psalm after psalm asks God questions like "How long, O Lord …?" and remonstrate over the suffering of the innocent and the apparent ease of the wicked (e.g., Pss. 10; 12; 13; 28; 30; 38; 56; 69; 88).

But I cry to you for help, LORD;
in the morning my prayer comes before you.
Why, LORD, do you reject me
and hide your face from me?…
You have taken from me friend and neighbor –
darkness is my closest friend.

—Psalm 88:13–14, 18

It surely cannot be accidental that in the divinely inspired book of Psalms there are more psalms of lament and anguish than of joy and thanksgiving. These are words that God has actually given us. God has allowed them a prominent place in his authorized songbook. We need both forms of worship in abundance as we live in this wonderful, terrible world.

I feel that the language of lament is seriously neglected in the church. Many Christians seem to feel that somehow it can't be right to complain to God in the context of corporate worship when we should all feel happy. There is an implicit pressure to stifle our real feelings because we are urged, by pious merchants of emotional denial, that we ought to have "faith" (as if the moaning psalmists didn't). So we end up giving external voice to pretended emotions we do not really feel, while hiding the real emotions we are struggling with deep inside. Going to worship can become an exercise in pretence and concealment, neither of which can possibly be conducive for a real encounter with God. So, in reaction to some appalling disaster or tragedy, rather than cry out our true feelings to God, we prefer other ways of responding to it.

It's all part of God's curse on the earth.
It's God's judgment.

It's meant for a warning.
It's ultimately for our own good.
God is sovereign so that must make it all OK in the end.[2]

But our suffering friends in the Bible didn't choose that way. They simply cry out in pain and protest against God – *precisely because they know God.* Their protest is born out of the jarring contrast between what they know and what they see. It is *because* they know God that they are so angry and upset. How can the God they know and love so much behave this way? They *know* that "the LORD ... has compassion on all he has made" (Ps. 145:9). Why then does he allow things to happen that seem to indicate the opposite? They *know* the God who says, "I take no pleasure in the death of the wicked" (Ezek. 33:11). How then can he watch the deaths of hundreds of thousands whom Jesus would tell us are not necessarily any more sinful than the rest of us? They *know* the God whom Jesus says is there when even a sparrow falls to earth (Matt. 10:29–31); where is that God when the ocean swallows whole villages (and churches)?

Such radically inexplicable disasters fill biblical believers with desperate, passionate concern for the very nature of God. So they cry out in vertigo above the chasm that seems to gape between the God they know and the world they live in. If God is supposed to be like *that,* how can the world be like *this?*

For us who share the faith of these biblical believers, this is an agonizing emotion precisely because we too love God. In such moments we can even understand those who hate God, and our anger and pain could easily make us shake our fists with them. But we don't, because our whole lifetime of trust and love for God and gratitude for his limitless goodness and mercy toward us in Christ cannot be overthrown in the day of disaster. But the pain remains, and the pain is acute.

Lament is the voice of that pain, whether for oneself, for one's people, or simply for the mountain of suffering of humanity and creation itself. Lament is the voice of faith struggling to live with unanswered questions and unexplained suffering.

God not only understands and accepts such lament; God has even given us words in the Bible to express it! An overflowing abundance of such words. Why, then, are we so reluctant to give voice to what God allows in his Word, using the words of those who wrote them for us out of their own suffering faith?

Therefore, I join the psalmist in lament. I voice my suffering, naming it and owning it. I cry out. I cry out for deliverance: "Deliver me, O God, from this suffering. Restore me, and make me whole." I cry out for explanation, for I no more know in general why things have gone awry with respect to God's desire than did the psalmist. "Why is your desire, that each and every one of us should flourish here on earth until full of years, being frustrated? It makes no sense." To lament is to risk living with one's deepest questions unanswered.[3]

In the wake of something like the tsunami, then, I am not ashamed to feel and express my anger and lament. I am not embarrassed to shed tears watching the news or worshiping in church after such terrible tragedies have struck again. I tell the God I know and love and trust, but don't always understand, that I just can't get my head around the pain of seeing such unspeakable destruction and death. I will cry out on behalf of the wretched of the earth, "Why those poor people, Lord, yet again? Haven't they suffered enough of this world's gross unfairness already?"

I am not waiting for an answer, but I will not spare God the question. For am I not also made in God's image? Has God not planted a pale reflection of his own infinite compassion and mercy in the tiny finite cage of my heart too? If there is joy in heaven over one sinner who repents, are there not also tears in heaven over thousands swept to their death?

So for the moment, I grieve and lament, I weep and I feel intense anger, and I do not hesitate to tell God about it and to file my questions before his throne. The same is true when I hear news of some dear loved one who has been stricken with some inexplicable and incurable illness. Whether on a grand scale of massive loss of human life or the intensified intimacy of the suffering of somebody personally known and deeply loved, the response is often the same: you have to pour out your true feelings before God, feelings that include anger, disbelief, incomprehension, and the sheer pain of too many contradictions.

Only then can I come back to *praise* God with integrity. Praise does not eliminate or override all such emotions. Rather, it is the safe framework of total acknowledgment of God and utter dependence on him within which they can be given their full expression.

However, I express all this protest within the framework of a faith that has *hope and a future* built into it. For the present state of creation is not its final state, according to the Bible. And in the resurrection of Christ we have the first-fruits of a new creation in which the old things will have passed away. I cannot claim to understand this great biblical hope terribly well either, but I draw enormous comfort from the earthiness of the Bible's vision of the ultimate destiny of creation – to which we will turn in the next chapter. So my cry against the disasters of the present is not just a candle in the dark or spitting into the wind.

It is much more akin to that agonized longing of the psalmists: "How long, O LORD, how long?" They were certain that God *would* do something, but they were consumed with longing that he *should* do it, sooner rather than later.

> The cry [of lament] occurs within the context of the *yet* of enduring faith and ongoing praise, for in raising Christ from the dead, we have God's word and deed that he will be victorious in the struggle against all that frustrates his desire. Thus, divine sovereignty is not sacrificed but reconceived. If lament is indeed a legitimate component of the Christian life, then divine sovereignty is not to be understood as everything happening just as God wants it to happen, or happening in such a way that God regards what he does not like as an acceptable trade-off for the good thereby achieved. Divine sovereignty consists in God's winning the battle against all that has gone awry with respect to God's will.[4]

Before we move on, however, let's keep ourselves on track by summarizing the two biblical responses to suffering and evil that we have surveyed in these first two chapters:

- The Bible compels us to accept that there is a mysteriousness about evil that we simply cannot understand (and it is good that we cannot).
- The Bible allows us to lament, protest, and be angry at the offensiveness of evil (and it is right that we should).

But if that were all, life would be bleak and depressing in the extreme, and faith would be nothing but gritting our teeth in the face of unexplained and unrelieved suffering. Thankfully the Bible has a lot more to say to lift our hearts with hope and certainty. That is where we are headed in chapter 3.

Notes

1. "God, 9/11, the Tsunami, and the New Problem of Evil", a lecture presented at the Seattle Pacific University in May 2005.
2. Nicholas Wolterstorff, in a profound reflection on lament (arising from the personal experience he and his wife suffered after the accidental death of an adult son), attributes some of this Christian reticence to Calvin's teaching on the importance of patience under suffering since it ultimately comes from God for our own good. Calvin's points have validity within a holistic biblical theology of God's providence, but they do not seem to allow for the equally valid biblical profusion of lament and protest; see Wolterstorff, "If God Is Good and Sovereign, Why Lament?" *Calvin Theological Journal* 36 (2001): 42–52.
3. Ibid, 52.
4. Ibid.

3

THE DEFEAT OF EVIL

Karl Marx said, "The philosophers have only *interpreted* the world ... the point, however, is to change it."[1] The Bible might similarly tell us that theologians try to *explain* evil, while God's plan is to *destroy* it. God will win. God will finally be just, and justified, in all his doings. And the justice and justification of God will ultimately involve the exposure and destruction of all that is evil.

This is the vital third perspective we must add to what we have said so far about evil and suffering. In chapter 1 we saw that the Bible compels us *to accept* the mystery of suffering as something that is beyond our final understanding (and thankfully so). In chapter 2 we saw that the Bible allows us *to protest and lament* at the offence of suffering as something that seems inexplicably to contradict the goodness and purpose of God himself. But the Bible takes us further, much further, and calls us *to rejoice* at the prospect of the defeat and final destruction of evil. Evil will be eradicated from God's creation. That is the hope and the promise of the Bible.

The whole Bible, indeed, can be read as the epic account of God's plan and purpose to defeat evil and rid his whole creation of it forever.[2] That, it can be argued, describes everything between Genesis 3 and Revelation 22. We cannot here retell or even summarize that great narrative, but we can unequivocally say that the cross and resurrection of Jesus of Nazareth stand at the centre of it. Here is the central and decisive moment of the victory of God over evil and the guarantee that it will ultimately be destroyed.

Let's probe three ways in which the cross helps our understanding of the problem we are addressing here and provides God's final answer to it.[3]

The Cross and Three Great Biblical Truths

In his profound study of this topic, *Evil and the Cross*,[4] Henri Blocher argues that there are three fundamental biblical affirmations that we must hold together in wrestling with the problem of evil. Each of them is an essential part of the teaching of the Bible. Each of them is clear and comprehensible when considered on its own, but our main challenge is in holding them together in our minds and in our faith when our struggles with suffering and evil in this world seem to contradict one or another of them. They are: the utter "evilness" of evil; the utter goodness of God; and the utter sovereignty of God.

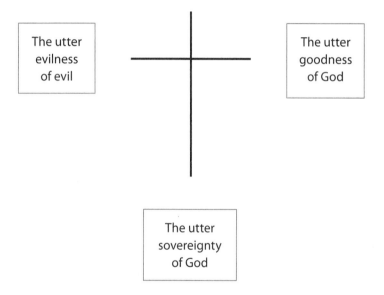

Blocher suggests that they can be arranged like a great capital T, or in the shape of a cross.

As we struggle with the problem of evil, we are tempted to compromise on one or another of these three absolute biblical convictions. We may, for example, reduce the severity of the Bible's diagnosis of evil—it's not really as bad as it seems and may even be all for the best. Or we may compromise God's goodness by making God complicit in some way with evil. Or we may try to "protect" God from being the cause of evil by limiting his sovereignty—there are some things that even God simply cannot control. But all of these moves will betray the Bible's teaching and reduce the full impact of its redemptive message. "Against these three temptations, Scripture raises the triple affirmation: that evil is evil, that the Lord is sovereign, and that God is good."[5]

The Utter Evilness of Evil

The Bible simply has no truck with evil. The Bible does not accommodate evil into a framework of acceptable realities, as many forms of religious worldview did and still do. Evil is never "just the way things are". It is never "all for the best in the end". Nor is it the best we can hope for in "the best of all possible worlds". Evil is not intrinsically "necessary" (in the sense that the world never was or never could be free from evil), even though the Bible certainly allows for the fact that in a fallen world evil sometimes necessarily has to be done.

Now, although we may be right to point out that moral freedom only makes sense when we have a real possibility of choosing evil rather than good, that does not make our free will the *cause* of evil's origin. In my days as a high school teacher I used to explain this as follows. If (risking my career) I were to tie up all my pupils and put gags on their mouths and then instruct them not to leave the room or make a noise while I was away, I would happily come back and find them all following my orders. But it would be meaningless to commend them for being "*good* children". They had no free choice to do otherwise. Their behaviour was not really moral at all.

If, however, I leave the room telling them to stay there and be quiet, and then I come back to find that some have run out, others are shouting, while a few are getting on with their work, I have a rational foundation for moral judgment of blame or praise, for distinguishing good and evil behaviour. My gift of freedom to the class has made that distinction possible. But the gift of freedom was not the *cause* of the bad choice that led some to disobey the instructions. It was merely the condition in which that bad choice was exercised. The cause lies somewhere else within them.

Evil cannot be dismissed simply as "the price God was willing to pay" or "the risk God was willing to take" for allowing us the gift of free will. This provides no explanation for the origin or cause of evil, and it tends to reduce the evilness of evil by giving it a validated place in God's moral universe.

On the contrary, evil is uncompromisingly rejected and denounced, and categorically doomed to ultimate destruction and eradication. It is the total negation of all that God is and wishes, hostile to the life, blessing, and goodness that God creates. Any "solution" to the problem of evil that makes evil less evil than the Bible says it actually is, is no solution at all for the Christian. So there must be no compromise or confusion at this point.

> Woe to those who call evil good
>   and good evil,
> who put darkness for light
>   and light for darkness,

who put bitter for sweet
　　and sweet for bitter.

—Isaiah 5:20

The Utter Goodness of God

Habakkuk, who struggled mightily with the problem of evil and the justice of God, declares that God cannot even look upon evil, let alone compromise with it.

Your eyes are too pure to look on evil;
　　you cannot tolerate wrongdoing.

—Habakkuk 1:13

John agrees: "God is light; in him there is no darkness at all" (1 John 1:5).

Many other Bible texts affirm this about God. There is no admixture of evil within him. Evil has no foothold in the person or character of God. On the contrary, he is utterly, primally, exclusively, and eternally good. As African Christians rejoice to repeat, "God is good: all the time!"

He is the Rock, his works are perfect,
　　and all his ways are just.
A faithful God who does no wrong,
　　upright and just is he.

—Deuteronomy 32:4

Therefore, although the Bible clearly indicates that God is sovereign over the reality and operation of evil within creation in such a way that he can include existing evil realities within the accomplishment of his purposes, God himself is not the origin, author, or cause of evil in itself. This is an important distinction. God's sovereign *use* or *control* of things, events, or people who are evil does not compromise his own essential goodness. For as we will see, all such overriding exercise of God's power over evil is for purposes determined by his goodness.

The Utter Sovereignty of God

The will of God remains sovereign over all created reality. This is a repeated biblical affirmation. It generates much mystery and theological struggle, particularly in relation to the equally biblical affirmation of human responsibility for the choices we make as free moral agents. Nevertheless, the Bible affirms that nothing happens in the universe *outside* the sovereign knowledge of God, whether by his decree or his permission. That single will of the one Creator God, indeed, is what constitutes the fact that we live in a *uni*verse, not a chaos. And that sovereign will of God can encompass even the alien force of evil, ruling and overruling it in such a way that in the end God's will prevails.

This is affirmed in the Bible even when the things that happen include disaster and many things that we would see as evil. Theologians at this point usually need to make distinctions between the decretive will of God (what God directly wills and wishes to happen) and the permissive will of God (what God permits to happen even if it includes the reality of evil in our fallen world). This is not the place to get into the finer points of that discussion, for the ultimate point still stands. Either way, God remains in overall sovereign charge of the outcomes of history and its final goal.

> When a trumpet sounds in a city,
> > do not the people tremble?
> When disaster comes to a city,
> > has not the LORD caused it?[6]

> —Amos 3:6

> I form the light and create darkness,
> > I bring prosperity and create disaster;
> > I, the LORD, do all these things.

> —Isaiah 45:7

In the context of the terrible judgment of God on Jerusalem, the author of Lamentations struggles with precisely the agony of knowing that what has happened is under the will of God, and yet has brought so much suffering that God himself grieves over.

> For people are not cast off
> > by the Lord forever.
> Though he brings grief, he will show compassion,
> > so great is his unfailing love.
> For he does not willingly bring affliction
> > or grief to any human being.
> To crush underfoot
> > all prisoners in the land,
> to deny people their rights
> > before the Most High,
> to deprive them of justice –
> > would not the Lord see such things?

> Who can speak and have it happen
>> if the Lord has not decreed it?
> Is it not from the mouth of the Most High
>> that both calamities and good things come?
> Why should the living complain
>> when punished for their sins?

—Lamentations 3:31 – 39

This agonizing series of questions shows that the writer is desperately holding together the goodness of God (he is filled with compassion and unfailing love), the terrible evil of injustice, and the overruling sovereignty of God.

All Three Truths in the Story of Joseph

There are some places in the Bible where these three great affirmations are woven together to show how closely they are related. One is the story of Joseph. It illustrates human wickedness at its worst—brothers planning a brother's murder and then betraying him into slavery; sons lying to a father. These are terrible evils and there was no excuse or justification for them. But the same story also illustrates the goodness of God in using these circumstances to good ends, preserving life and bringing blessing in spite of constantly contrary circumstances. And above all, the whole narrative is explicitly interpreted as a display of the sovereign will of God behind human choices and actions. So in this one story we have the evil of evil, the goodness of God, and the sovereignty of God, all operating in the same arena.

At the moment when Joseph made his identity known to his shocked brothers, Joseph utters these remarkable reflections:

> Then Joseph said to his brothers, "Come close to me." When they had done so, he said, "I am your brother Joseph, the one you sold into Egypt! And now, do not be distressed and do not be angry with yourselves for selling me here, because it was to save lives that God sent me ahead of you. For two years now there has been famine in the land, and for the next five years there will not be plowing and reaping. But God sent me ahead of you to preserve for you a remnant on earth and to save your lives by a great deliverance.
> "So then, it was not you who sent me here, but God."

—Genesis 45:4 – 8

Later, when the brothers are still fearful that their initial crime will rebound on their heads (ironically compounding it with yet another lie), Joseph sums up the situation in this profound theological affirmation: "Joseph said to them, 'Don't be afraid. Am I in the place of God? You intended to harm me, but God intended it for good to accomplish what is now being done, the saving of many lives'" (Gen. 50:19 – 20).

There is no softening of the evil intent and action of the brothers or of their moral responsibility. Their actions are inexcusably evil. Yet the goodness and sovereignty of God not only overruled their intentions but used them for the ultimate good of saving life.

It is important not to suggest that God "turned the evil into good", or that because it all worked out in the end, it wasn't really so bad after all. The actions of the brothers were evil. Period. Evil in intent and evil in execution. But God demonstrated his sovereignty by showing that he can take what is done as an existing evil in the world and use it to bring about his own good purposes. God remains good, and God remains sovereign.

All Three Truths Converge at the Cross

When we come to the cross, we find the same three great truths supremely at work. The powerful combination shows us just how essential it is to put the cross at the centre of all our wrestling with the problem of evil.

Like Joseph, Peter sums up what happened at the cross by seeing the wicked actions of morally responsible people under the sovereign knowledge and will of God, and by seeing the goodness of God's saving love whereby even those who perpetrated the act can find God's forgiveness:

> "People of Israel, listen to this: Jesus of Nazareth was a man accredited by God to you by miracles, wonders and signs, which God did among you through him, as you yourselves know. *This man was handed over to you by God's deliberate plan and foreknowledge; and you, with the help of wicked men, put him to death by nailing him to the cross.* But God raised him from the dead, freeing him from the agony of death, because it was impossible for death to keep its hold on him."

> —Acts 2:22–24 (my emphasis)

A moment later Peter holds out the good news of God's grace and forgiveness:

> "Therefore let all Israel be assured of this: God has made this Jesus, whom you crucified, both Lord and Messiah."
>
> When the people heard this, they were cut to the heart and said to Peter and the other apostles, "Brothers, what shall we do?"
>
> Peter replied, "Repent and be baptized, every one of you, in the name of Jesus Christ for the forgiveness of your sins. And you will receive the gift of the Holy Spirit."

> —Acts 2:36–38

So all three central truths are summarized here as Peter explains the cross in terms of human evil, God's sovereignty, and God's goodness. First, the cross exposed the utter depths of human and satanic evil – in hatred, injustice, cruelty, violence, and murder. All of this was hurled at Jesus, with no justification or excuse. Jesus died at the hands of "wicked men". At the cross, evil is seen at its worst for what it is and does.

Second, the cross happened fully in accordance with God's sovereign will from eternity. It is the supreme moment in history (which defines and enables all other such moments) in which God caused the wrath of human beings to praise him, somehow building the evil intent and actions of free creatures into his own sovereign purpose of loving redemption.

Third, the cross also expressed the utter goodness of God, pouring out his mercy and grace in self-giving love. At the cross God drew the worst sting of human and satanic evil and concentrated it on himself in the person of his Son, in order that it should be borne in the full depth of all its consequences and thereby release forgiveness. We will say more on this later.

The Cross and Christ's Government in History

The crucifixion of Jesus was an event in history. But the crucified Jesus is the one whose reign spans history. Indeed, it is the crucified Christ through whom God's sovereign government of the universe is exercised. This is the message of the amazing, mind-boggling, neck-stretching vision of John in Revelation 4 – 7, which should be read as a connected whole vision. It may seem remote and symbolic, but it is urgently relevant to the issue we are tackling here – the problem of evil in the world of human history.

The book of Revelation not only presents a vision of the ultimate future; it also exposes the hidden reality of the world we live in. It "uncovers" (the meaning of the world "apocalypse") what is really going on and how we are to live in the midst of this world while affirming the lordship of Christ. The world John lived in was filled with suffering, injustice, and evil – just as much as ours is. It was the world of the Roman Empire. We need to remember that as the backdrop to the whole book.

In such a world, who is in charge? Revelation 4 proclaims the answer: God is.

Room with a View

In Revelation 4:1 John is invited to go through a door into a room with a view – a view of the whole universe from God's perspective. This is our world from the perspective of God's throne. What does John see? It is like a series of concentric circles around the central focal point:

- the throne of God at the centre of the whole universe (4:1–2)
- twenty-four elders of God's people seated on their own thrones (4:4)
- four living creatures (4:6–8)
- countless hosts of angels (5:11)
- every creature in all creation (5:13)

This is a God's-eye view of reality. It includes the world we can see with the eyes in our heads (people and creatures), but also the world we can see only with the eyes of faith (the angelic hosts). John's vision binds it all together and says, "This is the real world. Everything in heaven and earth; everything past, present, and future; everything in the whole space-time universe is seen from the throne of God and is ruled over by the God on the throne, and it all exists to give him worship and praise."

This is a truly cosmic worldview, with a radically transforming perspective for someone living in a world where everybody saw Rome as the centre of the known world and the Roman emperor as the one seated on the throne of imperial power and government. No, says John, the throne of the living God is at the centre, and empires and emperors are among the creatures of the outer circle who exist to give praise to God.

The Lamb with the Plan

John then shifts our gaze from this "room with a view" to the Lamb with the plan. As Revelation 5 begins, John sees that the living God on the throne is holding a sealed scroll with writing on both sides. This is a closed book, as it were, a story that cannot be read and understood until it is opened. It stands for the meaning and purpose of history, the great plan of God for all time. But it is sealed with seven seals. History is a closed book in the sense that none of us who live within it has the stance or leverage to open the scroll—that is, to determine God's will in history. John weeps to realize that we cannot by ourselves understand the whole meaning of history within the plan of God (5:4).

Who can then? Who is worthy to govern history, to interpret and carry out the plan of God? The elders and the four living creatures give the answer: "The Lamb who was slain!" whom we know from elsewhere means the crucified Jesus. Thus, John now sees the crucified Jesus sharing the throne of God and taking the scroll and opening it, seal by seal (Rev. 5:5–7).

Jesus, the Lamb of God, holds the scroll of God's purpose, the key to the meaning and goal of all history. To confirm this, the living creatures and elders sing out this great affirmation:

> You are worthy to take the scroll
>   and to open its seals,
> because you were slain,
>   and with your blood you purchased for God
>   members of every tribe and language and people and nation.
> You have made them to be a kingdom and priests to serve our God,
>   and they will reign on the earth.

—Revelation 5:9–10

Why is Jesus worthy to open the scroll? The song gives three clear reasons: first, because he was slain (referring of course to the cross, through which he redeemed humanity); second, because through the cross Jesus fulfilled God's purpose, ever since Abraham, to bless people from *every* nation; and third, because through the cross Jesus has achieved victory for his people who will reign with him on the earth. Or, to put it in summary form: The cross is the key to all human history because it is *redemptive* (humanity will not go down the drainpipe of history into some cosmic sewer), *universal* (the cross is for people of all nations and cultures throughout all human history), and *victorious* (the Lamb wins! Victory is guaranteed for Christ and those redeemed by him).

In other words, the unfolding and meaning of history flow from the cross, just as the scroll unrolls in the hands of the Lamb who was slain. Like John, living in the horrors of the Roman Empire of his day, stuffed with evil, cruelty, and suffering, we too can only make sense of the world and all the terrible events that fill its history, past, present, and yet to come, if we look at them all from the perspective of the cross of Christ and all it accomplished.

But John isn't finished. The scroll starts to unroll, seal by seal, and the opening of the first four seals shocks us even further.

The Horsemen of History

Revelation 6:1–8 is a scary vision, but it is important that we read it now only in the light of what we have just witnessed in chapters 4 and 5.

> I watched as the Lamb opened the first of the seven seals. Then I heard one of the four living creatures say in a voice like thunder, "Come!" I looked, and there before me was a white horse! Its rider held a bow, and he was given a crown, and he rode out as a conqueror bent on conquest.
>
> When the Lamb opened the second seal, I heard the second living creature say, "Come!" Then another horse came out, a fiery red one. Its rider was given power to take peace from the earth and to make people slay each other. To him was given a large sword.

> When the Lamb opened the third seal, I heard the third living creature say, "Come!" I looked, and there before me was a black horse! Its rider was holding a pair of scales in his hand. Then I heard what sounded like a voice among the four living creatures, saying, "Two pounds of wheat for a day's wages, and six pounds of barley for a day's wages, and do not damage the oil and the wine!"
> When the Lamb opened the fourth seal, I heard the voice of the fourth living creature say, "Come!" I looked, and there before me was a pale horse! Its rider was named Death, and Hades was following close behind him. They were given power over a fourth of the earth to kill by sword, famine and plague, and by the wild beasts of the earth.

What on earth is going on here? It seems to me that these horses and their riders are intended to be symbolic of realities in John's own day (and ours). They picture the release of disasters that we see in repeated cycles all through human history.[7] Through bow and crown the white horse speaks of invasion and conquest. The red horse speaks of war, probably civil war and rebellion especially, in which people slaughter one another. The black horse speaks of famine, or rather famine for some but continuing luxuries for others. And the pale horse speaks of disease, plague, epidemic, and death of all kinds.

These are constant realities in human history. These four horsemen are not apocalyptic nightmares of the distant future. They are the stuff of the world in which we live. These four riders thunder through the pages of every history book of every era. It takes only a moment's thought to identify the horsemen of conquest, war, famine, and disease in multiple forms all over the world today.

Conquest still goes on, sometimes by military might (there used to be a country called Tibet), sometimes by economic or cultural aggression. War dominates everyday news. A single five-year period (1990–1995) saw 93 wars involving 70 states that left 5.5 million people dead. Famines still recur, in spite of all human efforts and sometimes caused by human folly or cynical neglect. HIV-AIDS is sucking the life out of swathes of Africa at the rate of a tsunami a month, though malaria actually kills even more. These are precisely the kind of evils we are struggling to understand in relation to the God we know and trust but often don't understand.

What about John's own day? George B. Caird[8] lists some of the terrible events that convulsed the Roman Empire during the last thirty-five years of John's life—earthquakes in AD 60; defeat of Roman armies by the Parthians in AD 62; the fire of Rome in AD 62 and the persecution of Christians that followed; the suicide of Nero in AD 68, followed by chaos, civil war, and four rival claimants to the throne; the four-year horror of the Jewish war, which ended in the destruction of Jerusalem and the temple in AD 70; the eruption of the volcano Vesuvius in AD 79, obliterating several towns in the Bay of Naples; the serious grain famine of AD 92.

From the first to the twenty-first century, these horsemen wreak their devastation through history. The point is that John sees the horsemen ride out from the scroll *in the hand of the Lamb*. That is to say, "John's vision of the four horsemen is intended to assert Christ's sovereignty over such a world as that." Indeed, "unless Christ can be said to reign over the world of hard facts in which Christians must live their lives, he can hardly be said to reign at all."[9]

But is this not all rather disappointing, something of an anticlimax? There we were with John in the throne room of the universe. We listened to choirs of all creation singing praises to the Lamb. We watched as the Lamb began to open the scroll of God's plan in history. And out come only these four wretched horsemen, representing disasters as old as the book of Genesis. Is this all there is to the reign of Christ? Nothing more than a kind of cosmic supervision of devouring evils rampaging out of control?

Ah, but that is precisely the point. They are *not* out of control.

Who summons them? Notice the word "Come". Each one is summoned under the sovereign authority of the throne. God rules the world, not the horsemen.

Who gives them power? Notice that to each of them something "was given" (e.g., a bow, a sword). This is a way of saying that all their powers are merely deputed by the sovereign God. They have power, but it is temporary, provisional, and subject to God's right to give and take away.

Above all, who is opening the seals? The Lamb who was slain! He is in charge of the unfolding of history within which these horrors take place.

The Lamb who was slain is the one who holds and opens the scroll. It was by his death on the cross that Jesus became worthy – that is, gained the right – to open the scroll. This means (and this is the absolutely pivotal, vital point to grasp), that *Christ's power to control these evil forces is the same power as the power he exercised on the cross.*

And what was that power?

We have begun to think of it this way already, but let's come back to it again. The cross was the worst that human evil and rebellion against God could do. At a purely human level it plumbed the depths of depravity, as the Gospels show with little need to embellish the facts. There were inflamed fanatics, corrupt religious leaders, lying witnesses, political conspiracy, vested interests, nationalist rage, morally bankrupt judicial process, excruciating torture, public shame, and taunting mockery; and even among the friends of

Jesus there was treachery, betrayal, denial, and cowardice. At a more profound level, we know that all the powers of evil, satanic allied with human, were ranged against Christ and hurled their worst at him.

But Jesus, the Lamb of God, doing the perfect will of his Father, transformed all this into the triumph of divine love, absorbing and defeating it simultaneously. But the crucial point is this: not only did Jesus defeat all the powers of evil, he made them into the agents of his victory and their own defeat. He turned evil against itself to its own ultimate destruction.

In the sport of judo, so I'm told, the essential idea is to take all the energy and force of your opponent's attack and turn it back on him in such a way that he is flattened by his own assault. If it is not too irreverent to put it like this, the cross was God's supreme judo. In the person of his Son he took all that sin and evil, human and satanic, could hurl at him and turned it back to its own ultimate destruction.

Henri Blocher also draws on this illustration from judo as he reflects on how the cross *used* evil for the defeat of evil:

> At the cross evil is conquered as evil: corruption, perversion, disorder, a parasite … evil is conquered as evil because God turns it back upon itself. He makes the supreme crime, the murder of the only righteous person, the very operation that abolishes sin. The manoeuvre is utterly unprecedented. No more complete victory could be imagined.... Evil, like a judoist, takes advantage of the power of the good, which it perverts; the Lord, like a supreme champion, replies by using the very grip of the opponent.... We have no other position than at the foot of the cross … God's answer is evil turned back upon itself, conquered by the ultimate degree of love in the fulfilment of justice.[10]

The Lamb who was slain is the Lamb on the throne

That, then, was the reality of the cross – the central moment in human history when God dealt with evil. *But now,* says John, *that same Jesus, the Lamb who was slain, reigns over the forces of evil that are loose in our world, in the same way as he reigned from the cross.* Ultimately, all that is evil and destructive will come under the sovereign power of the cross, to its own final destruction.

Once again, George B. Caird has a fine climax to his comment on this part of John's vision.

> He [John] is not asking us to believe that war, rebellion, famine and disease are the deliberate creation of Christ, or that, except in an indirect way, they are what God wills for the men and women he has made. They are the result of human sin; and it is significant that, out of all the apocalyptic disasters he could have chosen, John has at this point omitted the natural ones, like earthquakes, and included only those in which human agency has a part. The

point is that, just where sin and its effects are most in evidence, the kingship of the Crucified is to be seen, turning human wickedness to the service of God's purpose. The heavenly voice which says "Come!" is not calling disasters into existence. They are to be found in any case, wherever there are cruelty, selfishness, ambition, lust, greed, fear and pride. Rather the voice is declaring that nothing can now happen, not even the most fearsome evidence of man's disobedience and its nemesis, which cannot be woven into the pattern of God's gracious purpose.... The content of the scroll is God's redemptive plan, by which he brings good out of evil and makes everything on earth subservient to his sovereignty.11

Revelation 5 – 7, then, affirms this awesome paradox that is crucial to the way we should think about evil. All evil, disaster, and suffering stand under the sovereign control of God in Christ – and specifically under the authority of the *crucified* Christ (the Lamb who was slain, who is in the centre of the throne, sharing in the government of God over all creation).

If the first four seals speak of representative forms of evil and disaster, they are just as much under the authority of the one opening the seals as are the fifth and sixth seal. That means that whatever devastations may be included under the symbolism of the rampaging horsemen (first four seals), they are as much under God's sovereignty as the destiny of the martyrs (fifth seal, 6:9 – 11), the judgment of the wicked (sixth seal, 6:12 – 17), and the salvation of God's people from all nations (7:1 – 17, especially 9 – 10). In other words, if we believe that God is sovereign in his plan and power to protect his people, judge the wicked, and save people from all nations, we are summoned to believe also that he is sovereign over the very things that most seem to threaten those plans.

That sovereignty is exercised by the same one (the crucified Christ) and in the same way (through the paradoxical power of the cross) all the way to the end of history. The cross shows us that God can take the worst possible evil and through it accomplish the greatest possible good – the destruction of evil itself. Accordingly, under the governance of the crucified, nothing can happen in human history over which God is not ultimately sovereign and which he cannot, through his infinite power and wisdom, weave into the outworking of his universal purpose of redeeming love for the whole creation.

The Cross as Guarantee of the New Creation

It is fitting that we should close this chapter by turning to the closing chapters of the Bible itself: Revelation 21 – 22. For there we find the grand climax of the whole biblical narrative, which has been nothing less than the story of

God's triumph over evil. To do that great biblical story justice we would have to survey all the texts in the Old Testament that anticipate (and even celebrate in advance) the victory of God's kingdom over all forces of evil at work in history. We would need to observe how God's mission beginning with the call of Abraham was to bring about the blessing of the nations and their liberation from evil through the history of his people, Old Testament Israel, as the firstfruits of a new humanity. Then we would have to recognize the great battle that took place between the kingdom of God and the kingdom of the evil one in the Gospels. There, the Messiah Jesus, embodying Israel but remaining obedient where they rebelled, fulfils that mission of God and ultimately accomplishes it on the cross, as demonstrated by God's vindication of him in his resurrection.

However, taking all that grand narrative as read, we come to its climax: the arrival of a new creation. What do we find there? More importantly, what do we *not* find there? These two final chapters of the Bible repeatedly tell us about things that will *no longer* be part of universal reality. When God comes to establish the kingdom of his Christ, when he has made all things new and the old order of things has passed away, evil in all its forms will have been utterly eradicated. Look at the list:

- There will be no more sea (21:1). The sea represented chaotic, restless evil in Old Testament symbolism, the place from which the rampaging beasts in Daniel's visions had come to trample the nations. All such unruly rebellious hostility will have gone.
- *There will be no more death, mourning, crying, or pain (21:4).* All suffering and separation will be ended for there will be nothing any longer to cause them.
- *There will be no more sin,* for there will be no more sinners (21:7 – 8); the new creation involves exclusion as well as inclusion – exclusion of the unrepentantly and persistently wicked.
- *There will be no more darkness and night (21:25; 22:5),* in the sense of all that they represented. The light of God's presence will dispel the darkest evils.
- *There will be no more impurity, shame, or deceit (21:27),* characteristics that are among the original marks of our fallenness.
- *There will be no more international strife (22:2),* for the nations will find healing through the tree of life and the river of life.
- *There will be no more curse (22:3).* With the reproach of Eden lifted at last, earth will be freed from its subjection, and its redeemed inhabitants will be freed from bondage to its curse.

And all of this will be ruled over by, and filled with the presence of, the One who is repeatedly referred to as "the Lamb". All this is the reward of the crucified Christ.

All that will *not* be there in the new creation will not be there because of the victory of the cross of Christ through which they have been destroyed. And all that *will* be there in the new creation will be there because of the victory of the cross of Christ through which they have been redeemed.

This is our great hope and joyful expectation. In the midst of all our struggles now, as we confront evils we cannot understand and as we cry out to the God we cannot fully understand, we are urged by Jesus himself to pray, "Deliver us from evil". More than merely a prayer for daily protection, that is a cosmic request that will one day be cosmically answered. God will answer that prayer! It will be fully answered at the moment when God answers two other phrases in the Lord's Prayer: "your kingdom come, your will be done on earth as it is in heaven" (Matt. 6:10).

When the reign of God extends over every corner of the universe, when the earth is filled with the knowledge of God as the waters cover the sea, when the kingdoms of this world have become the kingdoms of our God and of his Christ, when heaven and earth are renewed and united under the righteous rule of Christ, when the dwelling place of God is again with humanity, when the city of God is the centre of all redeemed reality – then we will have been delivered from all evil forever.

The cross and resurrection of Christ accomplished it in history and guarantee it for all eternity. In such hope we can rejoice with incomparable joy and total confidence.

Notes

1. From the eleventh of his *Theses on Feuerbach,* to be found in Karl Marx and Friedrich Engels, *On Religion* (New York: Schocken, 1964), 72.

2. N. T. Wright: *Evil and the Justice of God* (Downers Grove, IL: InterVarsity Press, 2006).

3. In speaking of the cross in this chapter, I do not intend any neglect of the importance of the resurrection. Without the resurrection as God's vindication of all that Jesus said and did as the demonstration of God's power over death, and as the proof of the victory that Jesus won on the cross, the cross itself would have been just the final moments of one more wannabe-but-failed messiah. However, since the New Testament presents the cross as the moment of Christ's victory and accomplishment of God's mission, I concentrate on it in this section.

4. Henri Blocher, *Evil and the Cross: Christian Thought and the Problem of Evil* (Leicester: Apollos, 1994).

5. Ibid., 85.

6. Either this means that God caused the disaster as a form of his moral judgment (i.e., as an act of punishment) or that he *permitted* it (in the sense referred to above). The Israelites did not seem to have felt the need to make the distinction we make between "decretive" and "permissive" in the will of God; sometimes they use the causal form of verbs where we might want to make finer distinctions. If we were to translate the final line "has not the LORD permitted it?" we might feel more comfortable, but Amos would probably wonder what the difference was, since it still affirms that ultimately nothing happens outside God's sovereign will and purposes.

7. Some see the first, white horse and its rider as symbolic of Christ, by analogy with Rev. 19:11–16. This is possible, and if it were so, it would mean that Christ himself is the one who "leads" the "parade of disasters"—in the sense that he remains sovereign over them. But my own view is that it is more likely that all four horses in this sequence are similar in meaning.

8. G. B. Caird, *A Commentary on the Revelation of St. John the Divine* (London: A&C Black, 1966), 79.

9. Ibid.

10. Blocher, *Evil and the Cross,* 132–33.

11. Caird, *Revelation,* 82–83 (my emphasis).

PART TWO

WHAT ABOUT THE CANAANITES?

"The God I don't understand", for many people, is easily identified. It's the God of the Old Testament. Those who wish to deride the Christian faith in general find their sharpest ammunition ready made here. Richard Dawkins, for example, atheism's most prolific televangelist, minces no words in his assessment of Yahweh, the God of the Old Testament.

> The God of the Old Testament is arguably the most unpleasant character in all fiction: jealous and proud of it; a petty, unjust, unforgiving control-freak; a vindictive, bloodthirsty ethnic cleanser; a misogynistic, homophobic, racist, infanticidal, genocidal, filiacidal, pestilential, megalomaniacal, sadomasochistic, capriciously malevolent bully.[1]

For Dawkins and other atheists, of course, there is no problem of *understanding* involved. They have no desire at all to understand *God* as portrayed in the Bible since they consider him to be nothing more than a figment of the imagination anyway, and a warped imagination at that. Their only problem lies in understanding *people* who claim to believe in such a God.

But for Christians who do trust in God and have been taught essential truths about God's nature and character, there is a real problem. Some of us wince when we read Dawkins' words, not just because we find them offensive (which they are), but because, if we are honest, we sometimes find ourselves thinking the same thing when we read the Old Testament. Frankly, we find it embarrassing to be challenged about our belief in the Bible because we are embarrassed by the Bible's longest plot line (the story of Old Testament Israel) and by the Bible's most prominent character (Yahweh, the God of Old Testament Israel) – most prominent at least after Jesus (and all the more embarrassing because of Jesus).

What are we to make of texts that speak of God meting out horrific punishments on whole families, like Achan or Korah? Or a God who smites a man dead for touching a sacred object, like Uzzah, or for offering the wrong kind of sacrificial fire, like the sons of Aaron? How are we to understand the language of God's anger, jealousy, or vengeance alongside what we have been taught about God's love, mercy, and compassion? And what kind of God did the Israelites understand him to be when they cried out for him to curse people and avenge them on their enemies?

And most of all, *what about the Canaanites?* Is there any way to describe the conquest of Canaan by the Israelites other than religious genocide or ethnic cleansing? What possible connection can such violence have with the God we long to love, trust, and understand?

We are right to find such questions disturbing.

We are particularly disturbed by the violence of the Old Testament when we contemplate the way it has been used to justify violence down through the ages since. The centuries of Christendom have witnessed professing Christian leaders right up to modern times using the methods of conquest, torture, execution, horrifying punishments, and racist genocide – and claiming theological justification from their reading of the Old Testament. Crusades against Muslims, genocide of North American Indians or Aboriginal Australians, apartheid against black South Africans, discrimination and violence against African Americans, expropriation of land from Palestinians – even attitudes toward Roman Catholics in Northern Ireland: in all these cases the first step is to declare the "enemy" to be cursed by God, just like the Canaanites. After that, it becomes OK to just wipe them out (or to want to).

Now we cannot blame the Old Testament itself for such terribly deluded misuse of the Bible (for that is what it has been). But even if we exclude horrors that have been perpetrated by Christians with claimed sanction from the Old Testament, there are horrors enough within its own pages to disturb us. What kind of response can we make as we struggle to understand the God whom we believe we find self-revealed in the Scriptures?

The first thing we must do is to take a look at some of the ways people have tried to make this less of a problem than it seems at first sight. Unfortunately, I think we will find that some of the popular answers are dead ends that don't really help us find a way out. Still, when there are things you don't understand, it is at least helpful to remove the things that only make the problem worse! This is what we will attempt to do in chapter 4.

After that, I will outline in chapter 5 three frameworks of understanding the Old Testament as a whole, which I think will be helpful in putting this major problem into perspective. I don't claim to solve the problem – only to help us to grapple with it in the light of the perspectives that the Bible itself gives us for interpreting it.

Note

1. Richard Dawkins, *The God Delusion* (London: Bantam, 2006), 31.

chapter

THE CANAANITES – THREE
DEAD ENDS

W hat can you do about all the violence in the Old Testament? That is
the question, and we are right to struggle with it. If it is hard sometimes to understand God in the midst of the things that happen in our own
day or in our own lives, it is just as hard to understand why God said, did,
and commanded some of the things recorded in the Old Testament.

There are various ways in which people try to lessen the difficulty, but we
will limit ourselves to just three in this chapter. Some people are happy to leave
the problem in the Old Testament itself and imagine that the New Testament
gives us a very different and "right" approach. Some people like to think that
it was all a matter of mistaken zeal and primitive understanding of God on
the part of the Israelites, and we can thankfully discern their mistakes, leave
all that behind, and follow more enlightened ways. And there are those who
simply let their feet float off the surface of the text out of the real world and
into the much less troublesome world of spiritual allegories and nice moral
lessons. But none of these, I suggest, can really solve the problem and only end
up in partial or distorted understanding of the Bible as a whole.

It's an Old Testament Problem, Which the
New Testament Puts Right

Possibly the easiest and most popular way out of the difficulty is simply to pit
one Testament against the other. These things all happened in the Old Testament, but, thankfully, we are New Testament Christians and we now know

either that God was really never like that (though the primitive Israelites imagined he was), or that God has radically changed the way he deals with us now that Jesus has come and shown us a better way and fuller revelation.

This kind of solution goes along with one of the commonest misconceptions of the Bible that exists among believers and unbelievers alike, namely, the assumption that the so-called God of the Old Testament was all fire and brimstone, war and vengeance, blood and punishment. The so-called God of the New Testament is much nicer altogether. Jesus (for the first time, on this view), shows us that God loves us and cares for us, pardons and forgives us, and calls on us to do likewise.

Through this process we get over our embarrassment with the Old Testament by turning in relief to the New Testament. Perhaps, we might think, God had to do some of that Old Testament stuff at the time, but Jesus has shown that he really prefers to do things differently now. So we allow our New Testament simply to cancel out the Old Testament and consign its most unpleasant parts to the dustbin of history (and theology).

This, however, simply will not do—for three reasons. First, because the Old Testament has as much to say about the love and compassion of God as the New Testament does. Second, because the New Testament has as much to say (and more in fact) about the anger and judgment of God as the Old does. Third, because Jesus and the writers of the New Testament never seem to be embarrassed by Old Testament stories, nor do they reject or even correct them (though they do move beyond them).

Let's pick these up in turn. As we do, I think we will find that it is really a superficial and distorted view of the Bible to try to use the New Testament simply to reject the Old. Nevertheless, as we will see in chapter 5, there are ways in which the New Testament calls us to go beyond the Old in the light of the coming of Christ and his life, teaching, death, and resurrection. But first, let's correct the misunderstandings within this view.

The Old Testament and the Love of God

The popular idea (starkly summarized by the quotation from Richard Dawkins in the introduction to Part 2) that the so-called God of the Old Testament stands for unrelieved anger and violence ignores a massive amount of Old Testament teaching that seems never to have found its way into the popular consciousness, or seems to have been filtered out by the dominant prejudice. Here are just some examples.

Abraham, interceding with God on behalf of the wicked cities of Sodom and Gomorrah, found God willing to be far more merciful than he expected, only too eager to spare whole cities for the sake of a few righteous – if only they could be found, which clearly they could not. Abraham's confidence in God's justice was matched by his awareness that the justice of God was infused with mercy (Gen. 18).

Moses, even in a narrative that speaks of God's anger against his people, hears God declare his own name and character in these words:

> The Lord, the Lord, the compassionate and gracious God, slow to anger, abounding in love and faithfulness, maintaining love to thousands, and forgiving wickedness, rebellion and sin. Yet he does not leave the guilty unpunished; he punishes the children and their children for the sin of the parents to the third and fourth generation.
>
> —Exodus 34:6–7

This is one of the earliest and also most pervasive definitions of the character of God in the Bible. And it shows clearly that the "weight" of God's character is toward compassion, grace, and love. Love is "abounding"; anger and punishment are "slow". Love is for thousands; punishment is for "three and four".[1]

The psalmists knew full well the anger of God against the wicked, but they revel most in the compassion, forgiveness, love, grace, and generosity of God. Have those who think of the Old Testament God as all rage and violence ever read these texts?

> The Lord is compassionate and gracious,
>   slow to anger, abounding in love.
> He will not always accuse,
>   nor will he harbor his anger forever;
> he does not treat us as our sins deserve
>   or repay us according to our iniquities.
> For as high as the heavens are above the earth,
>   so great is his love for those who fear him;
> as far as the east is from the west,
>   so far has he removed our transgressions from us.
> As a father has compassion on his children,
>   so the Lord has compassion on those who fear him;
> for he knows how we are formed,
>   he remembers that we are dust.
>
> —Psalm 103:8–14

> The Lord is good to all;
>   he has compassion on all he has made....
> The Lord is trustworthy in all his promises
>   and faithful in all he does....

> The Lord is righteous in all his ways
>> and faithful in all he does.

> —Psalm 145:9, 13, 17

Jeremiah and Hosea, who both had uncompromising words to say about the anger of God against Israel's wickedness, had even more moving words for the love of God that drew his people back into his warm embrace. They talk about the self-sacrificial love of God, willing to pay the cost of forgiveness and restoration.

> I have loved you with an everlasting love;
>> I have drawn you with unfailing kindness.

> —Jeremiah 31:3

> "Is not Ephraim my dear son,
>> the child in whom I delight?
> Though I often speak against him,
>> I still remember him.
> Therefore my heart yearns for him;
>> I have great compassion for him,"
>> declares the Lord.

> —Jeremiah 31:20

> The Lord said to me, "Go, show your love to your wife again, though she is loved by another and is an adulteress. Love her as the Lord loves the Israelites."

> —Hosea 3:1

Ezekiel probably had the most sensationally severe portrait of Israel's sin among all the prophets. But he balanced it with the most poignant evangelistic appeals for repentance, based on the loving heartbeat of God himself.

> "As surely as I live," declares the Sovereign Lord, "I take no pleasure in the death of the wicked, but rather that they turn from their ways and live. Turn! Turn from your evil ways! Why will you die, O house of Israel?"

> —Ezekiel 33:11

Deuteronomy, the very book in which the conquest of the Canaanites is anticipated and commanded, also has some of the clearest teaching about the love of God, not only for his own people Israel (Deut. 7:8–9), but also in a universal sense for the needy (10:17–18).

So we cannot dismiss the problem just by saying that it's typical of the hateful God of the Old Testament. For the Old Testament defines Yahweh as gracious and compassionate and not only teaches us about God's forgiving love but even provides us with the vocabulary to understand and appeal to it.

The New Testament and the Wrath of God

We must turn to the other side of the coin, however. Is it true that the New Testament speaks only of a God of love? Are all concepts of divine wrath and punishment now superseded? Far from it.

The fact is that Jesus spoke more about hell than anybody else in the New Testament. "Hell" usually translates the Greek *gehenna*—a Jewish term for the burning rubbish dump outside Jerusalem. The word is only used twelve times, and eleven of them are in the Gospels spoken by Jesus as a metaphor for the fate of the unrepentant wicked. But Jesus also spoke the most sober warnings about the day of judgment (Matt. 10:15), eternal fire (25:41), terrible remorse (13:40–42), outer darkness (22:13), and tormenting imprisonment (18:34). This language comes from Jesus as the language of loving warning, but it shows how seriously he understood God's anger against sin.

Outside the Gospels, other New Testament writers graphically describe God's judgment as the terrifying context for understanding the good news of God's redeeming love. Paul explains it in the devastating logic of Romans 1:18–2:16. James and Peter are both equally emphatic (James 2:13; 1 Peter 4:17; 2 Peter 2–3). And Revelation uses all the Old Testament imagery available to depict the final exposure, defeat, and destruction of all that is evil and of all who unrepentantly persist in doing evil. Indeed, if we are thinking about comparing the Old Testament and the New Testament, the writer to the Hebrews compares God's judgment with the punishments prescribed in the Old Testament law and says it will be much worse!

> If we deliberately keep on sinning after we have received the knowledge of the truth, no sacrifice for sins is left, but only a fearful expectation of judgment and of raging fire that will consume the enemies of God. Anyone who rejected the law of Moses died without mercy on the testimony of two or three witnesses. How much more severely do you think those deserve to be punished who have trampled the Son of God underfoot, who have treated as an unholy thing the blood of the covenant that sanctified them, and who have insulted the Spirit of grace? For we know him who said, "It is mine to avenge; I will repay," and again, "The Lord will judge his people." It is a dreadful thing to fall into the hands of the living God.

—Hebrews 10:26–31

So the idea that the New Testament has left behind some primitive perception of an angry Israelite deity for a more congenial view of a nice loving Christian God is simply false. Indeed, as John Wenham puts it, the New Testament goes beyond the mainly historical, "this-life" perspective of the Old Testament and speaks of God's judgment mostly in terms of eternity.

> It is fallacious to regard this as essentially an Old Testament problem, and to set the "bloodthirsty" Old Testament over against the "gentle" New Testament. Possibly the phenomenon is more crude in the Old Testament than in the New, but of the two the New Testament is the more terrible, for the Old Testament seldom speaks of anything beyond temporal judgments ... whereas the Son of man in the Gospels pronounces eternal punishment.[2]

The New Testament Accepts the Stories of the Old

A third reason why it won't do to set the New Testament over against the Old (at least as regards the stories in the Old) is that the New Testament itself never does so. Of course, Jesus went beyond the Old Testament in his teaching. Yes, he did bring new wine that could not simply be contained in the old wineskins. But never did Jesus or any of the New Testament writers critique the words or actions of God in the Old Testament or suggest that the stories were immoral in their own context. On the contrary, even some of the horror stories are included in the lessons of faith in Hebrews 11 (a fact that does not whitewash evil actions done by some of them; people who are models of faith were also sinners and failures in many respects). Others are recalled as examples and warnings: the flood (Matt. 24:36–41; 2 Peter 3:3–7); Sodom and Gomorrah (Matt. 10:15, 11:23–24); Korah (Jude 11); the wilderness plagues (1 Cor. 10:6–10), and even the conquest itself (Heb. 11:31). In all these cases, the historical, earthly judgments of God in the Old Testament are used as case studies and warnings in relation to the even worse judgment to come. The New Testament also teaches us about the jealousy and vengeance of God (Rom. 12:19; 1 Cor. 10:22) and can utter the most solemn curses (1 Cor. 16:22; Gal. 1:9).

So as we struggle to understand this problem, let's at least agree that it will never be helpful to set the New Testament antagonistically against the Old. Admittedly we must take into account the historical dimension of God's self-revelation. There are many ways in which we will find that the New Testament sets the Old Testament in a preliminary or provisional place as compared with the finality of what God said and did through Jesus Christ. But we cannot dodge difficult problems with a casual, "Oh, but that's only in the Old Testament." If we do, we will probably be guilty of misunderstanding not only the Old Testament but also the New Testament.

The Israelites Thought It Was What God Commanded, but They Were Wrong

Another way "around" the problem of the violence in the Old Testament is to dissociate God from it altogether. It was the *Israelites themselves* who attacked and drove out the Canaanites and then took over their land. This was a necessary action from their point of view, since they had to live somewhere and could hardly survive indefinitely in the wilderness. So either they conquered the Canaanites first, and then, naturally enough, they later rationalized it as the will of their God, Yahweh; or they believed in advance that it was the will and command of Yahweh that they should take such action. Either way, all the talk about "God commanding" the conquest comes from the Israelites' own understanding, not actually from God himself. They did what they thought God had commanded – but they were wrong.

The neat thing about this "solution" is that we can now blame the Israelites for the slaughter of the Canaanites but not blame God. God is implicated only by the Israelites, but we need not accept their interpretation.[3]

At first sight this approach appears to have some biblical support. There are certainly cases in the Old Testament where people thought something was what God wanted and then found out later they were mistaken. Sometimes this may be rather ambiguous in the text – as, for example, when Moses killed the Egyptian, probably thinking it was the right thing to do, and ended up fleeing for his life. But sometimes God explicitly corrects a wrong interpretation of his mind – as, for example, when Nathan told David that God was happy for him to build a temple, only to have God correct him that same night (2 Sam. 7:1 – 4). Furthermore, there are examples in the Old Testament where God rebukes excessive violence, even when the one doing it thought he was acting on God's command. Jehu, for example, was anointed by Elisha with a commission to destroy the apostate house of Ahab and Jezebel (2 Kings 9:6 – 10). He turned it into a bloodbath and exterminated all the priests of Baal. Later, Hosea condemned this action (Hos. 1:4).

So we might think there is some justification for this view – blame the Israelites and keep God's hands clean.

But again, this really won't work. First, when people did get it wrong (as in the isolated cases mentioned above), the Old Testament does include the record of God correcting the misinterpretation of his will. If the conquest of Canaan had actually been such a massive and mistaken misinterpretation of God's will, we should surely read some corrective word later in the Scriptures – if not within the Old Testament itself (where the other corrections occur), then at least in the New. But we find none. There is no hint anywhere in the Bible that the Israelites took the land of Canaan on the basis of a mistaken belief in God's will. On the contrary, the *refusal* of the exodus generation to go ahead and do it (in the great rebellion at Kadesh Barnea in Numbers 14), and the *failure* of the following generations to complete the task properly, are condemned as *disobedience* to God's will (Ps. 106:24–35).

But the main problem with this view is that everywhere else in the Bible the conquest is never explained away as a colossal mistake; on the contrary, it is anticipated, commanded, achieved, and remembered as something that *accomplished* God's will.

God promised Abraham that he would give the land of Canaan to his descendants (Gen. 15:18–21). So the conquest is linked to the Abrahamic covenant. God promised the Israelites in Egypt that he would not only rescue them out of that oppression but also bring them into the land promised to Abraham (Ex. 6:6–8). So the conquest is linked to the exodus redemption. God gave Israel promises and warnings about their future life in the land, depending on their response to his law (see Deuteronomy). So the conquest is linked to the Sinai covenant.

The book of Joshua finishes the story of the conquest by saying that it was Yahweh himself who fought for the Israelites and gave them the land (Josh. 23:3–5, 9–10). Psalmists affirm that the conquest was not really the work of human hands at all, but the power of God (Ps. 44:1–3). Prophets saw the conquest as one of the great acts of God and used it to accuse Israel of ingratitude (e.g., Amos. 2:9) or to woo Israel back to a restored covenant relationship with God (e.g., Hos. 2:14–15). Even in the New Testament both Stephen and Paul refer to the conquest simply as an act of God's sovereignty (Acts 7:45; 13:19).

So the conquest is placed firmly within the whole unfolding plan of God in the Bible.

We cannot simply say that Moses and Joshua made a sincere but serious error of judgment in thinking (wrongly) that the attack on Canaan was a matter of obedience to God's command, and then imagining that their success in the conquest was the victory of God himself. For if *they* were so misguided about it, then so were all the other Old Testament speakers and writers who describe it in the same way. You simply can't surgically remove the conquest alone from the great sweep of Bible history, saying that it was merely the bloody actions of deluded warriors, while leaving all the rest of the story intact within the sovereign will of God. At least, you can't if you treat the Bible seriously as a whole.

It Is All Meant as an Allegory of Spiritual Warfare

Finally, we can always resort to a piece of fancy footwork that many preachers use to dodge the offence of the Old Testament. To be honest, many of us do the same when reading the Old Testament by ourselves or in a Bible study group. *You can always get a spiritual lesson out of it somewhere.* The Old Testament is simply there as a big storybook from which we are meant to learn spiritual truths, perhaps about Jesus, or about heaven, or about the Christian life. For example, the exodus can be a picture of God releasing us from the slavery of sin, the wilderness a picture of the trials and temptations of our spiritual pilgrimage, and the conquest a picture of our battle with Satan and the spiritual hosts of darkness. In this way, the language of "conquering the land", "drawing swords", and "tearing down strongholds" can all be sanitized for spiritual exhortation and even for writing vigorous songs with a good marching beat.

Now I don't want to dismiss such spiritualizing out of hand. Clearly the Bible itself makes use of its own great narratives for the purpose of warning, encouragement, challenge, and hope. Yes, the defeat of God's enemies is certainly used, in both Testaments, to strengthen believers in the face of hostility – human or satanic. Moreover, the New Testament uses the language of Old Testament warfare to describe the ultimate victory of God through Christ, both through his cross and resurrection and in his final cosmic reign. In addition, the destruction of the Canaanites is used in the Bible as one of several historical signposts pointing to the terrible final judgment. However, we must remember that this kind of spiritual use of Old Testament narratives is secondary and derivative. Their primary form is simply historical narrative. In other words, we are not really dealing with allegory here at all.

An allegory is a totally fictional narrative, deliberately and consciously created and written for the primary purpose of illustrating some spiritual truth or truths. The spiritual truth is primary, and the narrative content of the allegory is secondary. When you read *Pilgrim's Progress*, you know that John Bunyan is teaching you spiritual lessons about the "journey" of the Christian life, that the story itself comes entirely from his imagination, and that it breaks even the possibilities of any normal factual history. But as we read the down-to-earth narratives of the conquest of the Israelites over the Canaanites, we know we are not reading allegory but an unvarnished account that the writer asks the reader to receive as a portrait of events that took place on the soil of Palestine. The people in the stories are not allegorical fictions but are presented as historical. *It was not allegorical Israelites who attacked or allegorical Canaanites who died.*

So whatever spiritual lessons we may choose to draw from the narratives of the conquest (and there are plenty, as the Bible shows), we are still left with the earthy realism of the story itself, and we need better ways of looking at the problem it creates in our minds. In the next chapter we will see if there are more helpful frameworks in which to tackle it.

Notes

1. "Thousands" here probably means "thousands of generations" as it clearly does in Deuteronomy 7:9-10. The contrast is between God's faithful love that is virtually limitless as it flows through human history, and the temporal nature of his acts of judgment. Most Israelite families would have been three-generational and some would have four generations living together. When the head of a household sins (especially in idolatry, breaking the second commandment), the whole family is affected. God's punishment similarly affects the whole family. This is a principle of divine judgment, not for human courts (see Deut. 24:16).

2. John W. Wenham, *The Goodness of God* (Leicester: Intervarsity Press, 1974), 16 – 17.

3. This is the view expounded with great power by C. S. Cowles in "The Case for Radical Discontinuity", in Stanley N. Gundry, ed., *Show Them No Mercy: Four Views on God and Canaanite Genocide* (Grand Rapids: Zondervan, 2003), 13 – 44.

THE CANAANITES – THREE FRAMEWORKS

In chapter 4 we looked at some common approaches to the problem of the conquest of Canaan, but we found that none of them is really satisfactory. What are we to say then? Is there any "solution"?

I have wrestled with this problem for many years as a teacher of the Old Testament, and I am coming to the view that no such "solution" will be forthcoming. There is something about this part of our Bible that I have to include in my basket of things I don't understand about God and his ways. I find myself thinking, "God, I wish you had found some other way to work out your plans." There are days I wish this narrative were not in the Bible at all (usually after I've faced another barrage of questions about it), though I know it is wrong to wish that in relation to the Scriptures. God knew what he was doing – in the events themselves and in the record of them that he has given us. But it is still hard.

Nevertheless, there are a number of considerations that certainly help me cope with the destruction of the Canaanites and understand at least some things about it in the light of what the Bible as a whole says. I have to say immediately that the points I'm going to share with you in this chapter are not really "solutions". That is, they do not neatly remove the emotional and moral pain and revulsion generated by the conquest narratives. However, I do find these perspectives helpful for my own faith, and I pass them on in the hope they may help you too.

One of the problems is that we so often read this story, or horrible little bits of it, in *isolation*, and then try to find some meaning, justification, or excuse for it. But what we really must do is what we should do with every part of the Bible, namely, *to put it in the wider framework of our whole Bible.* We must get into the habit of doing that when we read any Bible text, and never more so than here.

So we will look at three frameworks that help to put the conquest in perspective—not in such a way as to make it "nice" or to take away all the nasty questions it raises, but at least in such a way as to help us connect it to the rest of what we know about God and his ways. We need to see the conquest narrative in the framework of the Old Testament story, in the framework of God's sovereign justice, and in the framework of God's whole plan of salvation.

The Framework of the Old Testament Story

The conquest of Canaan is indeed part of the Old Testament. Now I have not suddenly forgotten what I said in the last chapter. I am not pointing out its Old Testament location simply in order to dismiss it for that reason. Rather, we must understand the conquest within the context of ancient Near Eastern culture (and not by the standards of the Geneva Convention), and also within the limited span of history that it actually occupies (and not magnify it into the story of the whole Old Testament).

The Culture and Rhetoric of Ancient Warfare

The kind of warfare described in the conquest stories should, first of all, not be called "holy war" (a term never used in the Bible). It is called "a war of Yahweh". That is, it was a war in which the God of the Israelites won the victory over their enemies.

The main feature of Yahweh war was that it was sanctioned by Yahweh, who functioned as commander-in-chief (even above the human military leader), and the result was guaranteed by Yahweh, regardless of the size of the opposing human forces, or (in some cases) whether the Israelites even had to fight at all. The enemies were enemies of Yahweh, not just of Israel.

Within that context, the concept of *herem* (or "ban") was applied. This meant the total dedication of all that was being attacked—human, animal, or material—to God himself. In a battle or war in which *herem* was declared, there was to be no material profit for the Israelites, since no plunder was allowed. However, the rules of *herem* varied, as the Old Testament narratives show. Sometimes women and children were spared (Num. 31:7–12, 17–18; Deut. 20:13–14; 21:10–14); sometimes cattle could be kept (Deut.

2:34–35). But in the cases of nations living within the land of Canaan itself, the general rule was total destruction.

Now we need to know that Israel's practice of *herem* was not in itself unique. Texts from other nations at the time show that such total destruction in war was practised, or at any rate proudly claimed, elsewhere. But we must also recognize that the language of warfare had a conventional rhetoric that liked to make absolute and universal claims about total victory and completely wiping out the enemy. Such rhetoric often exceeded reality on the ground.

Admittedly this does not remove the problem, since the reality was still horrible at any level. But it enables us to allow for the fact that descriptions of the destruction of "everything that lives and breathes" were not necessarily intended literally. Even in the Old Testament itself this phenomenon is recognized and accepted. So, for example, we read in the book of Joshua that *all* the land was captured, *all* the kings were defeated, *all* the people without survivors (such as Rahab) were destroyed (e.g., Josh. 10:40–42, 11:16–20). But this must have been intended as rhetorical exaggeration, for the book of Judges (whose final editor was undoubtedly aware of these accounts in Joshua) sees no contradiction in telling us that the process of subduing the inhabitants of the land was far from completed and went on for considerable time, and that many of the original nations continued to live alongside the Israelites. The key military centres – the small fortified cities of the petty Canaanite kingdoms – were wiped out. But clearly not *all* the people, or anything like all the people, had in actual fact been destroyed by Joshua.

Even in the Old Testament itself, then, rhetorical generalization is recognized for what it is. So when we are reading some of the more graphic descriptions, either of what was commanded to be done or of what was recorded as accomplished, we need to allow for this rhetorical element. This is not to accuse the biblical writers of falsehood, but to recognize the literary conventions of writing about warfare.

Pondering *Herem* Further

One further thought about *herem* and "Yahweh war" is worth pondering, though I confess that I am not at all sure what conclusion my pondering leads to. That's often how it is when we struggle with things we don't fully understand about God. If such methods and practices in war were fairly standard in the ancient Near Eastern culture of that time, is there any sense in which God accommodated his will to such fallen reality within the historical earthing of his revealing and redeeming purpose?

We know that Old Testament law has to strike a balance between the ideals of God's creational standards and the realities of fallen human life. The clearest illustration of this tension within the Torah itself (meaning the whole first five books of the Bible, Genesis to Deuteronomy) comes from Jesus, in the divorce controversy. The argument was over the divorce law in Deuteronomy 24:1–4, which, as Jesus pointed out, did not *command* divorce, but permitted and regulated it for the sake of the woman. But Jesus takes his questioners further back and points to the creation ideal from Genesis 2:24. Lifelong monogamous marriage is God's best will for men and women. But in a fallen world God *allowed* divorce "because of your hardness of heart". The same Scriptures–drawn from the one Torah–both state God's creation ideal and also legislate God's concession to our sinfulness.

It seems to me probable that if Jesus had been asked questions about slavery or about polygamy, he would have answered similarly. From the beginning these things were not in God's intention; but in a fallen world of hardened hearts, they might be accommodated, with limiting and mitigating regulations, and with a strongly subversive critique that would eventually lead to clear recognition of their wrongness. That indeed is what we find in the Torah.

Is it possible (and as I say, I am not convinced I can answer this one way or the other to my own satisfaction), that in a fallen world where struggle for land involves war, and if the only kind of war at the time was the kind described in the Old Testament texts, this was the way it had to be if the land-gift promise was to be fulfilled in due course? If anything along these lines can be entertained–that is to say, if *herem*-style warfare can be even contemplated in the same moral framework as slavery and divorce (and many might reject the thought outright)–then we might be dealing with something God chose to accommodate within the context of a wicked world, not something that represented his best will or preference. In view of his long-term goal of ultimately bringing blessing to the nations through this people Israel, the gift of land necessitated this horrific historical action within the fallen world of nations at the time.

Is this a possible way of looking at *herem*? I can't say that I feel comfortable with it, but then neither can I (or should I) be comfortable with anything in our fallen world that is on the one hand a hateful evil, and on the other hand somehow permitted by God in given circumstances. Malachi tells us unequivocally that God hates divorce as a kind of violence (Mal. 2:16). Yet Jesus tells us that God permitted it in the context of our sin (Matt. 19:8).

The Conquest of Canaan as a Unique and Limited Event

Another aspect of this framework of the Old Testament story is that the conquest was a single episode within a single generation out of all the many generations of Old Testament history. Of course, it spans a longer period than that if one includes the promise and then the completion. The conquest of Canaan was promised to Abraham, anticipated as the purpose of the exodus, delayed by the wilderness rebellion, accomplished under Joshua, and brought to provisional completion under David and Solomon. Even including all this, though, it was limited in the specific duration of the warfare involved. Although the process of settling and claiming the land took several generations, the actual invasion and destruction of key fortified cities took place mostly within a single generation. And it is this event, confined to one generation, that constituted the conquest.

Now there are many other wars recorded in the Old Testament (as you might expect, since it covers about a thousand years of human history, so wars are pretty inevitable). Some of those other wars also had God's sanction – especially those where Israel was attacked by other nations and fought defensively to survive. *But by no means are all the wars in the Old Testament portrayed in the same way as the conquest of Canaan.* Some were clearly condemned as the actions of proud and greedy kings or military rivals. It is a caricature of the Old Testament to portray God as constantly on the warpath or to portray the conquest as simply "typical" of the rest of the story. It is not. The book of Joshua describes one key historical event, but it was finished. It should not be stretched out as if it were the background theme music for the rest of the Old Testament.

So the conquest of Canaan, as a unique and limited historical event, was never meant to become a model for how all future generations were to behave toward their contemporary enemies (whether future generations of Israelites or, still less, of Christians).

One way that the Old Testament resists the temptation to "apply" the conquest as a model for dealing with enemies forever after is that it is much more frequently referred to simply as an *act of God* rather than as the military achievements of the Israelites. The Israelite farmer, for example, when he celebrated the harvest in the land, was to declare, "I have come to the land that the LORD swore to our ancestors to give us" (Deut. 26:3) – *not* "to the land that I fought to conquer and obtain". Joshua reminds the people that it was "the LORD your God who fought for you" (Josh. 23:3). The psalmists and prophets lay all the stress on the conquest as *God's gift* of the land to

Israel (keeping his promise to Abraham). They hardly ever mention Israel's military exploits in the process. In fact they tend to discount them:

> With your hand you drove out the nations
> > and planted our ancestors;
> you crushed the peoples
> > and made our ancestors flourish.
> It was not by their sword that they won the land,
> > nor did their arm bring them victory;
> it was your right hand, your arm,
> > and the light of your face, for you loved them.

> —Psalm 44:2–3

The conquest, then, stood as a monument to *God's* faithfulness and mighty power. It was not a monument to *Israel's* military brilliance. It was not some great national achievement that could be replicated any time the Israelites felt inclined to do some Canaanite-bashing.

When we look at the conquest in this way, as a unique and limited event, a specific act of God located firmly within the narrative of Israel's early history of salvation, it also helps us understand why Jesus could prohibit his disciples from emulating the violence of the Old Testament, *without condemning the Old Testament itself*. Remember when the "sons of thunder", James and John, wanted Jesus to call down fire from heaven? Perhaps they were thinking of Sodom and Gomorrah, though they may have had Canaanites in mind too. They felt this should fall on a whole Samaritan village because they had refused to welcome Jesus. But Jesus roundly rebuked them. Such methods were not for Jesus or his disciples (Luke 9:51–56). We are not to behave in such ways now, nor should we ask God to.

But the fact that disciples of Jesus are not to emulate events or actions in the Old Testament does not mean that Jesus regarded those events or actions as inherently wrong in themselves at the time, or that he thought Moses and Joshua (for example) were utterly mistaken about God's will at the time, or that the Old Testament narrators, psalmists, and prophets were wrong to consider such events as having been accomplished or authorized by God. There is no indication that Jesus took such a view of the Old Testament narrative and much that suggests the contrary – that he accepted it at face value.

This leads naturally to one of the most important perspectives that the Bible itself offers in helping us to understand the conquest. This is a perspective that needs to be taken seriously since the Bible repeatedly affirms it. It brings us to our second major framework.

The Framework of God's Sovereign Justice

The conquest is consistently and repeatedly set within the framework of God's international justice and punishment. I believe this makes a major difference to how we read and understand the whole story. It is repeatedly portrayed as God acting in judgment on a wicked and degraded society and culture—as God would do again and again in Old Testament history, *including against Israel itself.* In that sense, although the story is unique and limited (as we have just seen), it is also entirely in keeping with the way the rest of the Old Testament shows God using nations as the agents of his anger against collective human wickedness.

The word "genocide" is sometimes used about Israel's conquest of Canaan in the Old Testament.[1] But this can be misleading. Technically it is correct, inasmuch as the term literally means the killing of a nation, and that is what Israel was commanded to do to the Canaanites (even if they manifestly did not actually carry it out fully). However, as used in the modern world, "genocide" goes along with vicious self-interest usually based on myths of racial superiority, and therefore it is sometimes also called "ethnic cleansing" (a euphemism if ever there was one—treating people like dirt). But the conquest of Canaan is *never* justified on ethnic grounds in the Bible, and any notions of ethnic superiority—moral or numerical—are resoundingly squashed in Deuteronomy, as we will see in a moment.

Nor is it right to argue, as some do, that there is an irreconcilable contradiction between Israel's celebration of their own release from oppression in Egypt and Israel's alleged oppression of the Canaanite nations a generation later. The action of Israel against the Canaanites is never placed in the category of oppression but of divine punishment operating through human agency.

The Wickedness of Canaanite Culture and Religion

As part of his covenant reassurance, God told Abraham that his descendants would possess the land of his temporary residence, but not immediately: "In the fourth generation your descendants will come back here, for *the sin of the Amorites has not yet reached its full measure*" (Gen. 15:16, my emphasis). What that last phrase means is that the Amorite/Canaanite society of Abraham's day was not yet so wicked as to morally justify God's acting in comprehensive judgment on it (as he was about to do, for example, on Sodom and Gomorrah). But that time would come. Eventually, the Canaanites would be so "fully" wicked that God's judgment would deservedly fall.

This interesting verse points to the justice of God, which Abraham totally believed in (see Gen. 18:25). All human beings and all nations are sinful in one way or another. But there are times when extremes of wickedness and degradation call down God's signal judgment, and there are times when God deems such action to be inappropriate or premature. God alone has such discernment. But God's words to Abraham indicate that judgment on the sin of the Canaanites still lay in the future, when it *would* be fully deserved.

Generations passed and Canaanite society did indeed fill up the pot of their sin. The degraded character of Canaanite society and religion is more explicitly described in moral and social terms in Leviticus 18:24–25; 20:22–24 and in Deuteronomy 9:5; 12:29–31. It includes the sexual promiscuity and perversion particularly associated with fertility cults as well as the callousness of child sacrifice. This is reinforced in the historical texts, with additional notes about social oppression and violence (1 Kings 14:24; 21:26; 2 Kings 16:3; 17:8; 21:2). Now if we take all these texts seriously as part of God's own explanation for the events that unfold in the book of Joshua, we cannot avoid their implications. The conquest was not human genocide. It was divine judgment.

The New Testament accepts the interpretation of the conquest that is so dominant in the Old–God's punishment of the wicked. Hebrews 11:31 describes the Canaanites as "those who were disobedient". This implies that the Canaanites had been morally aware of their sin but that they had chosen not to repent of it but to persist in it against the voice of their own consciences.

If we place the conquest of Canaan within the framework of punishment for wrongdoing, as the Bible clearly does, it makes a categorical difference to the nature of the violence inflicted. It does not make it less violent. Nor does it suddenly become "nice" or "OK". But it does make a difference. The consistent biblical affirmation that the conquest constituted an act of God's punishment on a wicked society, using Israel as the human agent, must be taken seriously by those who wish to take the Bible's own testimony seriously, and it must not be dismissed as self-serving disinfectant for the poison of Israel's own aggression. Punishment changes the moral context of violence. We can see this in other situations in life that involve violence at some level.

There is a huge moral difference between violence that is arbitrary or selfish and violence that is inflicted under strict control within the moral framework of punishment. This is true in human society as much as in divine perspective. Whatever our personal codes of parental discipline, there is surely a moral difference between a smack administered as punishment for disobedience and vicious or random child abuse. Similarly, there is a moral difference between the enforced captivity of someone imprisoned as punishment under due process of law for a defined criminal offence and the captivity of someone kidnapped as a hostage for no offence whatsoever.

The use of violence within a framework of justice and punishment may be problematic, but it is not simply indistinguishable from the use of violence in wantonly selfish, arbitrary, and malevolent ways. The fact that the Bible insists repeatedly that the violence of the conquest was inflicted as an act of punishment on a whole society puts it in a moral framework that must be differentiated from random or ethnocentric genocide. It does not make it "nice", but it does make it different.

The Conquest Did Not Mean That the Israelites Were Righteous

One of the strongest temptations in times of war is to demonize the enemy and placard your own side's righteousness. This is as true in modern times as ancient. It is all too easy to adopt the posture of the "knight in shining armour" and dress up the whole conflict in simplistic moral polarity as in Hollywood movies. If the enemies are "bad guys", then we must be "good guys". God knew that the Israelites would be tempted to fall into this kind of self-congratulation after they won their victories in Canaan, so he nipped it in the bud in Deuteronomy 9:

> After the LORD your God has driven them out before you, do not say to yourself, "The LORD has brought me here to take possession of this land because of my righteousness." No, it is on account of the wickedness of these nations that the LORD is going to drive them out before you. It is not because of your righteousness or your integrity that you are going in to take possession of their land; but on account of the wickedness of these nations, the LORD your God will drive them out before you, to accomplish what he swore to your fathers, to Abraham, Isaac and Jacob. Understand, then, that it is not because of your righteousness that the LORD your God is giving you this good land to possess, for you are a stiff-necked people."
>
> —Deuteronomy 9:4–6

The Israelites wanted to make a straightforward equation:

Our victory = our righteousness + the enemy's wickedness

But Moses says they've got the sum wrong. The Israelites would be right in their estimation of the Canaanites but utterly wrong in their estimation of themselves. The fact that God intended to use Israel as the agent of his punitive judgment on Canaan did not mean that the Israelites themselves were righteous. In fact, as Moses reminded them, their rebellions had made God angry enough to destroy *them* on more than one occasion (take a look at the rest of Deut. 9 for the evidence). So they had nothing to be proud and self-righteous about.

In later Old Testament history, turning the tables, God used Assyria and Babylon as agents of God's judgment on *Israel's* wickedness. But that did not make those nations righteous! Quite the opposite. Those nations would be condemned for their own wickedness.

God could and still can use the most deeply unjust nations as the agents of his own sovereign dispensing of historical justice in the international arena – and then deal with those nations too. This was the problem that Habakkuk wrestled with, and it still bothers us today. But the Bible asserts it. God can use one nation as a stick to punish another; but the stick he uses may itself be very bent.

But this brings us to a third point in relation to God's sovereign justice, and it is even more sharp.

God Threatened to Do the Same against Israel, and Did So

God warned the Israelites that if they behaved in the same way as the Canaanites, *God would treat Israel as his enemy* in the same terms as the Canaanites and inflict the same punishment on them using other nations (Lev. 18:28; Deut. 28:25 – 68). The land that had vomited out the Canaanites would be perfectly capable of doing the same with the Israelites, if they indulged in the same repulsive Canaanite practices. The same God who acted in moral judgment on Israel's enemies would act in precisely the same way on Israel. The Israelites needed to know (as do we) that the conquest was not some charade of cosy favouritism. Israel stood under the same threat of judgment from the same God for the same sins, if they chose to commit them.

But this was not left merely as a threat. In the course of Israel's long history in Old Testament times, God repeatedly did act in punitive judgment on Israel. And the language used to describe God's action on such occasions is exactly the same as the language of the conquest ("destroy", "drive out", "scatter", etc.). God thus demonstrated his moral consistency in international justice. It was not a matter of divine partiality (taking Israel's side no matter what). Quite the reverse: the Old Testament argues that Israel's status as God's elect people exposed them all the more to God's moral judgment and historical punishment than any of the surrounding nations, including those they conquered (cf. Ps. 78:59 – 64; Amos 3:2).

Indeed, we might point out that over the whole history of Old Testament Israel, far more generations of *Israelites* felt the judgment of God at the hands of their enemies than the single generation of *Canaanites* experienced the judgment of God at the hands of the Israelites.

And as has been mentioned, the conquest of Canaan stands in Scripture as one of those signal events that points to the final judgment (along with other catastrophes like the flood, Sodom and Gomorrah, the fall of Babylon, etc.). However, although the conquest may *point* to the final judgment, it was *not* the final judgment. It would be quite wrong to assume dogmatically that every Canaanite who perished automatically "went to hell". The story of Rahab, as we will see below, points strongly in another direction. God knows the hearts of all and his final judgment is discriminating, just, and merciful.

The Histories of Other Nations Also Directed by God

For many people there are probably two dimensions of the conquest narratives that most upset them and that they find hard to understand in relation to the God they know and love. One is the sheer horror of the bloodshed involved, as in any time of war. But the other is the fact that *God commanded it*. This is inescapable in Deuteronomy and the narratives.

As we have said above, it seems impossible to twist this into saying that Moses and Joshua thought up the whole grim scheme and then claimed God's support. We are well aware that political leaders sometimes do exactly that: plan an invasion and then claim to have God on their side. But as I have tried to explain, if we take that line, we make nonsense of a lot of the rest of the Old Testament (not just Deuteronomy and Joshua), and we part company with Jesus, Stephen, Paul, and the rest of the New Testament as far as we can tell, where the conquest is simply accepted in the way the Old Testament describes it: an act of God through human agents.

If we are troubled by the text saying that God commanded it, we have to ask: Would it actually make any difference theologically if there were no direct command of God in the text telling the Israelites to conquer Canaan, but he had simply allowed it to happen? Or would it make any difference if the driving out of the Canaanites had not been done by the Israelites at all, but by some other nation? After all, it is a central part of the biblical affirmation of God's sovereignty that *all things* happen in some way in accordance with his will—no matter who does them or whether he has given an explicit command or not. Nothing takes place outside the sphere of God's sovereign governance in the broadest sense.[2]

Deuteronomy, for example, in a much neglected chapter, puts Israel's driving out of the Canaanites on exactly the same footing as various other invasions and conquests that had taken place involving other nations in the region around the same time, and *it sees all of them as sovereignly managed by Yahweh, God of Israel.* This is clearly stated in Deuteronomy 2:10 – 12, 18 – 23, which is worth reading if you can cope with the unfamiliar names – indeed, precisely for that reason.

Actually, we are so unbothered by these statements about God driving out one bunch of foreigners at the hands of some other bunch of foreigners that some translations put these verses in parentheses! We read that God destroyed the Zamzummites by driving them out before the Ammonites, and we mutter, "Who? So what? Put that in brackets." But we read that God destroyed the Canaanites by driving them out before the Israelites and we exclaim, "*What? How terrible!* How could God *do* such a thing?"

Now we are not told that God *commanded* the Ammonites to drive out the Zamzummites, or that he *commanded* the descendants of Esau to drive out the Horites (Deut. 2:22), but the text makes it plain that these "drivings out" were as much the action of God as of the people who did them – just like the Israelites. Deuteronomy draws the comparison explicitly and intentionally. God is sovereign over the movements of *all* nations on the chessboard of history, and at one level, Israel's capture of Canaan is no different from these others, any more than their exodus from Egypt was any different from the migration of the Philistines from Crete or the Syrians from Kir, according to Amos 9:7. All of these are within the will of God – whether there are express commands or simply historical permission, so to speak.

So part of our difficulty may lie in the way the Old Testament makes little difference, as we seem theologically compelled to do, between the express or decretive will of God and the permissive will of God. That is to say, we affirm that all things happen within the sovereignty of God, but we find it necessary to distinguish conceptually between what God expressly wishes or effectively causes to happen and what he allows to happen, subject to his own final control. We have come to make that distinction as a necessary way of holding together all that the Bible itself affirms about the sovereign will of God being involved in all that happens. Stuff happens. And God is in the stuff, though we struggle to explain precisely how.

We are getting into deep water, which the greatest theological minds have never fully fathomed. But I hope we can at least see that merely reading that God *commanded* something does not put it into an essentially different box from what God *permitted* in all the other stories within the Old Testament, where it may appear that God stands back from the action and plays a less interventionist role (which is most often the case, actually). The whole biblical narrative, at every level, is an outworking in different ways of the sovereign providence of God in the complexities of human history.

The Framework of God's Plan of Salvation

We come to our third framework within which we need to place the conquest. We need to see it within the overall story of the Bible. The conquest of Canaan itself, of course, is a grim narrative of judgment and destruction. But it is part of the total Bible story, which is the story of salvation and ultimately a story of universal blessing. What light does that shed?

First of all, it reminds us that although the Bible contains stories of war, such as the conquest, it points toward God's ultimate plan, which is to bring peace among all nations and an end to war and all forms of violence. Second, when we trace the story back to Genesis, we recall that God's purpose declared to Abraham is to bring blessing to all nations. So we will look at how that long-term vision had some practical effects within the history and laws of Old Testament Israel in relation to foreigners. Finally, we must remember that the Old Testament points forward to God's accomplishing salvation for all nations through Jesus Christ and that this will be a cause for rejoicing among the nations, as indeed it has to be for us also, even if we struggle to understand the story that leads there.

The Vision of Peace

A major counterweight to the violence of the conquest is to hear a different voice within the Old Testament itself. It is the voice that condemns violence when it is the fruit of wickedness. This voice is heard early, when Jacob denounces his own sons Simeon and Levi for taking utterly disproportionate revenge (Gen. 34:30; 49:5–7). It is the voice that longs for an ending to all war and the coming reign of God's peace.

While the fact of war is acknowledged and while victory in war is seen as a gift of God (e.g., Pss. 18; 20), the excessive violence and bloodshed that are inevitable in wartime are critiqued. It was customary in the ancient world for conquering generals to honour the gods that had given them victory by building temples or statues of the gods in commemoration. The Old Testament narrative records that God had given David victory over his enemies. So David's desire to build a temple to his God might have been seen as the natural and expected outcome.

Yet we find the opposite. God unexpectedly blocks David from doing so, and among the reasons given was precisely the fact that he had been a man of war and bloodshed. The temple of Yahweh would not be built or characterized by such a life of violence (1 Chron. 28:3). The psalms complain regularly about violence, whether personal assault (Pss. 10; 59) or social oppression (37:12–15). Nations that readily resort to war and glory in it are also condemned (68:30). God's people are to trust in him for salvation, not in military muscle (33:16–19). At least one psalmist struggles with being a man of peace living in the midst of a war-hungry people (120:6–7)–a position believers often find themselves in.

Alongside such condemnation of the violence associated with injustice and oppression, there is the strong longing for an end to all war and the reign of God's peace. Psalm 46 looks forward to the day when God will make wars to cease to the end of the earth by abolishing all the weapons of war.

The same vision inspired Isaiah, who links this hope of an end to war with his promise of the coming of God's messianic king, who will reign over an era of cosmic peace between nations and between humanity and nature. Isaiah foresees all nations seeking justice under the government of God and needing neither to practise nor even to learn war anymore:

> He will judge between the nations
>   and will settle disputes for many peoples.
> They will beat their swords into plowshares
>   and their spears into pruning hooks.
> Nation will not take up sword against nation,
>   nor will they train for war anymore.

—Isaiah 2:4 (see also 9:2–7; 11:1–9)

War is part of the fallen world of violent human beings, but it will play no part in the new creation. War in the fallen world has also been part of God's international sovereignty, as an act of his historical justice (as the conquest is interpreted in the Bible), but even that too will be transcended. Peace, not war, is the mark of the reign of God. For the reign of God will mean the outpouring of God's Spirit and the triumph of righteousness and justice. As Isaiah foresaw, "the fruit of righteousness will be peace" (Isa. 32:17; cf. 32:1, 15–20). "Blessed," therefore, said Jesus, in harmony with this Old Testament perception, "are the peacemakers" (Matt. 5:9), along with those who hunger and thirst for justice and are persecuted for the sake of it.

Blessing the Nations

The second consideration to keep in mind when we put the conquest in a fully biblical framework is that it is part of a story that has as its ultimate goal the blessing of all nations. So important is this goal that Paul called it "the gospel in advance" (Gal. 3:8). It is the amazing good news that in a world characterized by the rebellion, sin, violence, corruption, and arrogance of Genesis 3–11, God still intends to bless all the nations on earth! That was his promise to Abraham in Genesis 12:3. So we have to see the whole story of Old Testament Israel as the first stage of that great project of God for world salvation.

In the Old Testament history of Israel there is a clear distinction between the people of Israel and the rest of the nations. Israel was the people whom God had chosen, called, redeemed, and brought into covenant relationship with himself. The nations did not yet enjoy that relationship. *But—and this is the utterly crucial point—the whole purpose of God in choosing Israel was so that the nations would eventually do so.* The overall thrust of the Old Testament is not Israel *against* the nations, but Israel *for the sake of* the nations.

There are many psalms and prophecies that speak about that, but we can look at two practical evidences of it: the conversion and inclusion of foreigners within Israel, and the care for foreigners in Israel's law. These provide interesting counter-testimony to the idea that Israel's only attitude to foreigners is the one we find in the story of the conquest.

However, before we turn to those positive angles, we have to face a difficulty that is probably already bubbling up in your mind: If God's plan was to bless the nations, then once again, what about the Canaanites? If Israel was supposed to be the means of God blessing the nations, how then could God use them to bring such suffering on the Canaanites? What we need to see is that the Bible feels no contradiction between the ultimate goal of universal blessing and historical acts of particular judgment.

It is important to see the blessing of the nations as God's *ultimate* (eschatological) purpose. It did not mean that God would therefore have to "be nice" to everybody or every nation, no matter how they behaved. The Old Testament makes it abundantly clear that God remains the moral judge of all human action and of all nations. God acts within history in judgment on the wicked, *including wicked nations*. As we have seen, that is how the conquest of Canaan is plainly interpreted in the Bible.

This was true for Israel as well. God's covenant promise of long-term blessing and protection did not prevent God from punishing particular generations of Israelites in their Old Testament history. So, God's ultimate purpose of blessing *all* nations does not eliminate his prerogative to act in judgment on *particular* nations within history, any more than parents' long-term and loving desire that their children should flourish prevents them from necessary acts of discipline or punishment in the meantime.

Conversion and Inclusion of Foreigners within Israel

It is amazing, and it cannot be accidental, that the opening narrative in the book of Joshua describes not a conquest but a conversion. The story of Rahab in Joshua 2 is prominent in position, length, and importance (see also 6:17, 22 – 25). Here is a Canaanite who recognizes the power of Yahweh, the God of the Israelites, as proved by the things she and her fellow Canaanites have heard about all he has done. But unlike the rest of the Canaanites, Rahab chooses not to resist this God and his people, but rather to change sides and put her trust in the first Israelites she meets.

This was not just a case of raw self-preservation. Rahab's words show a deeper theological awareness of the sovereignty of Yahweh in the exodus, in the gift of the land, and indeed over all creation. Rahab the Canaanite has come to believe what God spent a generation trying to teach the Israelites:

> [Rahab] said to [the spies], "I know that *the LORD has given this land to you* and that a great fear of you has fallen on us, so that all who live in this country are melting in fear because of you. We have heard how *the LORD dried up the water of the Red Sea for you when you came out of Egypt,* and what you did to Sihon and Og, the two kings of the Amorites east of the Jordan, whom you completely destroyed. When we heard of it, our hearts melted and everyone's courage failed because of you, for *the LORD your God is God in heaven above and on the earth below."*

> —Joshua 2:9 – 11 (my emphasis)

As a result, Rahab the Canaanite and her household are spared because she believed in Yahweh the God of Israel. Deuteronomy 7 makes it clear that the problem with the Canaanites was not ethnicity (which is why I dislike the word "genocide" with its ethnic overtones), but idolatry. Rahab shows that somebody who renounced the gods of Canaan and came to worship Yahweh the living God was spared. It also shows that there was a way for Canaanites to avoid the destruction, if they chose to. Were there other Canaanites who chose to believe in Yahweh, but didn't have Israelite spies dropping in to give their testimony to? Canaanite secret believers? We have no way of knowing of course, though we do know that some groups, like the Gibeonites, were spared and accepted into Israel and later even protected from other Canaanites – even though they had used deception to acquire that immunity (Josh. 9).

What we can say is that the very first Canaanite we meet in the narrative of the conquest of Canaan is a converted one who gets saved. And this story of conversion and salvation is so important that it is mentioned three times in the New Testament. Rahab enters into the genealogy of the Messiah (Matt.

1:5); she is included among the models of faith (Heb. 11:31); and she is held up as an example of proving faith by action (James 2:25).

Along with Rahab we can mention individuals like Ruth, who professes a conversion to the God of Israel that surpasses all others in the Old Testament for its rhetorical and emotional power (Ruth 1:16–17), Naaman (2 Kings 5, esp. v. 15), and the widow of Zarephath (1 Kings 17, esp. v. 24). All of these are foreigners who came to profess faith in Israel's God and receive his blessing, as Jesus controversially pointed out in his hometown (Luke 4:24–27).

Inclusion of foreigners was not merely for individuals. The Old Testament also points to the inclusion of whole peoples within the covenant people of God. This too can be very surprising. The Jebusites, for example, are regularly included among the standard list of nations in the land of Canaan that were supposed to be destroyed by Israel (e.g., Deut. 7:1). Yet they clearly were not destroyed in the original conquest, for even in Joshua's old age, we are told that "Judah could not dislodge the Jebusites, who were living in Jerusalem; to this day the Jebusites live there with the people of Judah" (Josh. 15:63).

It was David who eventually "dislodged" them when he finally captured Jerusalem, several centuries after Joshua (2 Sam. 5:6–10). But even then they were still not destroyed, but were rather absorbed into the tribe of Judah. The Jebusites seem to have moved from the "hit list" to the "home list" over the course of Israel's early history. From being among the nations destined for destruction, they came to be included within the covenant people as a clan in Judah.

This would be remarkable enough in its unpretentious way – another little piece of evidence that the conquest was not uniformly destructive and that not only individuals but whole peoples could change sides. However, the Jebusites feature once more in a far more powerful way, in a prophecy concerning – of all people – the Philistines. The prophet Zechariah, after describing God's judgment on the nations including the Philistines (Zech. 9:1–6), suddenly and surprisingly envisages a different future for the Philistines:

> It [Philistia] too shall be a remnant for our God;
>> it shall be like a clan in Judah,
>> and Ekron [a Philistine city] shall be *like the Jebusites.*

> —Zechariah 9:7 (NRSV, my emphasis).

The Philistines will have "a remnant" (a term normally associated with the saved remnant of Israel after judgment). And even the Philistines (historical archenemies of Israel) will come to be included within Judah itself as one of its clans—*just like the Jebusites, the original inhabitants of Jerusalem, no less!*

So the historical memory that the Jebusites had moved from being on the *herem* list of enemy nations before the conquest to being a clan within Judah living right in the city of David, is here used as a picture for what God's redeeming power can do for other enemy nations. What God had done for the Canaanite Jebusites, God could equally do for the Philistines! And if there is hope for the Philistines, there is hope for anybody. Psalm 87 caps this by including the Philistines and other historical enemies of Israel among those who will eventually be registered by God as native-born citizens of Zion. How much more included could you get?

Care for Foreigners in Old Testament Law

Another major counterbalance to the destruction of the Canaanites in the conquest narrative is the strength of practical concern for foreigners that is enshrined in Old Testament law. Many foreigners (whether former Canaanite population or immigrants) assimilated and became "resident aliens". But generally foreigners were vulnerable, because they lacked the natural protections of family and land. There was a strongly positive concern for their well-being and protection.

What did the Old Testament law have to offer such foreigners? A great deal. If you take time to read through the texts below, I think you will be impressed with an ethos that strongly modifies what we might think if we only read the conquest narratives. The Old Testament speaks of protection from general oppression (Ex. 22:21; Lev. 19:33) and from unfair treatment in court (Ex. 23:9; Deut 10:17–19; 24:17–18); inclusion in Sabbath rest (Ex. 20:9–11; 23:12; Deut. 5:12–15) and inclusion in worship and covenant ceremonies of Passover (Ex. 12:45–49), the annual festivals (Deut. 16), the Day of Atonement (Lev. 16:29), and covenant renewal ceremonies (Deut. 29:10–13; 31:12); the economic benefit of the triennial tithes (Deut. 14:28–29; 26:12–13) and access to agricultural produce (gleaning rights) (Lev. 19:9–10; Deut. 24:19–22); and equality before the law with native-born (Lev. 19:34).

Binding all such practical legislation together is the simple command, given twice: *love the foreigner*. In Deuteronomy, this command is based on the example of God himself. Yahweh is characterized by his practical love for the needy foreigner—a character trait that Israel knew well from their exodus experience:

> He defends the cause of the fatherless and the widow, and loves the foreign-
> ers residing among you, giving them food and clothing. And *you are to love
> those who are foreigners*, for you yourselves were foreigners in Egypt.
>
> —Deuteronomy 10:18–19 (my emphasis)

In Leviticus, the same command mirrors the earlier command in the same chapter to "love your neighbour as yourself" (Lev. 19:18).

> The foreigners residing among you must be treated as your native–born.
> *Love them as yourself*, for you were foreigners in Egypt. I am the LORD your God.
>
> —Leviticus 19:34 (my emphasis)

So there is a powerful pulse of legislative energy in Israel's law that is positively favourable and protective toward foreigners in their midst. Now of course this does not remove or even reduce the violence that we find in the narrative of the conquest. But it does show a counterbalancing force within the legal custom of Israel. And that in turn shows that the conquest was seen as a limited historical necessity, not as an ongoing paradigm for social attitudes or behaviour within Israel toward foreigners in general. When Paul told Christians to "practise the love of strangers", he was drawing on strong scriptural roots.[3] Hebrews 13:1–2 has a similar exhortation, with clear Old Testament allusion as precedent. There *philoxenia* is put right alongside *philadelphia* (love for brother/sister).

The Praise of the Nations

Finally, the third element in this "whole Bible framework" is to look to the ultimate future that the Bible envisages for the nations. What does God have in mind for the nations, as you read the Old Testament? Judgment, comes the answer, very quickly. Yes, but the same is true for Israel. Indeed, what is more prominent in the Old Testament than God's words of warning, threat, and then actual judgment on the covenant people themselves? The Old Testament is simply stuffed with the reality of judgment – *on Israel.* But beyond that judgment of Israel lay the indestructible hope that God would be faithful to his promise to them and once more bring them salvation and restoration.

And that same hope and promise is held out for the nations. God promised Abraham that through his descendants all nations on earth would be blessed, and that is the promise that drives the whole drama of the Bible toward its great climax in Revelation. So, just as Israel went through the purging fire of God's judgment but held on to his promise of ultimate restoration, so the nations will be sifted by the judgment of God, but there will be people from every nation who will be included within the redeemed humanity that God is already creating in Christ. His goal is that the new creation will be populated by people drawn from all the nations he has made. The quantity of biblical texts that affirm this is enormous, and it is rather scandalous that so many Christians are quite unaware of this great plan of God for the nations.[4]

Here is only the briefest outline summary of God's plans for the nations. It is worth pausing to take the time to read this sample of texts. They are amazing in their scope and vision.

- The nations will benefit from the Abrahamic blessing of Israel (Ps. 67).
- The nations will come to worship the living God (Pss. 22:27–28; 86:8–10; 102:15, 21–22; 138:4–5; 145:10–12; Isa. 2:1–5; 12:4–5; 42:10–12; 45:6, 14, 22–25).
- The nations will be included *within* Israel as the extended people of God. As such, they will be
  - registered in God's city (Ps. 87).
  - blessed with God's salvation (Isa. 19:16–25).
  - accepted in God's house (Isa. 56:3–8).
  - called by God's name (Amos 9:11–12).
  - joined with God's people (Zech. 2:10–12).

One text I have deliberately left to the end is Psalm 47. The reason for singling it out is that it specifically mentions the conquest of the Canaanites, *but it includes even that as a cause for praise among the nations themselves.*

> Clap your hands, all you nations;
> shout to God with cries of joy.
> For the LORD Most High is awesome,
> the great King over all the earth.
> *He subdued nations under us,*
> *peoples under our feet.*
> He chose our inheritance for us,
> the pride of Jacob, whom he loved.
>
> —Psalm 47:1–4 (my emphasis)

The writer of this psalm calls the nations to join in applause to Yahweh, God of Israel. Clapping is a form of physical and audible thanksgiving that goes beyond words. People clap because something has brought them pleasure or benefit, and they are grateful. What, then, does our psalmist invite the nations of the world to give a round of applause to Yahweh for?

The answer at first sight seems perverse (see v. 3):

> —*He [Yahweh] subdued nations under us [Israel],*
>   *peoples under our feet.*

The nations are being asked to clap to Yahweh because he is the God who defeated them through Israel! Is the psalm nothing more than military cynicism masquerading as worship? The only alternative to reading it in that way is to discern a deeper theological conviction about the meaning of the conquest.

The nations can be summoned to applaud Yahweh because even the historical defeat of the Canaanites by Israel will ultimately be seen to be *part of an overall history of salvation* for which the nations themselves will praise God. This means that we must read the single story of the conquest of Canaan within the larger story that will ultimately lead to all nations having cause to praise and thank God for the salvation he accomplished in Christ.

Canaanite culture at that point in history was degraded to the point of deserving divine judgment, as we saw. But the God who acted in historical judgment on them was also "the great King over all the earth". And when this great King takes up his reign, then *all* the nations will be the beneficiaries. Ultimately, then, the history of Israel, including even the conquest, will be the subject of praise among the nations, for whose saving benefit it happened. Deuteronomy 32:43, along with its use by Paul in Romans 15:7 – 12, points in the same direction.

Conclusion – the Road to Calvary

This thought brings me to a final reflection. As I struggle to understand God in relation to this nasty part of biblical history, I have to ask myself where I stand.

As I read Psalm 47, where do I find myself? I am not an ancient Israelite like its original author and hearers. Neither am I a Canaanite, one of the conquered nations of verse 3. But I do stand as an Irish believer among the redeemed from all the nations. I am among those who are summoned to clap my hands and give praise to Yahweh the God of Israel, the great King, the LORD Most High, and the God and Father of our Lord Jesus Christ. In that sense, because I am in Christ, I too am part of "the people of the God of Abraham" (Ps. 47:9; cf. Gal. 3:29).

For this history is part of the story of my salvation. This is *my* story; this is *my* song. This is the way in which God in his sovereignty chose to work within human history to accomplish his saving purpose for humanity and for creation, including me. I may not understand why it had to be this way. I certainly do not like it. I may deplore the violence and suffering involved, even when I accept the Bible's verdict that it was an act of warranted judgment. I may wish there had been some other way.

But at some point I have to stand back from my questions, criticism, or complaint and receive the Bible's own word on the matter. What the Bible unequivocally tells me is that this was an act of God that took place within an overarching narrative through which the only hope for the world's salvation was constituted.

Within that overall biblical perspective, the road to Canaan was one small stretch along the road to Calvary. From that point of view, I cannot do other than include it among the mighty acts of God for which all his people are called to praise him. I have to read the conquest in the light of the cross.

And when I do set it in the light of the cross, I see one more perspective. For the cross too involved the most horrific and evil human violence, which, at the same time, also constituted the outpouring of God's judgment on human sin. The crucial difference, of course, is that, whereas *at the conquest, God poured out his judgment on a wicked society who deserved it, at the cross, God bore on himself the judgment of God on human wickedness, through the person of his own sinless Son—who deserved it not one bit.*

As we draw this part to a close, note once again that humble submission to the biblical teaching on the sovereignty of God on the one hand, along with robust reflection on the mystery of the cross of Christ on the other, combine to strengthen our faith in the midst of things we do not understand. We will find the same thing as we move on to the next part to contemplate the cross itself.

Notes

1. As, for example, in Stanley N. Gundry, ed., *Show Them No Mercy: Four Views on God and Canaanite Genocide* (Grand Rapids: Zondervan, 2003).
2. I was started on this train of thought by an arresting comment of John Wenham: "Christians would find no great difficulty with the overthrow of the Canaanites had it taken place at the hands of their heathen neighbours" (*The Goodness of God* [Leicester: Intervarsity Press, 1974], 137).
3. The traditional translation of Romans 12:13, "practise *hospitality*", is too weak for the word Paul chose—*philoxenia,* which literally means "love of the stranger, the outsider". It is the diametric opposite of xenophobia.

4. I have explored this in considerable depth in my book *The Mission of God* (Downers Grove, IL: InterVarsity Press, 2006), ch. 14, and I cannot repeat all that detail here. The summary in the text gives some of the gist of it.

PART THREE

What about the Cross?

Are you perhaps surprised to find chapters on the cross in a book about "The God I Don't Understand"? "If this fellow doesn't understand the cross," you may be thinking, "how can he even be a Christian?" Well, you may remember that in the introduction I untangled several senses in which I am talking about not understanding. I pointed out that to say that there are things I don't fully understand about God is not the same thing as saying that I don't know God and that I don't love and trust him with all my being. I could make the same point talking about my wife, after all. I've known and loved her almost all my life (we were teenage sweethearts), but I doubt if I will ever fully understand her, and she would doubtless return the compliment (if that's what it is!).

I also pointed out that there are some things that I don't understand about God that leave me grieved or disturbed, and we have wrestled with some of those in parts 1 and 2. But there are other things that I don't understand, but I could not live without them, and they fill my heart and soul with immense gratitude, joy, and peace. That is where I put the cross of Christ.

I understand enough on the basis of what the Bible tells me to know that I owe everything I am now or ever will be to the love and grace of God supremely poured out at Calvary. But when I probe into why and how that is so, I join the multitudes who recognize depths and mysteries here that lie beyond our understanding – but not beyond our faith, praise, and worship.

After I was ordained in the Church of England I was asked during my first year of ministry in Tonbridge Parish Church to conduct the Three Hour Service on Good Friday. This traditional event in some Anglican churches was daunting enough for a young assistant pastor. But I treasured the privilege of preparing and leading it. My dog-eared notes still remind me of how I broke the time up into thinking about the cross and history, the cross and the universe, and the cross and us. Each hour included three sessions of Bible reading and meditation, some hymns, moving poems, and simple silence.

Over several decades of teaching ministry, I have lectured and preached on all kinds of subjects, Bible books, and themes. But it has always been true, and still is, that nothing gives me a greater sense of privilege, joy, and responsibility than preaching about the cross, and especially the simple Gospel narratives of it.

So, while it is true to say that I don't fully understand it, it is also true that of all the things my head doesn't understand about God, this is the one in which my heart delights most. This is the one that outweighs in positive glory everything else that puzzles me with negative problems. I pray that by the time we reach the end of this part of the book, you will be able to join me in that.

chapter

THE CROSS – WHY AND WHAT?

As I ponder the cross, three fundamental questions sum up our struggle to understand it: Why? What? and How? Why did God ever consider sending Jesus to die on the cross? Why was it necessary from our point of view? Why was he willing to do it, from his point of view? And then, What did God actually accomplish through the death of his Son? What was it all for? And finally, How did it work? How did one man's bleeding body stretched on two pieces of wood for six hours of torture and death on a particular Friday one spring outside a city in a remote province of the Roman Empire change everything in the universe? How did the cross of Christ accomplish all that the Bible tells us it did?

In this chapter we will take up the Why and the What. Then in chapter 7 we will ponder the How. That will lead us on in chapter 8 to an exploration of Paul's phrase that Christ died "according to the Scriptures", for that is primarily where our understanding must come from.

As in previous chapters, my hope is that while accepting there are things we *cannot* understand, we will at least be able to think a little more clearly about things we *should* understand – things that are often in danger of getting confused by false and unbiblical notions or popular caricatures of the truth. So my purpose is both to remove some false ideas as well as to do my best to explain what the Bible teaches clearly, without trying to give answers where the Bible itself seems to withhold them.

Struggling to Understand Why

"Why me?" We are used to hearing these words on the agonized lips of people who have suffered some terrible tragedy or accident. But they are just as much at home on the lips of those who have received some outstanding or undeserved blessing. "I don't deserve this!" can be a response to bad news or good news, and be equally true in both cases.

When we extend the question and ask it on behalf of the human race in relation to the good news of what God has done for us through the death of his Son Jesus Christ, it becomes even more impossible to answer. *Why us?* I sometimes picture the angels that surround God's throne shaking their celestial heads in amazement as they ponder two extreme facts that go beyond any comprehension: on the one hand (or wing), the utter degradation of the human race on this polluted planet, and on the other hand the terrible extremity of suffering that their Lord chose to endure for the sake of saving such appalling creatures. *Why them?* Charles Wesley had the same thought.

> —*In vain the first-born seraph tries*
> *To sound the depths of love divine.*
> *'Tis mercy all! Let earth adore,*
> *Let angel minds inquire no more.*[1]

Who are we, after all? What are we?

We are the creatures whom God has made in his own image, to love him, to love one another, and to care for the earth he put us in. Instead, we have used the capabilities inherent in bearing that image to deface it and to dethrone the one whose image it is. We reject God's authority, distrust God's Word, mock God's love, break God's laws, and trash God's world. In the process, we deceive, cheat, exploit, brutalize, crush, and kill one another.

We twist everything God made good, and we think good what God calls evil. We bless what God has cursed and curse what God has blessed. We boast of our moral autonomy as free rational individuals but languish in the bondage of collective craziness. We claim to have no need of God, yet we slavishly grovel at the feet of more idols and gods than we even recognize as being what they are. And that is just the faintest whisper of what we are, multiplied several billion-fold and by as many generations as there have been since Cain and Abel.

Yet Jesus died for us! God sent his Son into the world to save sinners! Hallelujah, *but why?* Why Bethlehem? Why Calvary?

Because God loves us!

This, of course, is the right answer. Right, biblical, true, terrific.

And totally inexplicable.

"God so loved the world that he gave his one and only Son …" (John 3:16). We know the most famous verse in the Bible so well that we can easily lose the awesome surprise of its truth. We sing our songs about the cross, with perhaps more familiarity than is good for us.

> —*Inscribed upon the cross we see,*
> *In shining letters, "God is love";*
> *He bears our sins upon the tree,*
> *He brings us mercy from above.*[2]

Yes, but *why* did God love us? This question was asked long before Jesus died on the cross. For the love of God is one of the strongest affirmations of the Old Testament, and it was just as baffling back then. Let's spend some time thinking about God's love in the Old Testament. It's always worth doing that! It will not *answer* the question Why? But it will certainly deepen it. And it will prepare us for chapter 8, where we discuss some important ways in which the Old Testament helps understand the cross. So come with me back to the Old Testament and the God of love we find there.

Why Did God Love the Old Testament Israelites?

Deuteronomy has a lot to say about God's love and about loving God back. It was clearly at the core of Israel's faith. But while every reason and motivation is given to encourage Israel to love God, nothing is ever explained as to any possible motive for why God loved Israel other than his own character and faithfulness. Deuteronomy ruthlessly corrects any false assumptions that the Israelites might have been tempted to make about the "Why?" of God's love. These are all assumptions that are still around today. Here are some of those false ideas.

Perhaps God loved the Israelites because they were a rather important people? Not a bit of it, says Moses. Israel was a mere tadpole among the big fish. Most of the big nations wouldn't even have known they were there at all.

> The LORD did not set his affection on you and choose you because you were more numerous than other peoples, for you were the fewest of all peoples. But it was because the LORD loved you and kept the oath he swore to your ancestors that he brought you out with a mighty hand and redeemed you from the land of slavery, from the power of Pharaoh king of Egypt.
>
> —Deuteronomy 7:7–8

Do you notice the circularity in that statement? "God did not love you because you were great." "Why did he love us, then?" "Because he loved you …" God loved you because God loved you. Period. You cannot go further back than that. God's love is axiomatic. That is, it is the starting point of all explanation, not something that can itself be explained by anything above or behind it.

Perhaps God loved them because he was, after all, their special Israelite god? Wasn't Yahweh their own national deity, whose job and duty it was to love and care for them? That's what national gods are for. A friend of mine in the United States told me how, in the days after 9/11 when posters and bumperstickers declaring "God bless America" appeared everywhere (was it a prayer or a boast?), someone turned up at their church in a car with a bumper-sticker saying, "God bless the rest of the world too." Apparently they weren't popular. Unpatriotic, they were told. God belongs to us, so we're the ones he's got to love and protect.

Not a bit of it, says Moses. God is universal, the God of the whole earth, the owner of every nation upon it. So why on earth he loved you Israelites of all people is a mystery, even though it's true. It should be a matter of repentant humility, not national pride.

> To the LORD your God belong the heavens, even the highest heavens, the earth and everything in it. *Yet* the LORD set his affection on your ancestors and loved them, and he chose you, their descendants, above all the nations – as it is today. Circumcise your hearts, therefore, and do not be stiff-necked any longer.

> —Deuteronomy 10:14–16 (my emphasis)

Or perhaps God loved the Israelites because they were a bit more righteous than the rest of the nations? Again, not a bit of it, says Moses. The fact is, Israel was a stubborn bunch of rebels from the start and rarely changed much throughout their history, except to get worse. So if they thought they were God's special favourites they were dead wrong – so wrong that God corrects the idea repeatedly.

> After the LORD your God has driven [the nations] out before you, do not say to yourself, "The LORD has brought me here to take possession of this land because of my righteousness." No, it is on account of the wickedness of these nations that the LORD is going to drive them out before you. It is not because of your righteousness or your integrity that you are going in to take possession of their land.

> —Deuteronomy 9:4–6

I have been an Old Testament teacher almost all my professional life, and I cannot count the number of times I get asked something along the lines of, "What was so special about the Jews that God chose them and not some other nation?" And my answer is always: "Nothing. Absolutely, definitively, unequivocally, nothing at all." This is not the expected answer, and so it usually leads to some protest or additional questioning. Surely there must have been some reason, right? So I turn to these ruthless texts of Deuteronomy for support. The love of God for Israel was motivated only from within God's own self, not by anything in the Israelites—numerical or moral. He loved them because he loved them, for reasons known only to himself.

Now you may wonder why I am placing so much stress on the mysterious and unexplained love of God for Old Testament Israel. What about the rest of humanity? Ah, but that is the very point. God's love and choice of *Israel*, in and through Abraham, was the opening phase of his loving plan for *all humanity*.

God loved Israel, not because they stood out as *better* than the rest of humanity, but precisely in spite of the fact that they exemplified (and amplified) all that is *worst* about humanity in general. The prophets told them so again and again. Far from being any better than surrounding nations, said Ezekiel, the people of Judah had sunk below the level of even the worst nations they could think of in their proverbial taxonomy of wickedness—Sodom and Gomorrah.

> As surely as I live, declares the Sovereign LORD, your sister Sodom and her daughters never did what you and your daughters have done.
> Now this was the sin of your sister Sodom: She and her daughters were arrogant, overfed and unconcerned; they did not help the poor and needy. They were haughty and did detestable things before me. Therefore I did away with them as you have seen.... You have done more detestable things than they, and have made your sisters seem righteous by all these things you have done.... Because your sins were more vile than theirs, they appear more righteous than you.

> —Ezekiel 16:48–52

So the persistent love of God for Israel, carrying them from one generation to another for all the centuries of their ingratitude, rejection, and disobedience, concentrates in one story the much larger story of the love of God for the human race for all the generations of their rebellious ways. And it was that love of God for the world that would ultimately lead him to the cross.

Thus, the sense of mystery and surprise carries over from the one (God's love for Israel) to the other (God's love for the world). This link between Old Testament Israel and the rest of humanity in the redeeming plan of God is a crucial part of the way the Bible portrays the atonement, so we must bear it in mind later when we think about the "How" of the cross. For the moment it is enough to remember that the way God in his patient love bore the sins of

Israel is a historical microcosm of the way God, in his infinite love, bore the sins of the world on the cross. Why he did either is at the very heart of the mystery that "God is love".

Surprised by Love

Those who know God best seem the most surprised by the undeserved generosity of his love. David was literally floored by it. When God made his great promise to David and his descendants (which Ps. 89:1–3 celebrates twice as an action of God's great love), David sat down in utter amazement and said, in effect, "God, I don't understand you! Why me?"

"Then King David went in and sat before the Lord, and he said: 'Who am I, Sovereign Lord, and what is my family, that you have brought me this far?'" (2 Sam. 7:18). *"Who am I?"* This, I suggest, is the right and healthy response to the outpouring of God's love. David was rather fond of it (see 1 Chron. 29:14–15).

We will never understand why God has chosen to love us, other than the revealed truth that God is love. It is simply and essentially God's character and nature to love. That states the truth, but it doesn't explain it. Or rather, it does not explain it in relation to anything that we can state about ourselves, other than that we are the creation of this God whose being is defined by love. The love of God is generated and motivated within God's own being, just as the light and warmth of the sun that we feel on planet Earth is generated within the sun itself and owes nothing to anything the earth or its inhabitants can do – other than to be orbiting within reach. No wonder Jesus used the sun as an image for the love of God (Matt. 5:43–45).

Who am I? Who are we? There is an awesome mystery about the self-sacrificing love of God for us.

> *My song is love unknown:*
> *My Saviour's love to me;*
> *Love to the loveless shown,*
> *That they may lovely be.*
> *O who am I, that for my sake,*
> *My Lord should take frail flesh and die?*[3]

The fact that we cannot fathom the "Why?" should lead to an underlying gratitude, constantly tinged with surprise, every time we ponder the depths of the love of God that led to Calvary.

They say that some people walk around the place in a bubble of entitlement. That is, they think the world and everybody around them owes them something, and they jump to assert their rights if the bubble is pricked. I feel that I walk around under a rainbow of gratitude. Whatever life brings, nothing can top the unbelievable love of God and his constant mercy, goodness, and eternal saving grace. Such gratitude is a richly cleansing, calming, refreshing emotion. Indeed it is more than an emotion. It is a whole worldview, a whole philosophy of life, the universe, and everything, for it is the only proper response to the very being of God, that he is love, amazing love.

> *Died he for me, who caused his pain?*
> *For me, who Him to death pursued?*
> *Amazing love! How can it be*
> *That Thou, my God, shouldst die for me!*[4]

This is a dimension of the God I don't understand that leads to overwhelming thankfulness, counterbalancing those dimensions of nonunderstanding that lead to overwhelming grief or anger that we pondered in Part 1.

Struggling to Understand What

What happened at the cross? At one level, the New Testament offers us the narrative of the cross itself, clear and profound in all four Gospels. But it is also summarized by Paul (or an even earlier creed that he is quoting): "For what I received I passed on to you as of first importance: that Christ died for our sins according to the Scriptures, that he was buried, that he was raised on the third day according to the Scriptures" (1 Cor. 15:3–4).

And it is captured in the childlike simplicity of Cecil Frances Alexander's hymn:

> *There is a green hill far away*
> *Outside a city wall*
> *Where the dear Lord was crucified*
> *Who died to save us all.*
> *We may not know, we cannot tell*
> *What pains he had to bear;*
> ***But we believe it was for us***
> *He hung and suffered there.* (my emphasis)

Dimensions of Sin and Atonement

At another level, the New Testament then goes on to tell us all that God has accomplished for us by this single act. Now already, in Part 1, we have thought about the cosmic achievement of the cross. That is to say, the death of Christ was the climactic victory of God that achieved the ultimate defeat of Satan and spells the final destruction of all that is evil in the universe. And in Part 4 we will see that our wonderful future certainty of the new creation is also founded on the cross and resurrection of Jesus Christ. These are the great comprehensive, universal realities that the cross has achieved for the whole creation. We must never reduce the cross only to the small scale of our own individual salvation. Personal salvation is but one infinitely precious dimension of the total work of God's redemption of his whole creation.

In this section we are concentrating on the cross in relation to ourselves – as human sinners – and the atonement that the Bible tells us God achieved for us through the death of Christ. The New Testament has so many ways of telling us about that, and the list is breathtaking. It is hard just to touch on each point without ending in tears of thankful praise.

The effect of sin on each human person and on all human beings together is comprehensively described in the Bible, and the extent of what God accomplished for us on the cross is correspondingly extensive. It is so extensive, in fact, that it is impossible to describe in only one way. So the Bible uses several different metaphors to express the infinite reality of the atonement. These are all different ways of looking at the same fundamental thing.

However, it is important not to think or speak of these as "*just* metaphors" – as if they were not referring to something real. A metaphor is a way of trying to communicate what one thing is like by reference to something else that we are familiar with. If I say, "The president is a lame duck", my metaphor means he has become weak and vulnerable. I don't mean he isn't really the president at all. Metaphors help us to *grasp* some reality and focus on some dimension of its importance or significance.

The atonement is a great, cosmic *reality* – an achievement of God that stands as the greatest truth in the universe. But the breadth and depth of that atonement is greater than can be captured in a single way. We have to look at this massive reality from many different angles. That's what the New Testament does through its various metaphors and what theologians do as they try to explain the atonement.

Here are some of the ways that the Bible clearly teaches that human beings are in desperate need, and the corresponding ways in which the cross meets those needs. For the moment, we merely list these. In chapter 8 we will need to think about some of them a little more deeply, where they are open to misunderstanding.

Coming Home

Sin leads us away from God. Like Cain, we wander off into our own wilder-nesses, cut off from God and feeling increasingly separated from the good-ness, joy, peace, and fulfilment that were meant to be part of being human in God's world. *Alienation and exclusion* are among the most painful things that anybody has to bear, and at a fundamental level sin imposes them on all human beings. We are cut off and excluded from God, apart from his grace. But through the cross, *God brings us home.* Using the Old Testament story, Paul tells Gentile believers that in contrast to being far away from God and his saving work, they have now been brought right into it.

> Therefore, remember that formerly ... you were separate from Christ, excluded from citizenship in Israel and foreigners to the covenants of the prom-ise, without hope and without God in the world. But now in Christ Jesus you who once were far away have been brought near through the blood of Christ.... Consequently, you are no longer foreigners and strangers, but fellow citizens with God's people and members of God's household.
>
> —Ephesians 2:11–13, 19

Mercy

Our sinful rebellion against God's love incurs God's *anger,* which does not for a moment mean any cessation in his love, for love is God's very being and nature. All of us, says Paul, Jew and Gentile, stand under that anger of God, which is both a present and a future reality (as in "the wrath to come"). But because of God's own action through Christ at the cross, he has made us recipients of his *mercy and kindness.*

> Like the rest, we were by nature deserving of wrath. But because of his great love for us, God, who is rich in mercy, made us alive with Christ even when we were dead in transgressions – it is by grace you have been saved ... expressed in his kindness to us in Christ Jesus.
>
> —Ephesians 2:3–7

Redemption

Sin puts us into *slavery,* a bondage from which we need to be released. But *redemption* always comes at a cost. God chose to bear that cost himself in the self-giving of his Son, who came "to give his life as a ransom for many" (Mark 10:45). In him, therefore, we have "redemption through his blood, the forgive-ness of sins" (Eph. 1:7). The cross spells freedom and release for captives.

This aspect of the achievement of the cross (redemption) is linked to the earlier point about God's victory over evil itself. Whatever evil is and whatever the source and nature of its terrible enslaving power, God in Christ has dealt it the fatal blow that will ultimately destroy it forever. In that great victory of God lies our rescue, our redemption – modelled for us in the Old Testament in the exodus story when God delivered the Israelites from the oppression of Pharaoh in Egypt.

Forgiveness

We have offended God personally and relationally. A *broken relationship* can only be mended when there is *forgiveness* given and accepted. That too is costly, for the offended one who chooses to forgive chooses to bear the pain and cost of the offence rather than hold it against the one being forgiven. The New Testament always links the forgiveness that God offers us to the cross of Christ, for that is where God himself bore the cost of our offence against his love. The broken relationship can be healed, but only because God chooses to "bear" the offence, to carry it with all its pain and cost in himself through Christ, and not hold it against us. The earliest preaching of the cross and resurrection of Jesus in Acts twice presents the forgiveness of sins as the primary result of repentance and faith in the crucified Christ (Acts 2:23 – 24, 38; 3:15 – 19).

Reconciliation with God

Sin makes us *enemies of God*. There needs to be *reconciliation* in order to remove that enmity. That too was part of the accomplishment of the cross.

> For if, while we were God's enemies, we were reconciled to him through the death of his Son, how much more, having been reconciled, shall we be saved through his life! Not only is this so, but we also rejoice in God through our Lord Jesus Christ, through whom we have now received reconciliation.
>
> —Romans 5:10 – 11

Elsewhere, Paul makes it clear again that this act of reconciliation was not a cheap cover-up. It involved Christ identifying himself with our sin in his death in such a way that God no longer counts our sin against us and thus enables reconciliation to take place.

> All this is from God, who reconciled us to himself through Christ and gave us the ministry of reconciliation: that God was reconciling the world to himself in Christ, not counting people's sins against them.... God made him who had no sin to be sin for us, so that in him we might become the righteousness of God.
>
> —2 Corinthians 5:18 – 21

Reconciliation with One Another

Sin also makes us *enemies with each other*. After the fall, humanity explodes with enmities on all sides—right from the story of Cain and Abel. By the time of the New Testament, even the necessary distinction between God's people Israel and the Gentile nations had also turned into one of enmity. This was the great barrier between Jews and Gentiles, symbolized in the clean and unclean food regulations.

But God's plan of salvation, first promised to Abraham, extended to all nations. So eventually the barrier between Jews and Gentiles must also be destroyed. And that is exactly what the cross accomplished. Three times Paul uses the word "peace" in a short passage in Ephesians that describes this process. Christ *is* our peace; Christ has *made* peace; and Christ came and *preached* peace—and all of this is through the cross. So, a powerful part of the message of the cross is not just that it turns us from being enemies of God into his friends, *it also enables human enemies to be reconciled* to each other, through Christ.

> But now in Christ Jesus you who once were far away have been brought near through the blood of Christ. For he himself is our peace, who has made the two one and has destroyed the barrier, the dividing wall of hostility, by setting aside in his flesh the law with its commands and regulations. His purpose was to create in himself one new humanity out of the two, thus making peace, and in this one body to reconcile both of them to God through the cross, by which he put to death their hostility. He came and preached peace to you who were far away and peace to those who were near. For through him we both have access to the Father by one Spirit.
>
> —Ephesians 2:13–18

Justification

Sin makes us *guilty* before God and deserving of God's punishment. At the cross God took that guilt and punishment on himself in the person of his own Son. For "the LORD has laid on him the iniquity of us all" (Isa. 53:6), and "Christ himself bore our sins in his own body on the tree" (1 Peter 2:24). We thus stand before God *not* guilty, in the *righteousness* of Christ. Because of the cross we are justified and declared righteous; that is, we are put right with God and no longer face the painful consequences of our sin. We become "the righteousness of God" (2 Cor. 5:21).

Cleansing

Sin makes us *dirty*. Uncleanness in the Old Testament was a state in which it was impossible to come into the presence of God. Among the effects of the blood of animal sacrifices in Old Testament Israel was the removal of uncleanness and ability of a person to come back into fellowship with God and the assembly of his people. The New Testament speaks of the *cleansing* power of the sacrificial blood of Christ—which is one aspect of calling him "the Lamb of God".

> The blood of Jesus, his Son, cleanses us from all sin.... If we confess our sins, he is faithful and just and will forgive us our sins and cleanse us from all unrighteousness.... He is the atoning sacrifice for our sins, and not only for ours but also for the sins of the whole world.
>
> —1 John 1:7–2:2 (NRSV)

New Life

Death is the great invader and enemy of human life in God's world. Since the garden of Eden, we have been subject to death, both physically and spiritually. That is, not only do we die physically, but we are also spiritually dead in sin, cut off from the life of God (Eph. 2:1). So we need God to deal with the reality of death in its fullest sense—for it is obvious that we can do nothing about it ourselves.

And this too is what God accomplished and offers us through the cross. For by Christ's death he broke "the power of him who holds the power of death—that is, the devil" (Heb. 2:14). The cross thus also becomes the gateway to new life, that is, into the resurrection life of Christ, which is the life of God. "God, who is rich in mercy, *made us alive* with Christ even when we were dead in transgressions—it is by grace you have been saved" (Eph. 2:4–5, my emphasis).

What a catalogue of salvation! Because of the cross, the Bible tells us, we can be transformed from being wanderers, rebels, guilty offenders, slaves of sin, enemies of God and one another, filthy, and spiritually dead into being at home with God, under the smile of his mercy and pardon, rescued from captivity, at peace with God and former enemies, washed clean, and alive for all eternity.

Do any of these wonderful portraits of salvation have special meaning for you? Of course, every single aspect of the atonement brings unique joys and relief and can be particularly meaningful in different ways for us. I love them all, as we all should, for they are essential dimensions of the truth. They are not there for us to pick and choose our favourites and ignore the others. We need to grasp all that God has done for us with both hands of grateful faith and love.

Nevertheless, while believing and rejoicing in all these great truths, I have found that the cleansing power of the cross is especially precious. It is wonderful to know that God has forgiven my sin; it is somehow even more stunning to know that he has washed it all away like dirt in a warm bath. I'm a man, of course. They say that 90 percent of men have problems with lust, and the other 10 percent are lying. I don't know if it is a form of temptation that ever gets any less with age (not so far, is all I can say), but it troubled my conscience greatly in my young adulthood. I shared it with an older Christian counsellor one time as we walked around a lake for hours. At the end, we sat down and he laid his hands on my head and prayed these words, which have lived with me ever since:

"Dear Lord, thank you that Chris is your child and that he is clean because he is in your hands. For your hands will touch nothing unclean, except for the purpose of making it clean through the blood of Christ."

I was so released by those cleansing words that I went for a swim in the lake straight after, and it felt like a sacrament of washing to my soul. What I'd always believed in my head about the cross became a reality in my heart. That has not eliminated the temptation or meant that I never sin that way again, but I know where to go quickly for confession and fresh cleansing. Nor would I want to suggest in any way that lust is the only sin that makes us dirty before God, but it often most feels that way internally. How much more wonderful are the words of John that "the blood of Jesus Christ God's Son cleanses us from *all* sin" (1 John 1:9).

We Believe It Was for Us

But how did the cross make such a colossal difference in all these dimensions, and many more? What did God do? What did Jesus do (remembering, of course, as we must stress again shortly, that these ultimately constitute the same question for "God was in Christ reconciling the world to himself")?

The key to the answer is that God through Jesus was doing what we could not possibly do for ourselves. God put himself in our place and did what he did for our benefit. God in Christ substituted himself in order to bear in himself what we would otherwise suffer because of our sin, and to gain for us what we would otherwise eternally lose.

The cross was fundamentally, profoundly, *"for us"*.

One of the earliest summaries of the Christian message (probably coined even before the followers of the Way of Jesus were first nicknamed "Christians") crisply interpreted the cross in this way. Paul had received and preached this version of the essential Christian gospel:

> For what I received I passed on to you as of first importance: that *Christ died for our sins* according to the Scriptures, that he was buried, that he was raised on the third day according to the Scriptures.

> —1 Corinthians 15:3–4 (my emphasis)

Jesus had paved the way for this understanding by interpreting his own death in advance as the fulfilment of the Passover sacrifice, in which the sacrifice of the lambs spared the lives of the firstborn sons of the Israelites on the night of the exodus. The blood of the Passover lambs was "for" them. Jesus' action had the same significance, but his words made it plain that he himself was that sacrifice, with his own body and blood.

> And he took bread, gave thanks and broke it, and gave it to them, saying, "This is my body *given for you*; do this in remembrance of me."
> In the same way, after the supper he took the cup, saying, "This cup is the new covenant in my blood, which is *poured out for you*."
>
> —Luke 22:19 – 20 (my emphasis)

In Matthew's version, the last phrase reads, "poured out *for many for the forgiveness of sins*" (Matt. 26:28, my emphasis).[5]

Jesus also interpreted his own death in terms of the suffering of God's Servant in the book of Isaiah. In the central passage, the Servant's death is portrayed in the clearest possible way as vicarious and substitutionary – that is to say, on behalf of and in the place of others.

> But he was pierced for our transgressions,
>   he was crushed for our iniquities;
> the punishment that brought us peace was on him,
>   and by his wounds we are healed.
> We all, like sheep, have gone astray,
>   each of us has turned to his own way;
> and the LORD has laid on him
>   the iniquity of us all.
>
> —Isaiah 53:5 – 6

From the words of the prophet, through the lips of Jesus, to the pen of the apostle, the same message comes through again and again: *Jesus took our place.*

> God made him who had no sin to be sin for us, so that in him we might become the righteousness of God.
>
> —2 Corinthians 5:21

> Christ redeemed us from the curse of the law by becoming a curse for us, for it is written: "Cursed is everyone who is hung on a pole."
>
> —Galatians 3:13

> "He himself bore our sins" in his body on the cross, so that we might die to sins and live for righteousness; "by his wounds you have been healed."
>
> —1 Peter 2:24

A moment ago we were talking about how the Bible uses different metaphors as ways of conveying the multifaceted truth about what God accomplished through the cross of Christ and what that accomplishment can mean for us when we put our faith in him. This basic affirmation, however, at the heart of the Bible's interpretation of the cross, namely, that it was an act of God in which God in Christ put himself in our place in an act of substitution for our benefit, is not really a metaphor.

As I said, a metaphor is a way of using one reality in order to portray the truth of a different reality. Metaphors are a common and necessary part of human life and language. Thus, for example, we see the reality of a slave or a hostage being set free, and we say, "*That* reality of ordinary life expresses a truth about *this* reality of the cross. The cross is a form of redemption. Buying freedom for slaves provides a picture for what God has done for us by paying the cost of our redemption through the death of his Son."

But the act of substitution seems not to be a "something else" that we can use as one way of talking about a *different* reality – namely, what God did at the cross. Rather, there is something inescapably *essential* about this. Substitution is not a metaphor for what God did; it is what he actually did. God actually did choose to put himself in a place where we should be, to do for us what we could not do for ourselves. What John Stott has called the "self-substitution" of God on our behalf is not one metaphor among others, but the core reality that then presents itself to our understanding through the variety of metaphors and analogies that the Bible uses to appreciate the vast rich reality of all that God achieved by that self-giving, self-substituting act.

We must come back to this in the next chapter, for it is open to misunderstanding, but to close this one it would be hard to put it better than John Stott himself:

> The concept of substitution may be said, then, to lie at the heart of both sin and salvation. For the essence of sin is man substituting himself for God, while the essence of salvation is God substituting himself for man. Man asserts himself against God and puts himself where only God deserves to be; God sacrifices himself for man and puts himself where only man deserves to be. Man claims prerogatives which belong to God alone; God accepts penalties which belong to man alone.[6]

> *Bearing shame and scoffing rude*
> *In my place condemned he stood;*
> *Sealed my pardon with his blood;*
> *Hallelujah! What a Saviour!*[7]

Notes

1. From Charles Wesley's hymn: "And Can It Be".
2. From "We Sing the Praise of Him Who Died", by Thomas Kelly.
3. From "My Song Is Love Unknown", by Samuel Crossman. See www.cyber-hymnal.org/htm/m/y/mysongis.htm
4. From Charles Wesley's hymn: "And Can it Be".
5. The reason why there are variant accounts of Jesus' words during the Last Supper is probably that he did not merely intone a few sentences of liturgy, but repeated and expanded what he said and what he meant so that they could grasp the depth of what he was saying.
6. John R. W. Stott, *The Cross of Christ* (Leicester: Intervarsity Press, 1986), 160. John Stott was writing this at a time when "man" was still commonly used gender-inclusively. He himself would now use more widely preferable generic terms such as "humankind" or "humanity".
7. From " 'Man of Sorrows', What a Name," by Philip Bliss.

THE CROSS – HOW?

We turn from the Why and the What to the How of the cross. What we are doing is moving from trying to understand the motivation behind the cross and the achievement of the cross to trying to explain the mechanism by which it "worked".

There is a sense in which our answer is going to be somewhat similar. If we ask "Why did God love us enough to send Jesus to the cross?" the answer is: "Because he did." And if we ask "How did the cross achieve salvation for us?" the answer is: "Because it did."

But of course, we are not content to stop there, and neither is the Bible. As we saw, the New Testament gives us many metaphors to help us understand the cross. And all down through the ages, Christian theologians have struggled to find ways of explaining how the death of Jesus on the cross brought about atonement between God and us. This isn't the place to survey all the theories that have been put forward; plenty of books do that. Some of those theories have been culturally embedded in particular aspects of society at the time the theory was developed. Some of them fall far short of the Bible, and others go far beyond what the Bible says.

On the whole, however, the evangelical understanding of the cross has regarded its substitutionary dimension as fundamental. As we argued at the end of the last chapter, this is not just one metaphor among many; it is of the essence of what the Bible says happened at the cross. Whatever else we may affirm about the glorious complexity of that event, this stands at the heart of it: Jesus died in my place, bearing my sin as an act of self-sacrificial love flowing from the heart of God. This not only emerges from multiple biblical passages but it also flows on into Christian worship and devotion, expressed in countless hymns and songs. As Paul put it with timeless simplicity, "Christ died for our sins according to the Scriptures" (1 Cor. 15:3).

Questioning Penal Substitution

However, in recent days there has been significant disagreement even among evangelical Christians about one particular way of describing the nature of that substitution. The phrase "*penal* substitutionary atonement" adds a specific dimension to the concept of substitution in itself. It sees the suffering and death that Jesus endured on the cross as the punishment of God for our sin, which God in Christ bore instead of us. The language is drawn from the world of the law court. In that sense it could be said to be drawing on a forensic metaphor to further explain the significance of the substitution itself. God is the judge. Sinners are guilty of having broken God's law. The penalty is death. But God in Christ bore that penalty in our place, so that we can be pardoned by God, be declared righteous in the righteousness of Christ, and gain eternal life instead of eternal death – which would otherwise be the just penalty for our sin.

Those who now question or reject this interpretation of the atonement do so on a number of grounds.

- It is said that it works on an impersonal and mechanistic perception of God and his law – as if the law were some kind of tyrant above even God himself, such that he couldn't forgive us even if he wanted to, without the law being satisfied through punishment being extracted from the guilty.
- It is said that it makes God out to be violent, lashing out in anger at us and only being diverted from doing so by being "allowed" to lash out in anger against Jesus instead.
- It is said that by inculcating the idea that the only way to deal with sin is through violence (by God against Jesus), this theory has been used to justify acts of violence by the church and has fostered the "myth of redemptive violence" in popular Western culture (i.e., the Hollywood answer to all evil – blast it away with a show of more fire power from the good guys than the bad guys).
- It is said that because it portrays God as relentlessly angry, it obscures the greater truth that God loves us and wants to welcome, heal, and restore us.

- It is said that by doing so, it ends up being very off-putting and evangelistically counterproductive. This is a huge concern to those who are passionate about the church's mission and for the effective communication of the gospel.
- It is said that it arose out of a culture that was fixated on sin and guilt, whereas even these words have become meaningless or significantly changed in postmodern culture. Postmodern people have no sense of "sin", in the sense of having broken the laws of God or offended the holiness of God. There is no guilt or penalty to be "borne". Rather, there is only shame to be healed. A more therapeutic and less forensic approach is recommended for contemporary culture.
- It is said that the whole idea is in any case immoral, for normal judicial procedure recoils from the possibility of punishing an innocent person in place of a guilty one and letting the guilty go free.

The real problem is that many of the things that opponents of penal substitution complain about are indeed to be rejected, for they are not what the Bible (or evangelical theologians) actually teach about it. The danger, as in so many disputes like this, is that people paint a caricature and then attack that.

One of the worst such caricatures is that the idea of Jesus bearing the punishment of God upon our sin is nothing more than a form of "cosmic child abuse". It is portrayed as a viciously vengeful Father assaulting his innocent Son with torture and a violent death in order merely to appease his own fury against others (us). Quite rightly, such an appalling idea is rejected as a grotesque distortion of how the Bible speaks of God, the cross, and us.

But the trouble is that even those who concede that such a portrayal is nothing but a caricature sometimes go on to make rhetorical contrasts with it, which only serve to confuse or distort major biblical affirmations. That is, in colloquial terms, they sometimes seem to throw out a very precious biblical baby with the very muddy bathwater of misguided popular perceptions.

In the UK, the debate around this issue has gone on for some time, but it came to a sharp focus with the publication of Steve Chalke and Alan Mann's book *The Lost Message of Jesus*. The book makes a passionate and powerful case for the need to present the radical nature of Jesus and his message in ways that will engage with our modern and postmodern cultures. It is a book with a lot of important and needful things to say. However, what sparked the controversy was a single paragraph in which they argue that the penal substitutionary view is a contradiction of the Bible itself (they never actually use the words "penal substitution", but it is fairly obvious what is in mind).

The fact is that the cross isn't a form of cosmic child abuse – a vengeful Father, punishing his Son for an offence he has not even committed. Understandably, both people inside and outside of the Church have found this twisted version of events morally dubious and a huge barrier to faith.[1]

Immediately, of course, we want to agree wholeheartedly with the denial contained in the first sentence and to agree with the second sentence that such an idea is a "twisted version of events". But their surrounding sentences introduce *a contrast between God's anger and God's love*, which I believe is fundamentally false. Let's look at that point and then take up several other false contrasts that seem to me to be equally confusing in this whole debate.

God's Anger or God's Love – or Both?

Here is how Chalke and Mann surround the "caricature" quoted above:

John's Gospel famously declares, "God loved the people of this world so much that he gave his only Son" (John 3:16). How then, have we come to believe that at the cross this God of love suddenly decides to vent his anger and wrath on his own Son?

[after the two sentences quoted above] … Deeper than that, however, is that such a concept stands in total contradiction to the statement "God is love". If the cross is a personal act of violence perpetrated by God toward humankind but borne by his Son, then it makes a mockery of Jesus' own teaching to love your enemies and to refuse to repay evil with evil.

You see the alleged contradiction? If you really believe in God's love, you can't believe that he could be angry – or at any rate that he could be angry at Jesus. Actually, almost all Christian theologians have refused to describe the cross in the blunt terms: "God was angry with or at Jesus." But Chalke and Mann write it that way as if this is what those who affirm penal substitution actually do believe. But in ridiculing the idea that God lashed out in anger *at Jesus*, they seem to imply that *the whole idea of God being angry at all* is questionable.

But we have to protest that such a contrast is biblically false and superficial. It is simply impossible to read the Bible as a whole and not recognize the reality of God's anger. I could fill the rest of this book with texts from all over the Bible that speak about it (Old and New Testaments, as we saw in chap. 4). But immediately I would also insist, it is equally impossible to read the Bible as a whole and separate God's anger from God's love, for they are intrinsically connected to one another.

God is love. Love is God's being, nature, and character. God acts with faithful love in all that he does (Ps. 145:17; or, perhaps, toward all that he has made). Everything in the universe calls forth God's love and is the object of it. There is nothing in the whole created universe that God does not love, with one single exception.

Only one thing in the universe arouses God's anger, and that is – evil. Why? Because the very essence of evil is to resist, reject, and refuse the love of God. Evil is in essence rebellion against God's love. Evil seeks to frustrate all the good purposes that God's love seeks to achieve for his creation, and that makes God angry. What sort of God would he be if he were not angry with everything that tries to wreck his good creation?

It is precisely because God loves the world so much that he is angry against all who defy the goodness of what God wants for his world. If God didn't love the world, he wouldn't be angry with evil. If God were not angry with evil, he could not really claim to love the world. Anger is the totally justified reflex of love when it is betrayed and frustrated. Would you want to be loved by a God who was *not* angry against evil?

Miroslav Volf is a Christian theologian from Croatia. He says that he used to hold to the fashionable view that dismissed the wrath of God, that the idea of an angry God was somehow incompatible with the love of God. But then war came to his country. Terrible atrocities were done. He found himself exceedingly and justifiably angry. Then he thought – if *God* is not angry at such injustice and cruelty, then he is not a God worth worshiping. Only if God *is* angry against such evil is he worth loving, or being loved by us.

> I used to think that wrath was unworthy of God. Isn't God love? Shouldn't divine love be beyond wrath? God is love, and God loves every person and every creature. That's exactly why God is wrathful against some of them. My last resistance to the idea of God's wrath was a casualty of the war in the former Yugoslavia, the region from which I come. According to some estimates, 200,000 people were killed and over 3,000,000 were displaced. *My* villages and cities were destroyed, *my* people shelled day in and day out, some of them brutalized beyond imagination, and I could not imagine God not being angry. Or think of Rwanda in the last decade of the past century, where 800,000 people were hacked to death in one hundred days! How did God react to the carnage? By doting on the perpetrators in a grandfatherly fashion? By refusing to condemn the bloodbath but instead affirming the perpetrators' basic goodness? Wasn't God fiercely angry with them? Though I used to complain about the indecency of the idea of God's wrath, I came to think that I would have to rebel against a God who *wasn't* wrathful at the sight of the world's evil. God isn't wrathful in spite of being love. God is wrathful *because* God is love.[2]

A few years ago my wife and I sat round our table with a woman in great distress. Her husband was behaving in inexplicably hurtful ways and it was throwing their marriage into a turmoil of contradictory messages. She was visibly and expressly angry indeed with him for his unconscionable behaviour. But then she cried through her tears, "But I do love him so much. I just want him back."

That's it, isn't it? That's totally understandable and justified. Love and anger go together when love comes up against wickedness. If she had not loved him so much, she would not have been so angry with him for what he was doing. If she had not been angry at all at his behaviour, it would have meant she did not really love him but was indifferent. Her anger and love were simultaneous emotions within the same breast, toward the same person. Why, then, do we say they are contradictory in God?

Actually, Chalke and Mann leave out a vital piece of John 3:16 in the quote above. God gave his only Son, so that those who believe in him *should not perish,* but have eternal life. But why should we be in danger of perishing? Not just because we are mortal, but, as Jesus clearly teaches in all four Gospels, because perishing is what happens to those who remain in their wickedness under God's anger without ever coming to repentance and faith. God's love for the world in John 3:16 does not exclude God's anger but assumes it, knows the terrible consequences of it, and provides the remedy for it.

So, while it is undoubtedly right to avoid talking about the cross as if God was angry with Jesus himself, it is undoubtedly wrong to separate the death of Jesus from what the Bible says about God's anger with sin, since it was our sin that Jesus was bearing. In his helpful book on this subject, *Aspects of the Atonement,* Howard Marshall quotes from the great Scottish theologian P. T. Forsyth: "There is a penalty and curse for sin; and Christ consented to enter that region.... It is impossible for us to say that God was angry with Christ; but still Christ entered the wrath of God."[3]

The wonderful paradox, which lies beyond our understanding, is that the cross was simultaneously the outpouring of God's anger and the outpouring of God's love. For in his love for us, God was absorbing, in Christ, his anger against sin. For that reason, two of the lines in Stuart Townend's wonderful hymn "In Christ Alone" could be modified to a greater biblical fullness of meaning. Townend wrote,

> ...*till on that cross as Jesus died*
> *the wrath of God was satisfied.*

It would be equally biblical and truthful and probably better to sing,

...till on that cross as Jesus died
God's wrath and love were satisfied.

The Father or the Son – or Both?

The next false contrast that absolutely has to be resisted is the idea of an angry Father and a victim Son, as if they were set against one another. As we saw, this is hinted at in Chalke and Mann's book. This is where those who reject penal substitution are right to oppose what is unfortunately a common way of presenting the cross at a popular level.

In an attempt to find modern analogies for the truth that Jesus bore our sin, popular preaching, children's talks, and the like tend to work with three independent parties in the action. There is God – with his anger and death sentence. There are human beings – exposed to that anger and about to be punished. But then there is Jesus – who steps into our place and God punishes him instead. Then we can go free.

The problem is that this popular presentation, and all the variety of illustrations that are used to "explain" it, fundamentally destroys the unity of Father and Son in the total work of our salvation. It drives a wedge between an apparently angry Father and a loving Son, or a punishing Father and an innocent Son, or a demanding Father and a paying Son. In effect it portrays the atonement as a play with three actors (God, Jesus, and us), whereas in reality the atonement involves only two parties (God and us).

Now of course, at this point we drive ourselves further into the mystery of the Trinity, for we are right to distinguish the persons of the Father and the Son. But we cannot oppose them to one another in the way that popular preaching often does. The action of each constituted the action of both, and both together constituted the action of the one God. Both Father and Son acted together in perfect harmony in the work of atonement, both together bearing its cost. Paul's profoundly simple statement captures the truth: "God was in Christ reconciling the world to himself" (2 Cor. 5:19, NASB).

John Stott emphasizes this point most powerfully. And since it is such a vital point and I cannot say it any better, I quote him here at length. Referring to those who speak as though Jesus were "an individual separate from both God and us, an independent third party", Stott says that they "lay themselves open to gravely distorted understandings of the atonement and so bring the truth of substitution into disrepute." He goes on:

> They tend to present the cross in one or other of two ways, according to whether the initiative was Christ's or God's. In the one case Christ is pictured

as intervening in order to pacify an angry god and wrest from him a grudging salvation. In the other, the intervention is ascribed to God, who proceeds to punish the innocent Jesus in place of us the guilty sinners who had deserved the punishment. In both cases God and Christ are sundered from one another: either Christ persuades God or God punishes Christ. What is characteristic of both presentations is that they denigrate the Father. Reluctant to suffer himself, he victimizes Christ instead. Reluctant to forgive, he is prevailed upon by Christ to do so. He is seen as a pitiless ogre whose wrath has to be assuaged, whose disinclination to act has to be overcome, by the loving self-sacrifice of Jesus.

Referring to biblical texts such as Isaiah 53:6, where we read that "the LORD has laid on him the iniquity of us all", Stott points out that they all have matching counterparts with Christ himself as subject, as, for example, "He himself bore our sins in his body on the tree" (1 Peter 2:24). Likewise, "God so loved the world that he gave his only Son" (John 3:16) is matched by "the Son of God, who loved me and gave himself for me" (Gal. 2:20). The perfect combination of the self-giving of the Son and the will of the Father is captured by Paul when he speaks of "God our Father and the Lord Jesus Christ, who gave himself for our sins to rescue us from the present evil age, according to the will of our God and Father" (Gal. 1:3–4). Stott continues,

> We have no liberty to interpret [such texts] in such a way as to imply either that God compelled Jesus to do what he was unwilling to do himself, or that Jesus was an unwilling victim of God's harsh justice. Jesus Christ did indeed bear the penalty of our sins, but God was active in and through Christ doing it, and Christ was freely playing his part (e.g. Heb.10:5–10).
>
> We must not, then, speak of God punishing Jesus or of Jesus persuading God, for to do so is to set them over against each other as if they acted independently of each other or were even in conflict with each other. We must never make Christ the object of God's punishment or God the object of Christ's persuasion, for both God and Christ were subjects not objects, taking the initiative together to save sinners. Whatever happened on the cross in terms of "God-forsakenness" was voluntarily accepted by both in the same holy love which made atonement necessary.... If the Father "gave the Son", the Son "gave himself". If the Gethsemane "cup" symbolized the wrath of God, it was nevertheless "given" by the Father (Jn. 18:11) and voluntarily "taken" by the Son. If the Father "sent" the Son, the Son "came" himself. The Father did not lay on the Son an ordeal he was reluctant to bear, nor did the Son extract from the Father a salvation he was reluctant to bestow. There is no suspicion anywhere in the New Testament of discord between the Father and the Son, "whether by the Son wresting forgiveness from an

unwilling Father or by the Father demanding a sacrifice from an unwilling Son". There was no unwillingness in either. On the contrary, their wills coincided in the perfect self-sacrifice of love.[4]

Here is how Donald Macleod puts the same point, in even stronger language:

> Jesus and the Father are one (John 10:30).... On Calvary, Jehovah condemns sin. He curses it. He puts it outside (Hebrews 13:12). Equally, however, He bears it. He imputes it to Himself. He receives its wages. He becomes Himself its propitiation. He becomes the sinner's ransom. He becomes even the sinner's advocate—God with God. Certainly we must not ignore or obscure the distinction between God the Father and God the Son. Equally, however, we must avoid the more prevalent danger of regarding the Father and the Son as different beings. In the last analysis, God expresses His love for us not by putting another to suffer in our place, but by Himself taking our place. He meets the whole cost of our forgiveness in Himself, exacting it of Himself. He demands the ransom, He provides the ransom. He becomes the ransom. Herein is love.[5]

Guilt or Shame—or Both?

Another criticism of the concept of penal substitution comes from those who argue that it only makes sense in cultures with a developed sense of personal and objective *guilt*. This means that people have a sense of the law as something over and above them, such that if they break the law, they are objectively guilty, whether anybody ever finds out what they did or not. But in some cultures (e.g., in many parts of Asia and the Middle East), the real problem is not so much objective guilt as subjective and social *shame*. What counts in any set of behaviours or circumstances is not whether what I did was right or wrong according to some external law, before which I am therefore innocent or guilty, but whether what I did has brought shame to myself, my family, or those closest to me, within the structure of social relationships I inhabit. Guilt is experienced as an unbearable burden on the *conscience*, facing some external standard—whether the law or God; shame is experienced as an unbearable destruction of one's *self-esteem*, facing others in society—it is precisely "loss of face".

Now those who analyze these things in relation to Christian mission are highly motivated to communicate the message of the gospel in terms that people can understand and relate to. In the Western world, this means that we have to find ways of connecting with the thinking of people who are shaped within postmodernity. This is absolutely right and necessary. Wrestling with the cultural dynamics and shifting meanings of guilt and shame is a vital part of evangelism with integrity and relevance.

Postmodernity and Shame

One of the marks of the postmodern shift has been the loss of the transcendent, or at any rate, of any transcendent that looks like the God of the Christian worldview. People no longer have any awareness of a personal moral God whom they have offended. The biblical concept of sin has lost all currency or has been utterly trivialized. Naturally, therefore, guilt is no longer something objectively real in terms of our relation to God.

Guilt is either merely a *psychological* deficit to be addressed therapeutically, or a *legal* nicety to be decided judicially. Guilt is either subjective, but actually unreal and unhealthy; or it is objective, but purely horizontal within social relations. Guilt *before God* is a non-starter, perceived as a tool of religious oppression. For people who think like this, trying to explain the cross in terms of Jesus' taking on himself our guilt before God and suffering its consequences in our place makes no sense.

Now there can be no doubt that Western society has moved in this direction. There is a real cultural shift going on, which requires us, as always, to work hard at presenting the gospel in ways that "connect" with people where they are. The New Testament, after all, shows us how Paul framed his message in different ways when addressing Jewish audiences steeped in Old Testament Scriptures, or when addressing Gentile audiences steeped in polytheistic assumptions and practice. Likewise, given that many postmodern Westerners have virtually zero knowledge of the biblical story or awareness of the biblical God, we cannot speak to them in ways that make the same assumptions that could be made by evangelists in earlier generations, when they were addressing people who were familiar with the Bible and were shaped by its worldview, even as unbelievers.

Alan Mann is one of many who seek to find ways of understanding and communicating the atonement that make sense to this changed cultural reality. The subtitle of his book expresses precisely this very positive intention: *Atonement for a "Sinless" Society: Engaging with an Emerging Culture.*[6] By "sinless", Mann does not mean, of course, that society today does nothing wrong, but rather that most people have lost any sense of "sin" in its biblical sense. Their problem is, therefore, not a sense of guilt but of shame.

This postmodern, "chronic shame", however, does not mean being ashamed at having offended some *external* authority, but the shame that is caused *internally* by the inconsistency between the image of ourselves that we project on the outside and the real selves that we know ourselves to be on the inside. We are, almost literally, "ashamed of ourselves". We lack integrity and authenticity, and all our relationships are distorted and polluted by this inner shame. We fear exposure of the inner self to the outside world and the shame that would bring, so we construct ideal selves and project them instead.

Now it seems to me that Mann is very perceptive in his analysis of postmodern culture at this point. He describes in potent and haunting terms "the relational dysfunction – the debilitating, demoralizing and dehumanizing effects of chronic shame".[7] He is also right to ask how the atoning power of the narrative of the cross can engage with people in the grip of such forces. But once again, in order to emphasize the reality and pervasive power of shame, he seems to fall into the trap of falsely excluding (or, at any rate, radically deemphasizing) the reality of guilt (by which I mean not just guilty feelings but the objective fact of having offended God in the biblical sense). His chapter "From Sin to Shame", for example, has a subheading "Shame, Not Guilt". He says that we must "orientate our narratives of atonement so that they address the issues of shame, and not of 'sin' and guilt".[8] And while he rightly says we must use all the resources of the biblical narrative in relating the gospel to all the needs of people, he glaringly misses out on one key element of the biblical witness.

> The story of atonement needs to be rich and thick so that it can speak meaningfully and sufficiently to every storied-self it encounters: The lost need to be found. The socially excluded need to be welcomed. The sick need to be healed. The oppressed need to be liberated. The divided need to be reconciled. The chronically shamed need to become "shame-less".[9]

To all of which we can say, Amen! And the New Testament certainly portrays the gospel in all of these ways. But surely we have to add to the list: *The guilty need to be pardoned and forgiven*. That is not the *only* dimension of atonement (and Mann rightly condemns those who speak and preach as if it were), but it is surely an indispensable one if we are to be faithful to all dimensions of the biblical good news.

So once again, I find myself appealing for a "both-and" approach – because that is what the Bible itself gives us.

People sometimes speak about "shame cultures" and "guilt cultures", as if they were mutually exclusive. It is true, of course, that one or the other may be the dominant emphasis in different cultures. But the Bible speaks readily about both and about the need to deal with both. Shame is not just a postmodern phenomenon, even if it has taken on some peculiarly postmodern features. It is as old as the garden of Eden and was in fact the first effect of human disobedience. Having disobeyed God, Adam and Eve were ashamed in each other's presence. They covered themselves and they went into hiding. Postmodern people retain the horizontal shame but have lost the awareness of vertical disobedience, as Mann well points out. His description of chronic shame is not just a comment on social postmodernity but a picture of human culture ever since Genesis 3.

> The chronically shamed fear exposing the reality that the way they narrate themselves to others is not their real self. They are insecure in their relating, constantly aware of the need to cover the self from the "Other" for fear of being found socially unacceptable. The shamed person lives in a permanent state of hiding, even when interacting with others.[10]

Isn't that what we find in the garden of Eden?

The problem is that postmodern shame is entirely focused on the self and its inadequacy or incoherence, whereas the Bible insists that such disorder in the self (which is very real) is the fruit of a disordered relationship with God caused by sin and disobedience. You cannot deal with shame without addressing guilt. The Bible decisively tackles both.

So we do not need to stop talking about the reality of guilt in order to rightly talk about the reality of shame. Both are part of our human predicament and need. Both are addressed by the gospel.

Ezekiel on Shame

Ezekiel gives us a profound analysis of shame. He understands what it means to *be shamed*, and what it means to *feel shame*. Amazingly, he can even apply them to God. Ezekiel 36:16–32 is a key passage and worth reading in full.

Ezekiel begins with the fact of the exile and interprets it as the indisputably deserved punishment of God on Israel for their sins (vv. 16–19). But the scattering of his people among the nations brought shame on the name of Yahweh himself (vv. 20–21). There was contradiction between the true story (God was punishing his own people) and the story being told among the nations (Yahweh is just another weak god defeated by Babylon's gods).

Yahweh's reputation was at stake. He was being put to shame among the nations, so much so that he "felt sorry for his own name" (that's what v. 21 literally says). So God will act to bring his people back in order to restore his own name and remove the shame of misunderstanding (vv. 22–23). To do so, he will also restore Israel, cleanse them, remove their polluting idolatry, and give them a new heart and spirit of obedience (vv. 24–27).

Then comes the key reflection on our theme. This act of divine forgiveness and "at-one-ment" will not only deal with the sin that broke their relationship with God, it will also deal with the *shame* that was the consequence of God's displeasure. They will be once again "shame-less" among the nations, able to hold their heads up without reproach (v. 30; cf. v. 15). So they need have no shame in the presence of others. Yet, paradoxically, they *will* recall their sin with shame in the presence of God (vv. 31–32). There is no contradiction here. The first speaks of the removal of debilitating social shame. The second speaks of the healthy shame that flows from the grateful memory of all that God has saved us from. Here is what I wrote about this wonderful passage of Ezekiel elsewhere:

> Spiritually and psychologically there is profound insight in this chapter into the proper place of shame in the life of the believer. Israel were *not* to feel ashamed in the presence of the other nations (36:15), but they *were* to feel ashamed in the presence of their own memories before God (36:31–32). Similarly, there is a proper sense in which the believer who has been forgiven by God for all her sins and offences may rightly hold up her head in company.
>
> We may have no control over what other people think of us, but that need not destroy the proper sense of dignity and self-respect that comes from knowing the affirmation of God himself. In the Gospels Jesus seems deliberately to have given public affirmation to those who experienced his forgiving and re-instating grace—to remove their shame (E.g. Zaccheus, the woman who washed his feet, the woman healed of a menstrual disorder, cleansed lepers, the woman caught in adultery, etc.). The strong desire that Yahweh would protect the humble and sin-conscious worshipper from public shame and disgrace is often to be found in the Psalms. A favourite of my own for many years has been Psalm 25.
>
>> *— To you, O LORD, I lift up my soul; in you I trust, O my God.*
>> *Do not let me be put to shame, nor let my enemies triumph over me.*
>> *No one whose hope is in you will ever be put to shame (Ps. 25:1–3).*

And what relief it is to hear the word of God coming, as it did to Israel in exile, to address that fear with the words of assurance:

> *— Do not be afraid; you will not suffer shame.*
> *Do not fear disgrace; you will not be humiliated (Isa. 54:4).*

> With such a promise, and on the basis of the cleansing and restoring work of Christ, the believer can face the world, certainly not with pride, but equally certainly without shame.

But on the other hand, the same person, alone with God and the memories of the past, can quite properly feel the most acute inner shame and disgrace. It is not, however, a destructive or crushing emotion. Rather it is the core fuel for genuine repentance and humility and for the joy and peace that flow from that source alone. When *I* remember my sins I know that *God* does not. From his side they are buried in the depths of the sea, covered by the atoning blood of Jesus Christ, never again to be raised to the surface and held against me. And it is only in the awareness of that liberating truth that I can (or even ought) to remember them. For this is not the memory that generates fresh accusation and guilt – that is the work of Satan the accuser. Satan's stinging jolts of memory need to be taken straight to the cross and to our ascended High Priest, for,

> *When Satan tempts me to despair*
> *And tells me of the guilt within,*
> *Upward I look and see him there*
> *Who made an end of all my sin.*

No, this is the memory that generates gratitude out of disgrace, celebration out of shame. It is the memory which marvels at the length and breadth and depth of God's rescuing love that has brought me from what I once was, or might easily have become, to where I am now, as a child of his grace.

> *In the cold mirror of a glass, I see my reflection pass;*
> *See the dark shades of what I used to be;*
> *See the purple of her eyes, the scarlet of my lies.*
> *I said, Love, rescue me.*[11]

You may well detect some autobiographical emotion in that passage. Years ago there was a time when I allowed myself to persist in behaviour that was knowingly sinful and of which I was deeply ashamed. In God's mercy it ended; I repented deeply before God and trusted his forgiveness. Knowing myself forgiven, but still struggling with that sense of shame combined with relief that the depths of what we know of ourselves is not known by others, I found myself thinking again of the crucifixion narrative. And I suddenly exclaimed aloud to myself, "Jesus bore my shame – the shame that should be mine!" For indeed, the whole point of crucifixion as a means of execution was that it was unbearably, publicly, shaming.

The Gospels, even in the reserved way they describe how Jesus was treated, make it clear that he was excruciatingly humiliated before the mocking public gaze. But that shame should not have been his, for he had done no wrong. It was mine, deservedly mine, but undeservedly taken by him.

I had known this in my head before, of course–simply as part of my theoretical understanding of the atonement. But for the first time it became overwhelmingly real. "Jesus bore my shame!" I repeated to myself over and over again, with tears of gratitude. Enough, surely, that he had borne the just condemnation of God on my guilt. That much I knew, and I rejoiced in God's forgiveness. Enough, surely, that through his blood I could be washed clean from the dirt and pollution of my ways. That too I knew as a precious truth. But that he had borne the most fearful shame in my place, that he had borne for me what I could not even bear to think about for myself–that was beyond all understanding, though it rolled over my soul in waves of deep reassurance. The promise of Isaiah 54:4, quoted above, came as a direct word of comfort to my heart: "Do not be afraid; you will not suffer shame. Do not fear disgrace; you will not be humiliated"; though I knew I could claim it only because the shame had already been borne by Christ.

Bearing shame and scoffing rude
In my place condemned he stood;
Sealed my pardon with his blood;
Hallelujah! What a Saviour![12]

That is why I said that, of all the things that lead me to speak of the God I don't understand, the cross is top of the list. My overflowing thankfulness for my experience of God's love proved at Calvary far outweighs my pain and struggle with the baffling horrors we thought about in Part 1, and it helps me to cope with them within the security of knowing that God is love all the way down.

We have been thinking in this chapter about some of the false contrasts that easily arise when there is disagreement over the meaning of the cross. In each case I have urged that we need to hold closely together things that easily get set against each other. There is one more such contrast that I find just as troubling in the way it pulls apart what the Bible as a whole seems to hold together. That is, the question whether the cross was the supreme moment of God absorbing the worst that human evil could do to him and defeating it, or the supreme moment of God pouring out the fullness of his anger against sin and evil and bearing it in Christ. But to understand how these relate to each other we will need to dig deeply into our Bibles and move on to a fresh chapter.

Notes

1. Steve Chalke and Alan Mann, *The Lost Message of Jesus* (Grand Rapids: Zondervan, 2003), 182.
2. Miroslav Volf, *Free of Charge: Giving and Forgiving in a Culture Stripped of Grace* (Grand Rapids: Zondervan, 2006), 138–39.
3. P. T. Forsyth, *The Work of Christ* (London: Hodder & Stoughton, 1910), 201, quoted in I. Howard Marshall, *Aspects of the Atonement* (London, Colorado Springs, Hyderabad: Paternoster, 2007), 36.
4. John R. W. Stott, *The Cross of Christ* (Downers Grove, IL: Intervarsity Press, 1986), 150–52. The quote in the few lines is from I. H. Marshall, *The Work of Christ* (Exeter, Paternoster, 1969), 74.
5. Donald Macleod, *Behold Your God* (Inverness: Christian Focus, 1995), 184; as quoted in another fine book, Tim Chester, *Delighting in the Trinity* (Oxford: Monarch; Grand Rapids: Kregel, 2005), 65.
6. Alan Mann, *Atonement for a "Sinless" Society: Engaging with an Emerging Culture* (Milton Keynes: Paternoster, 2005).
7. Ibid., 47.
8. Ibid., 54.
9. Ibid., 97.
10. Ibid., 41.
11. Christopher J. H. Wright, *The Message of Ezekiel* (The Bible Speaks Today; Downers Grove, IL, and Leicester: Intervarsity Press, 2001), 301–2; the closing song is from "Love, Rescue Me", by U2.
12. From " 'Man of Sorrows', What a Name," by Philip Bliss.

THE CROSS – ACCORDING TO THE SCRIPTURES

We have been exploring the mystery of the cross. In chapter 6 we saw that while we may never be able to fully understand the Why of God's self-giving love for us, we can embrace with arms of gratitude the broad What of all that God accomplished for us through the cross of Christ. With multiple pictures, the New Testament portrays the rich comprehensiveness of the atonement. Then in chapter 7 we turned to the How of the cross, where there has always been controversy. Recently, the traditional understanding known as "penal substitution" has come under attack. Without getting embroiled in that whole debate, I am trying to untangle some false opposites that seem to lie at the heart of much misunderstanding. In chapter 7 we rejected confused and confusing polarization between God's anger and God's love, and between the Father and the Son, and between guilt and shame. In this chapter we explore one more.

Human Wickedness or God's Judgment – or Both?

One of the ways that some people describe what happened at the cross is to lay all the emphasis on the human and satanic evil that was hurled against Jesus and borne by him without retaliation. This is what Christ was really suffering, they argue – not the inflicted punishment of God. So they avoid the idea of penal substitution by arguing that on the cross Jesus was taking on himself, not God's wrath against us, but the wickedness of humanity against God. He took the worst that humanity could throw at him, and in absorbing it into himself defeated it. The cross was the way in which God in Christ absorbed and dealt with human evil and violence. Christ suffered at the hands of humanity and in bearing our sin in that sense, ultimately drew its sting and bore it away. He bore our wrath against God, not God's wrath against us.

Now there is enormous truth, of course – revelatory, exemplary, and redemptive truth – in what this view *affirms*, even though we must disagree about what it *denies*. As we have already argued in chapter 3, one of the essential elements of the meaning of the cross is that it was the point at which the awesome, terrible power of evil was exercised to its most extreme point. Human beings and Satan did their absolute worst in rejecting, violating, torturing, and murdering the Lord of life and creation. And Jesus not only bore it but he triumphed over it, praying for his Father to forgive his human executioners.

There is no doubt that this was an unfathomable dimension of the suffering of Christ, that he became the solitary target of unimaginable hatred, injustice, oppression, violence, torture, and murder. Equally there is no doubt that the New Testament marvels that in bearing such treatment, Jesus did not fight back or even curse back, but simply took it (1 Peter 2:23). Furthermore, the New Testament certainly affirms that in absorbing all that the power of evil could do to him at the cross, Jesus thereby triumphed over it. The cross, in other words, was not merely passive acceptance of evil, but supremely active victory over it (e.g., Col. 2:15).

All this, then, we can gladly affirm.

But in affirming the horrific depths of the cross as an act of sinful humanity, must we then exclude the idea that Christ's sufferings on the cross were also an act of God? Are we to deny that on the cross God in Christ was not only bearing the utmost expression *of our sin* against him, but also bearing for us the judgment of God *upon our sin*?

Once again, I have to say, this is surely another false opposite. To affirm that the cross involved Jesus bearing the worst of *human* wickedness does not lead us to deny that the cross also involved Jesus bearing the weight of *divine* judgment. We do not have to choose one against the other, for the Bible affirms both.

"According to the Scriptures"

At this point, I find it helpful to turn again to the Old Testament. Indeed, we should turn to the Old Testament as our initial resource for understanding the cross. For we can be sure that Jesus himself understood his own death in the light of the Scriptures that we now call the Old Testament, and so did Paul. Paul quotes what is probably the earliest summary of the gospel: "that Christ died for our sins *according to the Scriptures*, that he was buried, that he was raised on the third day *according to the Scriptures*" (1 Cor. 15:3–4, my emphasis).

Now I used to understand that repeated phrase ("according to the Scriptures"), as most other people I suppose, in much the same way as we do when we say, "as the Bible says". We have in mind some particular passage of Scripture that supports the point we are making. So we read Paul as if he meant, "Jesus died and rose again, as the Bible says (you can check it out in the Gospels)." But of course, Paul did not mean it like that, for the canonical Gospels were not yet written when he was evangelizing in Corinth and then writing to the church there. In other words, when Paul said that Christ died "according to the Scriptures", he was talking at a time before the New Testament was written, so "the Scriptures" he must have been talking about were the Old Testament.

What Paul meant was, "Jesus died and rose again, *in agreement with and in fulfilment of* what the Scriptures tell us." That is to say, it is not just that the death of Jesus is *recorded in* the Bible, but that the death of Jesus *accorded with* the Bible – the Bible that Jesus and Paul knew, which of course was what we now call the Old Testament. The significance of the death and resurrection of Jesus must be rooted in the Old Testament – the narratives, the law, the prophets, the psalms, and so on.

Above all, the life and death of Jesus the Messiah must be understood within the framework of the *story* of Old Testament Israel. For it was in fact the culmination, the climax, the destination of that whole story. That is certainly how Jesus understood it himself.

The Double Identity of Old Testament Israel

Please bear with me, then, as we step back and think about the Old Testament for a moment. I shouldn't have to apologize for asking you to do that, but so few people seem to bother! It will take a little time, but it will really help us when we come back to the question of the human and divine aspects of the cross. You see, part of the problem with so many theories of the atonement through the centuries is that they try to explain the death of Christ in terms of *other* stories or worldviews where it does not really fit, while ignoring the one story in which it is actually set – the biblical story of God's dealings with Israel and of God's mission through Israel to bring blessing and salvation to the world.[1]

Now in the Old Testament story the people of Israel displayed a terrible ambiguity. On the one hand, they represented God's *promise* to the world.

God promised Abraham that through his descendants all nations on earth would find blessing. Salvation would come to all the nations through what God would do in this one nation, Old Testament Israel. They were the people of promise. But on the other hand, Israel *rebelled* constantly against God, and in their sin and wickedness they sank even below the level of nations that had no covenant relationship with God or the benefit of God's law. They were a rebellious house. That's the double truth about Israel as the Old Testament presents them to us: a people of promise and a people in rebellion.

So Old Testament Israel both embodied God's promise of salvation for humanity and also exemplified humanity's history of rebellion. Israel was the focal point of God's love for the world and yet also the focal point of the world's sin against God. *Bear all this in mind as we remember that Jesus was the Messiah—the one who embodied Israel.*

So when Israel persisted in rebellion despite centuries of warning from the prophets, what happened? According to the Old Testament historians and prophets, God poured out his anger upon them in the event known as the exile, which happened in 587 BC. This involved three major elements: first, it was explicitly described as an act of God's *punishment* for their accumulated and covenant-breaking wickedness; second, it took the form of the most terrible *destruction*—the city of Jerusalem, the temple, and many thousands of lives; and third, it sent Israel off into exile in Babylon, away from their land, into deathly *separation* from the place of God's presence and blessing.

Now this awful event stands as a kind of historical model or microcosm in two ways. On the one hand, Israel in their rebellion against God, in their refusal to respond to his love and care towards them, is like a microcosm of humanity as a whole. The fate they suffered under God's judgment likewise models what the Bible says is the ultimate destiny of the unrepentant wicked. Indeed, the exile contained precisely the same three elements that are found in the most concise description of the fate of the wicked that the New Testament provides: *punishment, destruction*, and *separation* from God. "They will be punished with everlasting destruction and shut out from the presence of the Lord and from the glory of his might" (2 Thess. 1:9).

On the other hand, Jesus as Messiah was a microcosm of Israel. The Gospels show this clearly by illustrating again and again how the story of Old Testament Israel is recapitulated in the story of Jesus. Matthew shows this even in the infancy of Jesus. And as the Messiah embodied Israel in life, so he embodied them in death. Calvary was an infinitely intensified re-enactment of the terrible judgment of 587 BC. Jesus himself saw it that way when he linked his own death to the destruction of the temple (John 2:19–22), for the destruction of the temple had been the climax of the devastating horror of the fall of Jerusalem and the beginning of exile. But of course, there was one utterly crucial difference. For Israel, the exile was deserved on account of their sins. For Jesus the Messiah, the cross was totally undeserved for he was without sin.

But now we come to the key question. Who was responsible for the exile? Who caused it to happen? Was it an act of God, or an act of wicked men?

Nebuchadnezzar or God—or Both?

Remember, we are thinking about the cross and wondering if it should be seen primarily as an act of terrible human wickedness, inflicted on Jesus by his enemies and representing the worst that human evil could do to God; or as an act of terrible divine judgment in which Jesus bore the weight of God's anger against our sin. And I've been saying that it will help if we remember that the Bible sees Jesus in the light of the story of Old Testament Israel—or rather, as the climax and fulfilment of that story in which Jesus, as Messiah, embodied Israel and accomplished Israel's mission and destiny.

So the question is: Was the exile the result of appalling human wickedness and violence inflicted on Israel by their enemies, the Babylonians, for rebelling against them? Or was it the result of divine punishment inflicted on Israel by their God, Yahweh, for rebelling against him?

And the answer that the Bible itself gives us, of course, is that *it was entirely both at the same time.* Or, to be more precise and faithful to the way the Bible actually explains it, God in his sovereignty used the Babylonians as the agent of his own judgment. The actions were wholly theirs, and they bore moral responsibility for the extent of their cruelty and violence (and the prophets make that plain too). But behind the hand of Nebuchadnezzar was the hand of God. God was acting through the actions of men.

Now that is precisely how Peter describes the cross in Acts 2:23: "This man was handed over to you by God's deliberate plan and foreknowledge; and you, with the help of wicked men, put him to death by nailing him to the cross." Peter even uses the phrase "this man [Jesus] was *handed over* to you", which is frequently the way the Old Testament describes God acting in judgment on Israel by handing them over to their enemies (e.g., Ezek. 11:9).

I have to say at once that I don't understand this—in the sense that I can't hold both parts of it easily together in my head at the same time (God's sovereignty and human moral responsibility). Yet the Bible unquestionably affirms both. God acts through human actions—without turning people into puppets.

Just to make sure we really grasp the point as best we can, let's listen to some of the prophets wrestling with this paradox of divine action through human action. Remember that all this is crucial to understanding the mystery of the cross, to help us see it as simultaneously the action of human beings and an act of God.

Habakkuk, grieving over the sin of his own people, was astonished to hear God say that he was about to raise up the Babylonians as the agent of his punishment on Israel (Hab. 1:5–6). But even though Habakkuk struggled to understand God's ways, he realized that,

> *You*, Lord, have appointed them to execute judgment;
> *you*, my Rock, have ordained them to punish.
>
> —Habakkuk 1:12 (my emphasis).

The Babylonians would do their worst; but through them God would be doing what he planned.

Jeremiah, writing to the exiles themselves in the midst of their trauma, knew that he was writing to "all the people *Nebuchadnezzar* had carried into exile from Jerusalem to Babylon" (Jer. 29:1). But his letter begins with the words of God describing them as "all those *I [God]* carried into exile from Jerusalem to Babylon" (v. 4, repeated in v. 7 and 14, my emphasis). These are two complementary perspectives on exactly the same historical event. At "ground level" everybody knew who had destroyed Jerusalem and carried off the Israelites into exile–Nebuchadnezzar. You would have seen him and his armies doing it if you had been there. The TV news cameras would have recorded it. But the prophet knew that behind the human actors stood the mysterious sovereign Lord God. The eye of faith discerned what TV cameras could never record–the will and purpose of God. Nebuchadnezzar, like the Assyrians before him, was nothing more than a stick in the hand of God, the agent of his judgment against Israel (Isa. 10:5).

Ezekiel lived among the first group of exiles who had been taken to Babylon before the final destruction of Jerusalem. To show the exiles that there was no hope for the city, Ezekiel acted out the terrible final siege by lying down for days on end beside a model of Jerusalem on a clay brick (you can read the whole bizarre story in Ezek. 4). All around it he put little models of siege works. They were clearly the Babylonian armies, the enemies of Israel.

But whom did Ezekiel himself represent, lying there glaring at the besieged city? He tells us. He was portraying God himself who was the *real enemy* behind the human enemies. The fire and sword, the bloodshed, death, and destruction, physically inflicted by the Babylonians, were all at the same time acts of God. And when Ezekiel brought the whole acted prophecy to an end by shaving his own head and beard with a sword, the message was clear: the sword was Nebuchadnezzar, but the hand that wielded it was the hand of God, and the body being shaved was the people of Israel under God's wrath. "Therefore this is what the Sovereign LORD says: I myself am against you, Jerusalem, and I will inflict punishment on you in the sight of the nations" (Ezek. 5:8). Read all of Ezekiel 5 to feel the full force of this declaration of God's judgment, carried out through human enemies.

So then, in suffering the worst violence and cruelty that the Babylonians could inflict on them, the Israelites were, *in those very circumstances*, bearing the weight of God's condemnation of their accumulated wickedness. This is the consistent prophetic interpretation that the Bible gives us of the destruction and exile of Israel in 587 BC: divine judgment executed through human agency.

And that event with its double significance provides precisely the model that the New Testament picks up for understanding the human and divine dimensions of the death of Messiah Jesus on a Roman cross outside Jerusalem. In bearing the worst that the Roman and Jewish authorities could do to him and all that it represented of *human* rage against God expressed through injustice, rebellion, and violence, Jesus was simultaneously bearing the weight of *God's* condemnation and judgment on the accumulated sin, not just of Israel but of the world.

This is what it means to say, with Paul, that Christ died "according to the Scriptures". It means his death is to be understood in line with, in the light of, the Old Testament story. We do not have to choose one or the other — human wickedness or divine judgment. It was both. In fact, it was divine judgment operating sovereignly through the agency of human wickedness.

To return to an earlier point, there is a crucial and transforming difference between the two events. Israel suffered on account of their own sin, whereas Jesus' sufferings were wholly undeserved. The sins whose judgment he bore were not his own but ours — which is why every word in Paul's definition of the gospel is important: "Christ died for *our* sins according to the Scriptures."

Recognizing the Truth

Eventually, with the help of their prophets, the Israelites came to recognize both sides of this truth. That is, they came to see the truth about themselves (that they were punished justly for their own sins), and they were given a prophetic prospect about the coming one (that he would suffer innocently for the sins of others). So in this way too the Old Testament Scriptures prepare the way for our understanding of the meaning of Christ's death.

The Truth of God's Punishment

Jeremiah explained the exile from God's point of view, as clearly as it could be put, as an act of God himself:

> I have struck you as an enemy would
>   and punished you as would the cruel,
> because your guilt is so great
>   and your sins so many.
> Why do you cry out over your wound,
>   your pain that has no cure?
> Because of your great guilt and many sins
>   I have done these things to you.
>
> —Jeremiah 30:14–15

Isaiah saw the same thing and wondered why Israel would not accept it:

> Who handed Jacob over to become loot,
>   and Israel to the plunderers?
> Was it not the Lord,
>   against whom we have sinned?
> For they would not follow his ways;
>   they did not obey his law.
> So he poured out on them his burning anger,
>   the violence of war.
> It enveloped them in flames, yet they did not understand;
>   it consumed them, but they did not take it to heart.
>
> —Isaiah 42:24–25

They did come to accept it in the end, as *Ezekiel* witnessed at last, so that he was then able to bring them words of comfort and hope (Ezek. 33:10). The book of *Lamentations* is filled with the same painful acknowledgment (e.g., Lam. 1:5, 8, 14, etc.).

The Truth of God's Suffering Servant

But looking forward, as Isaiah invited them to contemplate the sufferings of the coming Servant of the Lord (who in other respects shared the identity of Israel), they realized in their shock that *his* sufferings and death would be utterly *undeserved*. On the contrary, he would suffer for all of "us" (Israel and the nations) so that we could find peace, healing, and righteousness.

Surely he took up our pain
  and bore our suffering,
yet we considered him punished by God,
  stricken by him, and afflicted.
But he was pierced for our transgressions,
  he was crushed for our iniquities;
the punishment that brought us peace was on him,
  and by his wounds we are healed.
We all, like sheep, have gone astray,
  each of us has turned to our own way;
and the LORD has laid on him
  the iniquity of us all.

—Isaiah 53:4–6

And at Calvary itself, this world-transforming truth was recognized by one of the terrorists crucified beside Jesus, to his own ultimate salvation. Luke almost certainly intends us to hear the echo of Isaiah 53 in his record of these words:

One of the criminals who hung there hurled insults at him: "Aren't you the Messiah? Save yourself and us!" But the other criminal rebuked him. "Don't you fear God," he said, "since you are under the same sentence? *We are punished justly, for we are getting what our deeds deserve. But this man has done nothing wrong.*"

—Luke 23:39–41, my emphasis

Indeed so. For the innocent man at his side was bearing not only the unjust punishment of Rome for crimes he had not committed, but was by that very means bearing the just judgment of God on our sins in our place. "Christ died for our sins *in accordance with the Scriptures.*"

Does Sin Have Consequences?

As I have tried to follow the debate over the penal substitutionary theory of the atonement, struggling to understand the good points that its detractors make against a distorted version of it and struggling to think carefully through what the Bible as a whole teaches, I keep coming back to one fundamental question. Does sin have consequences? Everybody in the debate, as far as I can see, agrees that it does. But the deeper core of that question lies in asking if those consequences include God's punishment. Or most simply put: Does wickedness deserve to be punished?

There is a fundamental issue at stake here, and I am well aware that there are all kinds of philosophical, theological, and ethical debates over exactly what punishment is, why it is a good or bad thing, and the like.[2] But is there some kind of legitimate retributive principle built into the way our good Creator God has designed his good universe? Is there some objective, God-related foundation for what we sometimes call "just deserts" – that is, that there is a proper suffering that is deserved as a form of just retribution for wickedness deliberately perpetrated and totally unrepented? And can this be carefully and clearly distinguished from mere lust for vengeance and ungodly escalating retaliation?

Without being able to substantiate it here, I believe that the answer is yes, and that as human beings we have some deep and primal instincts (not merely derived from our sinful fallenness) that recognize this to be so. Wrongdoing has painful consequences that are deserved. Wrongdoing that goes completely unpunished leaves us deeply unsatisfied – and as I said, this is not merely a lust for vengeance but reflects a deep moral truth about God and his universe.

If this is true, it is true because God intended it to be so. In other words, we cannot remove our discomfort with the idea of God's anger against evil and sin by "distancing" the consequences of sin from God's personal reaction. Some people try to do that by saying that the Bible's language of "the wrath of God" is not a matter of God's personal anger, but only a way of saying that we live in a moral universe in which evil acts have built-in painful consequences that will eventually catch up with us. We pay the cost in the end because judgment operates inevitably in the moral system.

To such a view, I have to say, first, that it can sound more like the impersonal iron law of *karma* within Hindu philosophy than the way the Bible repeatedly describes God's anger against sin in very personal and relational terms indeed. But second, if judgment is a process that operates within the moral universe (as it clearly does), *who made the moral universe to be like that?* If wrongdoing has consequences at all, then whether we locate those consequences in the direct action of God or in a more abstract moral system at work really makes no ultimate difference. For the Bible clearly teaches that God is as sovereign in his governance of the way the "moral universe" works in general as he is over his own direct actions in particular. We cannot blame the painful consequences of sin on "the system" and exonerate God from all intentionality or involvement.

So as I ponder all aspects of the cross and try to assess what it means to include the word "penal" in our understanding of Christ's substitutionary death, I cannot escape asking the question again, *Does sin deserve to be punished?* And is such proper retribution part of God's sovereign, holy, loving justice in ruling the universe he created?

If not: then great swathes of the Bible make no sense or are clearly in error. For the Bible affirms from cover to cover that there is a dimension of just and proper punishment with which God in holy, loving justice responds to human wrongdoing.

If not: then we would seem to be adrift in a universe of ultimate moral indeterminacy. We can have no confidence that justice will finally be done, that God himself will be vindicated, or that all the evil in the history of the world will ever be fully dealt with.

If not: then the very concepts of grace and mercy seem to be emptied of meaning. It has been said that grace is God giving us what we don't deserve, while mercy is God not giving us what we do deserve. Certainly, in the Bible grace and mercy override all that we could ever, or actually do, deserve. But if there is no such thing as "what we deserve" at all, no moral relationship between our behaviour and its consequences, then it seems vacuous to speak of grace or mercy.

But if so: then it seems inescapable that we should include this dimension in the great cosmic achievement of the cross of Christ. To say that "Jesus bore my sin on the cross" must mean not only that he bore the worst that my sin could inflict on *him* (though it truly does mean that), but also that he bore the consequences of what my sin would otherwise incur for *me*. It means not just that Christ bore my unjust deeds, but also that he bore my just deserts. He not only took what I did to him; he took what I deserve from God.

And so, yet again, I find myself pleading for balance and against rhetorical contrasts and exclusions. I agree that Jesus spoke words of love and compassion, not accusation, to marginalized victims of oppression. I agree that it can be distasteful to hear evangelists hammering only a single drum, "You're not a victim; you're a rebel." I agree that God's heart bleeds for the broken and abused multitudes of our world who desperately need love, acceptance, compassion, and justice, and that he offers them exactly that in Christ. But according to Jesus and the whole Bible, they also need forgiveness. Every victim of sin is also a sinner. There is none who is *only* sinned *against*. The Old Testament Israelites thought of themselves as the victims of other people's cruelty—and they were. But they also needed to realize that they were guilty before God for their sinful rebellion, and so they must repent and turn to God for his forgiveness.

The extent of God's love is not only that he has entered with compassion into our suffering and proved (from the exodus to Galilee) that he is the God who stands with the weak and poor and oppressed—all this is gloriously and gratefully true. God has identified himself with *our* suffering and knows what it is to bear the pain of human injustice and violence. Yes, but the even greater extent of God's love is that he also took our sin and rebellion—of the oppressed and the oppressor – and bore all its just consequences on himself, in the mysterious unity of the Trinity at the cross.

We began the previous chapter by agreeing that there is a twisted version of penal substitution that is rightly to be rejected – the idea of an angry God making a victim Son the whipping boy for his brutality. Such a picture of "cosmic child abuse" is indeed a grotesque caricature. But it is equally a grossly deficient caricature to reduce the cross to nothing more than a cosmic sympathy card, in God's handwriting saying, "I share your pain". God did more than merely share our pain. God in Christ bore the pain of the just consequences of our sin, bore them "for us", such that we need never have to bear them ourselves, for all eternity.

Bringing It All Home

How can I bring all this back down to my own struggle to understand the cross at a personal level? It seems to me that it is utterly right to do what some of our most profound hymns do and to acknowledge for myself both sides of the truth we have been thinking about.

On the one hand, at the cross Christ bore the weight of all *my sin against him*. All my hatred and rejection of God, all that I have been, or could be capable of, in my sinful rebellion against my Creator was part of what Christ suffered. I stand among the enemies of God as one of those whose sin nailed Jesus to the cross.

> *Ashamed I hear my mocking voice call out among the scoffers*
> *It was my sin that held him there, until it was accomplished.*[3]

On the other hand, at the cross, Christ bore the weight of *God's judgment on my sin*. He bore not merely the brunt of my sin against him but the consequences of my sin upon me. He took not only what my sin could do, but also what my sin deserves.

At this point, whether in devotional struggle to understand or in the professional duty to preach and explain, or more often in songs and prayers of public worship, I find myself again and again overwhelmed with tears at the deep down truth of the cross that can never be fully grasped, but can only be gratefully embraced.

> *My sin, oh, the bliss of this glorious thought!*
> *My sin, not in part but the whole,*
> *Is nailed to the cross, and I bear it no more;*
> *Praise the Lord, Praise the Lord, O my soul!*[4]

What sin deserves, the Bible tells us, is to be utterly excluded from the presence of God. And that indeed is what Christ experienced at the height (or depth) of his suffering on the cross. His terrible cry of abandonment, "My God, my God, why have you forsaken me", plumbs the depths of this mystery and drives us to wrestle with what Paul meant in saying, "God made him who had no sin to be sin for us" (2 Cor. 5:21).

> In the moment of the Son's greatest need and greatest pain, God is not there. The Son cries and is not heard. The familiar resource, the ultimate resource, the only resource, is not there. The God who was always there, the God who was needed now as He had never been needed before, was nowhere to be seen. There was no answer to the Son's cry. There was no comfort. Jesus was left God-less, with no perception of His own Sonship, unable for the one and only time in His life to say, "Abba, Father." He was left with no sense of God's love and no sense of the operation of God's purpose. There was nothing but that *"Why?"*, trying vainly to bridge the Darkness. He was sin. He was lawlessness, and as such He was banished to the Black Hole where lawlessness belongs and from which no sound can escape but, *"Why?"* That was the Son's only word in His final agony as He reached out to God whom He needed so desperately but whom as Sin He couldn't discern and from whose presence He was outcast. There could be no accord. "God his Son not sparing"! He had to be dealt with not as Son but as Sin.[5]

What saving significance there is in that cry of Jesus! Because he went through that experience of utter abandonment by God, I will never need to. That is what inspired this sonnet of D. A. Carson:

> *The darkness fought, compelled the sun to flee,*
> *And like a conquering army swiftly trod*
> *Across the land, blind fear this despot's rod.*
> *The noon-day dark illumined tyranny.*
> *Still worse, abandonment by Deity*
> *Brought black despair more deadly than the blood*
> *That ran off with his life. "My God, my God,"*
> *Cried Jesus, "why have you forsaken me?"*
> *The silence thundered, Heaven's quiet reigned*
> *Supreme, a shocking, deafening, haunting swell.*
> *Because from answering Jesus, God refrained,*
> *I shall not cry, as he, this cry from hell.*
> *The cry of desolation, black as night,*
> *Shines forth across the world as brilliant light.*[6]

Notes

1. The crucial importance of interpreting Jesus – his life, identity, self-understanding, teaching, aims, and especially his death and resurrection – in relation to the story of the mission of God for the whole world through Old Testament Israel, has been thoroughly argued by N. T. Wright. See especially *Jesus and the Victory of God* (London: SPCK, 1996). My own *The Mission of God: Unlocking the Bible's Grand Narrative* is based on the same understanding of the necessity of reading the Bible as a whole for our understanding of the breadth of God's redemptive accomplishment in Christ.

   Unfortunately, whereas for me this comprehensive biblical framework for understanding the cosmic scope of God's accomplishment through the cross only enhances my profound appreciation for the personal heart of substitutionary atonement, there are those who seem to find it strangely threatening to their concern for the latter. I find this puzzling and disturbing, since it has always seemed to me that it is of the essence of evangelical identity and commitment to strive for the broadest and deepest understanding of the whole Bible and to interpret the Bible in the light of the Bible. That is the ambition as well as the humble limit of all our research.

   Few if any evangelicals have done more to champion the penal substitutionary understanding of the atonement, or to articulate it with such erudite clarity, as J. I. Packer. So I am grateful for the book in which he and Mark Dever have assembled some of the best of their own and others' writings on this subject over many years (*In My Place Condemned He Stood: Celebrating the Glory of the Atonement* [Wheaton: Crossway Books, 2007]). And yet, I am saddened by Dr. Packer's apparent suspicion of the wider biblical setting of understanding the cross, expressed at the end of his introduction to the volume:

   > In recent years, great strides in biblical theology and contemporary canonical exegesis have brought new precision to our grasp of the Bible's overall story of how God's plan to bless Israel, and through Israel the world, came to a climax in and through Christ. But I do not see how it can be denied that each New Testament book, whatever other job it may be doing, has in view, in one way or another, Luther's primary question: how may a weak, perverse, and guilty sinner find a gracious God? ... And to the extent that modern developments, by filling our horizon with the great metanarrative, distract us from pursuing Luther's question in personal terms, they hinder as well as help in our appreciation of the gospel (pp. 26–27).

   I simply fail to see how gaining the widest possible biblical perspective, from the whole biblical narrative, can hinder our appreciation of the gospel – *unless* it is accompanied by *denial* of the personal and substitutionary nature of Christ's death (which readers can see is certainly not true in my own case). But I am disturbed that it is possible for the reverse to happen – namely, that some theologians and preachers are so obsessed with the penal substitutionary understanding of the cross that they either ignore or seem scarcely aware of the total biblical story in which it is set and the vast cosmic and creational dimensions of the cross that the New Testament itself also spells out so clearly.

2. Howard Marshall has a fine and careful discussion of the nature of punishment and retribution in biblical perspective, and particularly on the threat of *exclusion* from God as its primary element, in *Aspects of the Atonement: Cross and Resurrection in the Reconciling of God and Humanity* (London: Hyderabad; Colorado Springs: Paternoster, 2007), ch. 1, "The Penalty of Sin".

3. From Stuart Townend's hymn: "How Deep the Father's Love for Us".

4. From the hymn, "When Peace Like a River", by Horatio Spafford.

5. Donald Macleod, *A Faith to Live By* (Inverness: Christian Focus, 2002), 130–31; as quoted in Tim Chester, *Delighting in the Trinity* (Oxford: Monarch; Grand Rapids: Kregel, 2005), 61.

6. D.A. Carson, *Holy Sonnets of the Twentieth Century* (Grand Rapids, Baker; Nottingham, Crossway: 1994), 51. Used by permission.

PART FOUR

What about the End of the World?

Theologians tend to make rather bad jokes. Like the one about the theology student approaching his final exams who was heard to say, "I don't know much about eschatology, but it's not the end of the world."

Well, many of us, myself included, don't claim to understand more than the tip of the iceberg about the end of the world. And although there are many people who will confidently sell you a detailed timetable for how it will all unfold – complete with "End Times" websites and video games to rehearse it and T-shirts to show you're ready for it – the truth is that none of us can possibly understand fully all that God has in store for the universe he created and for this planet Earth in particular.

I sometimes think it is like a creature whose eyes and brain can only see things in black, white, and shades of grey, trying to imagine what a world of colour is like. Or for us who live in a world of three dimensions trying to imagine what it might be like to live in a world of four (or five or fifty) dimensions. Or for a baby in the womb trying to imagine life after birth in a world that he experiences indirectly, but has not yet entered. Or twins in the womb having a conversation: "Do you believe in life after birth, then? 'Air', and 'Light', and all that stuff we hear voices about?" "Of course not. It's all wishful thinking. Amniotic fluid is all there is. When you're born, your born – finished, that's it. Kick around while you can."

We simply have no means of conceiving the realities of life in the new creation – yet.

Of course, as with everything else these days, if you really want to know the answer, you can always Google it. I tried that, and found there were 846 million entries for "End of the World" – which is rather a lot to survey, even if you cut out the towns and pubs actually called "World's End". At a rough count there seem to be eight movies, eighteen songs, and a band in New York with that name. There are over three million websites making end of the world predictions, including several that urge us to believe it will happen in 2012, for reasons not entirely clear to me. But since that is the year of my retirement I needn't worry about my pension plans.

There are so many cranks and controversies that grow like weeds around this question. If we started trying to deal with all of them, it would take another book (which I wish somebody would write). But by way of introduction it seems good to try to tackle at least some of the more dominant examples of what I think are misleading (though hugely popular) ways of thinking about the end of the world. We will do that in chapter 9. Then we can move on more happily in the final two chapters to the certainties that the Bible clearly does teach about this great event and what lies beyond it, and to the consequences for our own lives and behaviour here and now.

chapter

9

CRANKS AND CONTROVERSIES

It is hard enough struggling with the God we don't understand when we only have the Bible in front of us. It gets even worse when we are assailed by dozens of theories on all sides, in very persuasive glossy books, telling us what the Bible supposedly teaches about the end of the world – and a lot more besides. You might say that is a bit rich coming from me, when I'm trying to do the same thing! Well, this is a very personal book, and I can only speak from where I stand and say how it seems to me. And it seems to me that some of the most popular beliefs around this subject are a long way from what the Bible, taken in a comprehensive and balanced way, actually teaches.

However, I am well aware that you might be convinced of one or another of the viewpoints I am going to criticize – and that's fine. All I ask is that you do what the Bereans did (Acts 17:10 – 11) and search the Scriptures for yourself to see what is true. And if you don't like controversy or if you don't wish to have your favourite views put in doubt, feel free to skip this chapter for the moment and go on to the next one. I do not want you to miss the last two chapters, which are far more positive and enriching for our souls.

You're still there? Well, let's tackle some of the hard stuff.

Last Things, Last Days, and End Times

Traditionally (for the sake of the muddled theological student above), *eschatology* is the name given to that branch of Christian systematic theology that deals with "the last things". That was the term commonly used for the seven things that the Bible says lie ahead of us all – either in terms of our personal experience or in terms of cosmic reality. Classically, the seven last things are listed as:

- death
- the intermediate state[1]
- the return of Christ
- the resurrection of the dead
- the day of judgment
- heaven
- hell

The Bible also speaks about "the last days". But as it is used in the New Testament, this term clearly does not refer only to some far off future era, thousands of years after the apostles' own times. No, it is used repeatedly to describe the whole time from the first coming of Christ until his return. "In these last days he has spoken to us by his Son", writes the author of Hebrews (Heb. 1:2), speaking about the earthly life of Jesus (see also 1 Peter 1:20; 1 John 2:18).

So, the last days were launched by Jesus himself, and we have been living in them ever since. The New Testament does not think of the last days as a period that still lies ahead, immediately before the Lord Jesus returns. No, the last days have already arrived with Jesus. We are already living in them – and will continue to do so until Christ returns. So when somebody anxiously asks me, "Do you think we are living in the last days?" I cheerfully reply, "Yes. But so was the apostle Paul, and so were Augustine, Francis of Assisi, Martin Luther, or Mother Theresa. We've all been living in the last days, since the New Testament."

The phrase we hear most nowadays, though, is "the end times". And that has become a whole speculation industry. In spite of Jesus' warning that we would not know the day or the hour of his return (since even he did not), and in spite of his telling us that our prime task is simply to be ready for it by getting on with faithfully doing what he has told us to do, people still insist on defying Jesus' warning. So they produce all kinds of fanciful theories, predictions, and timetables about exactly how and when the world will end, in what order things will happen, and where it will all take place. It's as if they have the script in front of them, with the CNN cameras ready to roll when the action starts. "Have your 'End of the World' experience, folks, in the comfort of your own home." Then others build whole layers of fantasy and fiction on top of their speculation, producing books that are so popular they seem, if not to outsell the Bible itself, to be read more voraciously.

Such speculation is not new, of course. For many centuries Christian groups have come up with predictions of the end of the world–all of them as mistaken as they have been frequent (you can find fascinating lists of them on Google or Wikipedia). Often there is a surge of such frenzy at times of great stress and panic.

Around the turn of the first millennium, AD 1000, Europe was awash with expectations that the world would end then, since the millennium had clearly come and gone, had it not?

The times of the great plagues that swept Europe from the fourteenth century onward produced similar fears. Civilization was doomed and Christ must come back soon.

Martin Luther was totally convinced that the world would come to an end within or very soon after his own lifetime–in an Armageddon-style war with the Muslim Turks (not a lot has changed).

At the height of the Cold War in the 1970s, Hal Lindsey's *Late Great Planet Earth* spawned widespread certainty that the 1980s would see conflagration in the Middle East, with communist hoards fulfilling Ezekiel's vision of Gog and Magog on the soil of the modern state of Israel, ushering in Armageddon and the return of Christ (on a premillennial dispensationalist schedule).

The turn of the third millennium in AD 2000 produced the Y2K frenzy, with a range of more secular (and some religious) apocalyptic predictions.

Today, the so-called war on terror has been the catalyst for more recycling of those kinds of apocalyptic scenarios, based on deceptively simplistic and distorted polarizing of world politics–with profoundly shortsighted and one-sided perceptions of realities in the Middle East.

I discovered that the fathers of Anglicanism were not so bothered about such things. The Book of Common Prayer gives you tables to find the date of Easter until AD 2299! This is handy if you are planning an Easter conference for your church with two centuries' advance notice. There's even another table with complicated formulae enabling you to work it out for every century until AD 8500–and there is even a little box next to that date, with "etc." in it! So if there are any Anglicans still around in AD 8599, we will have great fun filling in that next little box with the date of Easter AD 8600–and probably still arguing with those who will be confidently predicting Christ will return in AD 8601.

As I said, this is not the place to deal with all the contemporary "end times" theories, except to urge you to be cautious and discerning not to believe everything you read or hear from popular "end times prophecy specialists", and to check all that you do hear by careful study of the Scriptures. Such caution, I would urge, is particularly important in relation to those who build detailed and dogmatic predictions around three particular favourites of the end times speculators: the millennium, the rapture, and the modern state of Israel.

The Millennium

This word means a period of one thousand years. When you think of the amount of controversial theological and popular theories that surround it, it may come as a surprise to learn that the term is actually found in the Bible in six verses of only one single chapter – Revelation 20. The book of Revelation is filled with symbolic and metaphorical imagery, and it seems most likely that this expression also is being used in that way, to imply a long but indefinite time period.

Yet people have built whole timetables, theologies, and complicated schemes of interpreting the rest of the Bible upon their understanding of a phrase that comes just six times in six verses in its final book. Whole denominations have formed around the differences of opinion! It all hinges on whether you think Jesus will return before the millennium starts (premillennialism) or after it has ended (postmillennialism), or whether you think (as I am inclined to) that the term refers to the whole period between the first and second coming of Christ (amillennialism). Then, I am told, there are the panmillennialists – those who think it will just all pan out in the end.

Now this is not the place to solve these disputes, and people are sincere in holding to one or another viewpoint, as I am sure you probably are. Nor am I questioning the importance of seeking a sensible theological understanding, based on careful exegesis and hermeneutical tools, of what Revelation 20 was intending to communicate, in the context of the whole message of that book. Many people never do that, however, but just take their theories off-the-peg from the latest book or the dogmatic stance of their denomination.

My point is simply that we need to avoid getting sidetracked into a whole jungle of arcane interpretations, built on shaky assumptions about a term that *occurs in one single short passage and nowhere else in the Bible.* That does not mean that it doesn't matter. It means that the millennium probably is not such a central part of what we need to focus on when thinking about the end of the world as some people make it out to be.

The Rapture

At least the term "millennium" or "thousand years" is a word that actually occurs in the Bible. Contrary to what you would think from the avalanche of rapture theories and predictions, the word "rapture" isn't in the Bible at all. Nor, in my view, is the event that the word is popularly supposed to describe – at least, not as it is usually portrayed.

The currently most popular view of the rapture (known as "pretribulation rapture") is that it will be a moment when all the Christians on earth will be suddenly, silently, and secretly snatched away from earth up to heaven, leaving behind not only their unbelieving loved ones, but also their clothes and spectacles and anything they happened to be in at the time – like cars and planes (causing untold chaos). The rest of humanity will be left behind to struggle on for another seven years of "the tribulation", before the millennium starts. All kinds of appalling calamities (drawn from a fairly literal reading of Revelation) will fill that time.

Yet again, the idea of a rapture is drawn from a single Bible text – two verses in particular (which are almost certainly being misunderstood). Then, as with the millennium, other texts that actually say nothing about a rapture are drawn in to support the original idea. That is, once you have interpreted this one text in terms of the rapture, as popularly conceived, you then tend to "find rapture" all over the place where it is not actually mentioned.

Yet on this slender biblical foundation, a vast edifice of speculation has been built into a kind of "folk Christianity", accepted without question by millions of believers. The most prominent example is the *Left Behind* series of novels (along with the movies, websites, games, and merchandizing surrounding it) – a mammoth marketing success that builds wholly imaginary fiction on top of a questionable and relatively recent[2] interpretation of the Bible, in an area that Jesus warned us not even to speculate about. Then there are websites that provide "rapture-o-meters", so that you can calculate how close we are to its happening. Never mind that Jesus said the coming of the Son of Man would be when we least expect it. These websites presume to tell us how close we are to the hypothetical event itself!

1 Thessalonians 4:16 – 17

The key text for the rapture theory is 1 Thessalonians 4:16 – 17. Paul is seeking to encourage the believers in the young church in Thessalonica that their loved ones who have died believing in Christ are perfectly safe and will not lose out when Christ appears. Whether dead or alive at that moment, all believers will be united in welcoming the Lord's coming.

Paul then brings his encouragement to a climax with a portrayal of the return of Christ that seems to draw on two metaphors – one from the

Old Testament, the other from his own contemporary world. This what Paul says:

> For the Lord himself will come down from heaven, with a loud command, with the voice of the archangel and with the trumpet call of God, and the dead in Christ will rise first. After that, we who are still alive and are left will be caught up[3] [*this is the single word that has generated the rapture concept*] together with them in the clouds to meet the Lord [*lit., "for a meeting with the Lord"*] in the air. And so we will be with the Lord forever.

In verse 16, Paul is probably using the memory of Mount Sinai, the greatest theophany (i.e., appearance of God) in the Old Testament, when God came down to the top of the mountain for a meeting with his redeemed people, with a loud voice and a supernatural trumpet call (Ex. 19:17 – 19). Similarly, says Paul, only even more majestically, the Lord himself will come down again, not just to a mountain, but to the earth itself. And not just to dwell in a tabernacle, but to take his rightful residence as Lord of the whole earth.

In verse 17, Paul is probably drawing on the common practice of cities in the Roman Empire when the emperor came to visit. The dignitaries of the city would go out partway "for a meeting" with the emperor on the road as he approached and then accompany and welcome him into their city.[4] They did not meet the emperor and then go off with him somewhere else; they met him in order to offer their allegiance and to bring him into their corner of his empire. They were welcoming the emperor to the city over which he ruled. That, says Paul, is like believers welcoming their Lord on his return to his rightful place as Lord and King of the whole earth. We go to meet him in order to welcome and receive him back, not to disappear to some other place.

The motion and direction of Paul's imagery, then, is *not*: that Jesus comes down halfway, then we are snatched up to him, then *he* turns round and goes back up again, taking us with him back to heaven. In fact, heaven is mentioned only as the place *from which* the Lord comes. It is not referred to at all as the place *to which* we go. Rather, it is *we* who turn around, in Paul's imagery! The sequence of his description is: Jesus is coming back to earth; we are snatched up in the air for a meeting with him as he comes; and then we welcome him to his rightful home *here* – his kingdom, his inheritance, his renewed creation, his redeemed people. We will then be with the Lord forever, not because *we* will have gone to heaven, but because *he* will have come home to dwell with us (as Rev. 21:3 explicitly says).

So Paul is talking about the glorious *public* return of King Jesus, not about a *secret* rapture of the saints (and in any case, how could anything be *less* secret than what verse 16 describes?). It will be as public and unavoidable as when God thundered and trumpeted at Mount Sinai or when the Roman emperor came to visit his dominions.

Matthew 24:40–41

The other passage that is sometimes used as justification for a secret rapture is Matthew 24:40–41:

> Two men will be in the field; one will be taken and the other left. Two women will be grinding with a hand mill; one will be taken and the other left.

This is interpreted to mean that one will be taken (raptured to heaven), while the other is left behind to endure whatever comes next on earth (hence the title of the series, *Left Behind*).

But in the immediate context, Jesus refers to the suddenness of the flood (as a picture of the sudden and unexpected nature of the coming of the Son of Man). The ones "taken away" then were those *destroyed* in the flood (v. 39). Being "raptured" in that sense was decidedly not a welcome escape but an act of judgment.

In verses 40–41, Jesus is probably likening his coming to a sudden and unexpected enemy attack on a village (just as he also compared it to a thief coming in the night). Some unfortunate people will be captured and taken away (like the victims of the flood in the preceding verse); others – the *fortunate* ones – will be left behind (i.e., spared or saved). Rapture-gazers reverse the symbolism entirely by reading into these verses a meaning they have already mistakenly taken from 1 Thessalonians 4, namely, that Jesus is talking about taking people away to heaven. All he is doing is picturing the suddenness and decisiveness of the appearing of the Son of Man.

The Land of Israel

Ever since the occupation of Palestine by Jewish settlers in the early 1900s and the establishment of the modern state of Israel after the war of 1947–48, the land and state of Israel have figured prominently in some end times scenarios. Often these views are based on interpretations of Old Testament prophecies about the land of Israel that take no account of how such texts are related to Christ in the New Testament. That is, they skip happily off the pages of Ezekiel and land in the twentieth century, without reference to what the New Testament teaches about the fulfilment of Old Testament hopes in the life, death, and resurrection of Jesus.

In the Old Testament, of course, the promise and gift of the land form a major part of Israel's faith. Paul reminds us that all Old Testament promises have their "Yes and Amen" in Christ (2 Cor. 1:20). Whether Gentiles or Jews, believers in Christ constitute the spiritual seed of Abraham and are heirs to the covenant and promise (Gal 3:26–28; cf. Rom. 4:11–12). But that promise made to Abraham had the land as a major constituent. If all the great themes of Old Testament faith and ritual converge typologically on Christ, where does the land fit in?[5]

The New Testament gives no special theological place to the land of Palestine, simply as *territory*. The land as a holy *place* has ceased to have relevance for Christians. The vocabulary of blessing, holiness, promise, gift, inheritance, rest, and so on is never used of the territory inhabited by the Jewish people anywhere in the New Testament as it so frequently is in the Old. All these "landed" realities were transferred to Christ himself (just like the sacrifices, the priesthood, the temple, and the kingship).

Paul's teaching on the new status of the Gentiles in Christ (Eph. 2:11–3:6) is rich in Old Testament land imagery. Gentiles, before coming to Christ, were "excluded from citizenship in Israel and foreigners to the covenants of the promise"; that is, they had had no share in the land-kinship membership of Israel (2:12). But through the cross of Christ, Gentiles "are no longer foreigners and strangers [landless dependants], but fellow citizens with God's people and members of his household" (2:19). This speaks of permanence, security, inclusion, and practical responsibility (cf. 3:6). This is exactly what "being in the land" meant for Old Testament Israel. But now that same security is enjoyed by all in Christ–believing Gentiles as well as believing Jews. What Israel had through their land, all believers now have through Christ. Now Christ himself takes over the significance and the function of that old land-kinship qualification. To be "*in Christ*" carries the same status and responsibilities as to be "*in the land*".

The writer to the Hebrews wanted to reassure Jewish believers in Jesus that they had lost nothing of their great inheritance, but rather had it all the more richly and eternally in Christ. Look at what he tells them "*we have*": We *have* the land–described as "the rest", which even Joshua did not finally achieve for Israel, but into which we can enter through Christ (Heb. 3:12–4:11). We *have* a high priest (4:14, 8:1, 10:21). We *have* an altar (13:10). We *have* hope through the covenant (6:19–20). We *have* confident access into the Holy Place, so we have the reality of tabernacle and temple (10:19). We *have* come to Mount Zion (12:22). We *have* a kingdom (12:28). Indeed, according to Hebrews, the only thing *we do not have* is that here we have no earthly, territorial city (13:14). In the light of all the other positive "haves", this clear negative stands out all the more significantly. There is no "holy land" or "holy city" for Christians. We have no need of either. We have Christ.

We must also point out that nowhere at all does the New Testament build any of its teaching about the future of either Christians or Jews or the world around future events involving a renewed independent state of Israel in the land (in New Testament times, of course, there was no state of Israel; Judea and other parts of the land were subject parts of the Roman Empire. There had been no independent state called Israel on that soil since the fall of Samaria to the Assyrians in 721 BC). Of course, Paul does indeed talk about God's continuing love for the Jews and speaks of them being "grafted back" into their original olive tree, through faith in Jesus. But it is a categorical mistake to simply equate what the New Testament teaches about Jewish people in general with the modern state of Israel alone.

Now, of course, it is not surprising that many *Jews* have a deep attachment to the land of their ancestors, or that they continue to hold to a territorial understanding of the land promise to Abraham, since they do not accept the fundamental Christian premise that, as Paul says, "what God promised our ancestors he has fulfilled for us, their children, by raising up Jesus" (Acts 13:32–33). One has to say, though, that not all Jews have by any means supported the establishment of the state of Israel or approve of its continued actions over the past half century, and many sincere Jews reject Zionism politically and theologically; moreover, many are dismayed at the behaviour of Israel socially and militarily.

But no single land or city on earth has a special or holy significance *for Christians*. The centre of our faith is not a place but a person, the person of Jesus the Messiah. And he is Lord of all the earth and will return to claim the whole earth.

Some "end times" scenarios predict a localized return of Jesus to Jerusalem, or the rebuilding of the temple there, or the last great battle of Armageddon literally fought in the land of modern Israel.[6] These sensational predictions (some of which casually entertain scenarios involving *massive* loss of life) enter into popular Christian fiction and folk religion. But they also affect powerful political agendas, and that makes them much more potentially insidious. They give a privileged place in God's alleged final agenda for world history to the modern state of Israel on the basis of some questionable interpretations of Scripture. This, then, leads those who endorse such views to an unbiblical suspension of any prophetic critique of the oppressive policies and practices of that state.

For some Christians, the modern Israeli state is excused from any moral or international accountability because it is "fulfilling prophecy". Such an attitude of blind "support for Israel" stands in jarring contrast to the words of most of the actual biblical prophets themselves, and even of Jesus. It has always seemed strange to me that anybody who dares voice criticism of the modern Israeli state is quickly accused (by some Jews and Christians alike) of anti-Semitism. Yet, by that standard, Jesus, Paul, and the prophets would all have to be put on the same charge—which is wildly ridiculous, since all of them profoundly loved their own people, yet spoke the most trenchant words of prophetic accusation against idolatry, oppression, and racist nationalism within Israel itself. In fact, it is clear that Jesus point-blank refused to accept the agenda of Jewish territorial and political nationalism of his own day and spoke out against it. It is hard to see how he could endorse its modern equivalent.

Conclusion: Check It Out

Now you may well disagree with me on any or all of the last three points, and that's fine. There are very strong and very different convictions about these things held by many sincere people. And in my life as an Old Testament teacher I have come up against many of them one way or another. It is not easy to swim against the tide of such popular convictions. There is also a massive weight of popular assumptions, books, movies, websites, and multi-million dollar promotion—all of which give some end times scenarios an air of infallibility and inevitability. They are just so powerfully persuasive in the way they are dressed up.

But it is tragic if Christians take their beliefs more from fictional novels and even comics and Hollywood movies than from a careful study of the Bible itself and of the solid tradition of Christian faith through the ages of the church. We need to ask whether our beliefs in these matters are shaped by the recent popular "folk Christianity" in our surrounding culture, or by thoughtful understanding of the Bible for ourselves.

All I would urge, then (before you throw this book away if you disagree with me, and miss the last two chapters!), is to be careful and discerning and seek to be governed by what the Bible, interpreted as a whole, has to say.

So, rather than dig ourselves into ever deeper pits of probable disagreement over disputed opinions, let us move forward and think about what the Bible clearly and repeatedly teaches about the end of the world. Let's think about the biblical *certainties* that lie before us and the practical *consequences* that they have on how we should live now.

When the Bible talks about the end of the world (to go on using our loose phrase, which is actually not accurate), it draws our attention to two things: an ending and a beginning. The first is an event, the second is an ongoing new state of affairs. The event is the great climax of all history, when Christ returns. The new beginning is the new creation, which Christ's return will usher in – the new age of the eternal reign of God, when he takes up residence again among his redeemed humanity in a renewed creation.

We will look at each of these in the next two chapters.

Notes

1. This is the term used to describe the state of the individual person in the "interval" between their personal death and the return of Christ.
2. The teaching in its contemporary form dates from the mid-nineteenth century, particularly from the teaching of John Nelson Darby, from whom stemmed the scheme known as premillennial dispensationalism. The idea that the saints would be raptured before the great tribulation ("pretribulationism") is sometimes said to go back to a young Scottish girl, Margaret McDonald, who had prophetic visions in 1930 that she shared with Edwin Irving, but a direct link between her and the early fathers of dispensationalism is disputed. It gained its present popularity as the dominant assumption in much evangelical folk religion in America largely as a result of the Scofield Bible and the phenomenal success of Hal Lindsey's book *The Late, Great Planet Earth* (Grand Rapids: Zondervan, 1970).
3. This is the single word that has generated the rapture concept. The English word "rapture" is derived from the Latin (Vulgate) translation, which uses *rapiemur* (from *rapio, rapere, rapui, raptum,* "to snatch away").
4. The practice continued in many kingdoms after the Roman Empire fell. The great "Royal Progresses" of English monarchs included such protocols. A good description of one, when Henry VIII visited York in 1541, is found in C. J. Samson's historical novel *Sovereign*. (London: Pan Books, 2007).
5. I have discussed this issue in much more depth in *Old Testament Ethics for the People of God* (Downers Grove, IL: InterVarsity Press, 2004), chap. 6.
6. For all that is said, written, and imagined about the so-called battle of Armageddon, many people never notice that in Revelation *it is a battle that is never fought!* Every time it is mentioned, there is a great gathering of all the forces hostile to God, Christ, and his people, but each time, there is *no* battle, *no* great clash of armies – as in much popular fiction. Rather, the enemies of God are simply routed, destroyed by earthquake, or by the sword of his mouth, or by fire from heaven (see Rev. 16:12 – 21; 19:19 – 21; 20:7 – 10). Even the great original cartoon for all this speculation – Ezekiel 38 – 39 – never

describes an actual battle, but simply assures the reader that God himself will destroy all the armies of his enemies. God's people will not fight the last battle; only God himself will.

chapter

10

THE GREAT CLIMAX

"When's the Big Day?" That's a question we use often enough in everyday life. We might ask it of a young couple who have become engaged to find out whether they have fixed the wedding day yet. Or if there is a sportsman in the family, we might be enquiring about that grand finale of some exciting competition when everything will be decided.

The Bible has a "Big Day", and it was arousing interest from early on.

Waiting for God

"The day of the Lord" is a frequent expression in the Old Testament. At first, it described the hope of the Israelites that Yahweh, their God, would intervene to defeat their enemies and lift them up out of oppression. Amos, however, turned the concept on its head and said that when God intervened on "the day of the LORD", it would be darkness, not light (Amos 5:19–20). God was indeed coming to judge his enemies, but who were they? Not just the foreign nations. The shocking fact was that Israel and Judah, by their rejection of covenant obligations, by their idolatries, and especially by their social injustice and exploitation of the poor, had turned themselves also into God's enemies and were standing right in the blast path of his judgment – when the day of the Lord came. The Big Day was not one to look forward to.

Other prophets took up Amos's lead and built their own descriptions of that coming day of the Lord. In the sense of the imminent judgment of God, the day of the Lord was initially fulfilled in Old Testament history when

Jerusalem was destroyed and God's people were exiled to Babylon in 587 BC. But some prophets also used the term to look even further ahead and used it in a combined positive and negative sense. The day of the Lord would certainly bring judgment, but it would also mean deliverance and joy for those who remained faithful to God. Read, for example, Zephaniah 1:14–18 as a terrible picture of the day of the Lord as one of wrath and judgment; but follow it immediately by reading Zephaniah 3:9–17 for the sequel filled with healing, restoration, and joy–all as part of "that day".

In the New Testament, the day of the Lord gains a more clearly final sense with reference to the return of Christ, and indeed Paul turns it into "the day of Christ" (e.g., Phil. 1:6, 10; 2:16; cf. 1 Cor. 1:8). The day of Christ is the great climax, the grand finale, of all the work of God in history. It is the day that will bring to completion the whole story of salvation. This great event has a clear programme set in advance in the Bible. Three great actions will unfold: the return of Christ, the resurrection of the dead, and the final judgment.

These are usually presented in that order, which has a certain natural logic and sequence. But they must be held together as all part of the one great final event. This is "the end", but it includes all three elements. So we will think about each in turn. But keep in mind as we do so that these are all closely interconnected dimensions of the same great climactic event.

The Return of Christ

The New Testament teaches that Jesus Christ will return to complete the work he accomplished in his earthly lifetime. Since much earth time has elapsed since Christ's first coming and we are still waiting for his second coming, we tend to separate the first and second coming in our minds, in our liturgy, and in our church calendars. Indeed, in the traditional church's year, curiously, we think of his second coming at Advent before we celebrate his first coming at Christmas! The New Testament writers, however, held them together much more closely as two parts of a single great achievement of God.

Pause and read these three passages and you will see that in each case Christ's first and second coming are integrally linked together: Titus 2:11–13; Hebrews 9:26–28; 1 John 3:2, 5.

So how will it happen? What will it be like when Christ returns? Well, as you will not be surprised to hear by this stage of this book, there are depths that we surely cannot hope to understand in detail. If it is hard enough to understand God when we think about what he has done in the past or what he allows in the present, it is even more difficult to understand all that the Bible tells us about God's plans for the ultimate future. Even Jesus himself was reticent to spell it out and resorted to imagery and comparisons. So we should not press our questions beyond what is clearly taught.

But at least three things seem clear in the teaching of the New Testament. The return of Christ will be personal, visible, and glorious. We can at least understand what these words mean, even if we cannot understand the mechanics of how they will be true.

Personal

First of all, it will be the real Jesus who returns. The New Testament is not talking about a mystical presence or some subjective inner feeling that "Jesus is here", in the way that some people talk about the continuing presence of legendary heroes who are now dead. Nor is this the sentimental or emotional comfort that bereaved folk sometimes express when they say about a deceased loved one, "She will always be with us." No, the New Testament affirms that Jesus will be as recognizable when he returns as he was to his first disciples when they met him after his resurrection. When the disciples saw the risen Jesus, they knew for certain that it was he – the real Jesus, more real indeed than ever.

Recall the description of the ascension when Jesus, having blessed his disciples and commissioned them again to carry forward the mission of God, was raised up before their eyes and then disappeared in a cloud – symbolic of returning to the very presence of God in heaven. They stared into the sky. Where had he gone? Would they ever see him again? Luke continues:

> They were looking intently up into the sky as he was going, when suddenly two men dressed in white stood beside them. "Men of Galilee," they said, "why do you stand here looking into the sky? This same Jesus, who has been taken from you into heaven, will come back in the same way you have seen him go into heaven."

> —Acts 1:10 – 11

"This same Jesus . . ." Not his ghost, or his influence, or his memory, but the Jesus they knew and loved. The return of Christ will be personal, recognizable, and unmistakeable (see also James 5:7 – 9; 1 John 2:28).

Visible

Second, the return of Christ will be visible. It will not be secret or only for believers. It will be as "unsecret" as a flash of lightning. "For as lightning that comes from the east is visible even in the west, so will be the coming of the Son of Man" (Matt. 24:27). Lightning that streaks across the whole sky is visible to everybody underneath. So Jesus says his arrival will be unmistakably visible to all. Nobody will be unaware of it.

A few verses later Jesus reinforces this by saying that the impact of his coming will be felt by all nations on earth. His return will be universally witnessed: "At that time the sign of the Son of Man will appear in the sky, and all the nations of the earth will mourn. They will see the Son of Man coming on the clouds of the sky, with power and great glory" (Matt. 24:30)

In the same way, Revelation's opening picture of the exalted Jesus declares: "Look, he is coming with the clouds, and every eye will see him" (Rev. 1:7). Sometimes the New Testament says that Jesus will be "revealed", which means clearly seen by all for who he truly is (1 Cor. 1:7; 2 Thess. 1:7).

Because it will be visible, the second coming of Christ will also be public and universal. Nobody is going to miss it. His first coming would not have merited even a footnote in any newspaper in Rome. Even Herod in Jerusalem had to be told about it by foreign visitors. But when Jesus comes again, it will be an event of global, instant, total, and overwhelming public awareness. It will displace whatever else is happening at the time. Nobody is going to say, "Just wait till I finish this," or "Let me go fetch my camera." Absolutely everything will yield right of way to the returning King, irresistibly visible to all.

Thinking about this, of course, pushes our minds beyond our cognitive comfort zone. The normal laws of physics, we protest, do not allow any event to be simultaneously visible from every point on a spherical planet. Proposed solutions that involve satellites and TV screens (which some people give as the reason the event has waited so long!) seem laughably techno-obsessed. Even if we could imagine a day when everybody on earth actually had access to TV (a marketer's dream, no doubt, but a cultural nightmare), the thought of the second coming of Christ having to be dependent on everybody simultaneously watching a TV screen is absurd (and what if somebody decides to switch their TV off–do they then get excused from the event?).

No, I may not understand the mechanics, but I am certain that the Creator of the universe has the power and means to make the return of his Son instantly visible and compellingly real to every human being on the planet. Wherever you or anyone else may be on the surface of the earth on the day Christ returns, you will see him. For those of us who spend a lot of time travelling from one part of the earth to the other this is a greater comfort than our travel insurance document. There are many things I have missed back home by being away when they happened. This won't be one of them!

Glorious

In contrast to his first coming in humility and obscurity, Jesus will return in the full glory of his divine majesty (the references to clouds in several Bible passages are symbolic of this; clouds are often evidence of the presence of God). When Jesus first came, it was to a mother's womb, a borrowed manger, a carpenter's bench, and a cross. When he comes again, it will be to his rightful kingdom, his inheritance of all things in heaven and on earth, and in the fullness of his divine glory.

So Paul writes, "We wait for the blessed hope – the *glorious* appearing of our great God and Saviour, Jesus Christ" (Titus 2:13, my emphasis). Paul is probably making another startling echo of the protocol language of the Roman Empire. "Our great god and saviour" was a phrase used to describe the Roman emperors. Cities would look forward to a visit from "our great god and saviour". Paul says, as it were, "So do we, but a far greater and far more glorious one – the appearing of *our* great God and Saviour, Jesus Christ" (see also 2 Thess. 2:8).

Putting these three great biblical affirmations together, then, the return of Christ will mean the *personal presence* of the one who is now physically absent from us, the *visible presence* of the one who is now invisible to us, and the *glorious presence* of the one whose glory is now hidden from us. That is the scope and scale of the Bible's portrayal of this great event. Let's not waste time fantasizing and speculating about the *timing* of it. Let's trust and rejoice and prepare for the *certainty* of it.

What Does It Mean for Me?

I was preparing to preach on Isaiah 52:7 – 10 recently. It is that wonderful passage filled with excitement in which the prophet pictures the lonely sentries in devastated Jerusalem seeing a runner from the east bringing good news that God is at last returning; the exile is at an end and God is on his way home.

> How beautiful on the mountains
>   are the feet of those who bring good news,
> who proclaim peace,
>   who bring good tidings,
>   who proclaim salvation,
> who say to Zion,
>   "Your God *reigns*!"

> Listen! Your watchmen lift up their voices;
> together they shout for joy.
> When the Lord *returns* to Zion,
> they will see it with their own eyes.
> Burst into songs of joy together,
> you ruins of Jerusalem,
> for the Lord has comforted his people,
> he has *redeemed* Jerusalem.
> The Lord will lay bare his holy arm
> in the sight of all the nations,
> and all the ends of the earth will see
> the salvation of our God.

—Isaiah 52:7 – 10 (my emphasis)

I noticed, as any preacher might, the three words in our English text all beginning with "r" (in italics). And I preached on how the prophet was encouraging the exiles that their God was the reigning, returning, redeeming King. Then I drew the text through to the New Testament and pointed to the way it finds its next level of fulfilment there. For Jesus of Nazareth was (in his first coming), is now (in his sovereign government), and will be (at his second coming), God reigning, God returning, and God redeeming.

To think about how to apply the passage, I asked myself the question, *What does it mean for me here and now that Jesus is the reigning Lord, the returning King, the redeeming Saviour of the world?*

Christ Reigning

For me, to believe that Jesus is reigning means that when I reflect on the news of the world – with all the unpredictable complexities of international life, the claims and counterclaims, and the posturing and arrogance of military power and economic dominance – I must constantly ask how and where do I see the signs of the reign of God in Christ in the midst of it all.

But isn't that far too difficult in our mad and topsy-turvy world? Probably no more difficult than it would have been in the days of the prophets when Assyria, then Babylon, and then Persia seemed to rule the world. Or in the days of Jesus and the apostles, when the Roman Empire dominated their world as the single superpower, imposing its will by an ambiguous mixture of ruthless military superiority, economic self-interest, and positive achievements. Not a lot has changed. But in the midst of all that ambiguity, we are called to affirm, "Our God reigns; Jesus is Lord! (and not Caesar or Caesar's successors)." In that I rest my confidence and hope.

Christ Returning

For me, to believe that Jesus is returning means that when I think of the "waste places" of the earth (like the "ruins of Jerusalem") – the ruins of things God created beautiful; the destruction of our planet's diversity and beauty; the desolation of human suffering under the brutality of the wicked; the devastating wastage of life and hope through HIV-AIDS, etc. – then I remember that Jesus is also the returning King. And I remember the wonderful climax of Psalm 96:

> Let the heavens rejoice, let the earth be glad;
> let the sea resound, and all that is in it.
> Let the fields be jubilant, and everything in them;
> let all the trees of the forest sing for joy.
> Let all creation rejoice before the LORD, *for he comes,*
> he comes to judge the earth.
> He will judge the world in righteousness
> and the peoples in his faithfulness.

> —Psalm 96:11 – 13 (my emphasis)

The whole creation looks forward to God's coming, because when he does, he will put things right (the meaning of "he will judge the world in righteousness"). So there is hope. There will be justice and restoration when Christ returns.

Christ Redeeming

For me, to believe that Jesus is the redeemer God means that when I think of the vast numbers of the human race who live in slavery and oppression of all kinds – bondages created by poverty, hunger, and injustice; by violence, murder, and rape; by the tentacles of addiction; or by sheer ignorance of the liberating truth of the gospel – I look forward to the day when all the ends of the earth will see the salvation of our God. I look forward to the day when all those who turn to him in their need and despair and long for his appearing will see their Redeemer as he really is – the Lord, King, and Saviour of the nations.

Did you see the *Lord of the Rings* trilogy of movies? I went to all three, and I remember the crowds lining up to see Part 3. In fact, whether we'd read the book or not, we all knew how the story would end – with "The Return of the King". Well, we have read God's book, and we also know how the story of the universe will end. It ends with the return of the King and the salvation, not just of "the shire", but of the whole of creation and all God's redeemed humanity from every nation on the planet.

But how? I ask myself. How and when can these things be? How can I possibly understand the nature or the implications of such vast convictions? I can only answer in the words of a hauntingly beautiful hymn by W. Y. Fullerton, "I Cannot Tell".[1] Every verse balances what we cannot understand with what we assuredly know (see emphasis). The last two verses put it like this.

I cannot tell how he will win the nations,
How he will claim his earthly heritage,
How satisfy the needs and aspirations
Of east and west, of sinner and of sage.
But this I know, all flesh shall see his glory,
And he shall reap the harvest he has sown,
And some glad day his sun will shine in splendour
When he the saviour, saviour of the world is known.

I cannot tell how all the lands will worship,
When at his bidding every storm is stilled,
Or who can say how great the jubilation,
When all our hearts with love for him are filled.
But this I know, the skies will sound his praises,
Ten thousand thousand human voices sing,
And earth to heaven and heaven to earth will answer,
"At last the saviour, saviour of the world is king!"

Well, that's what it means for me. But what does it mean for *them*, I thought as I prepared my sermon on Isaiah 52:7 – 10 and took the text for a walk (as I often do). I was walking on Tottenham Court Road, near my home, and I thought, "What about these people on the streets of London in their thousands? What does it mean for them that Jesus is the reigning Lord of history, the returning King of creation, and the Redeemer and Saviour of the world?"

The answer seemed to bounce back off the walls of the buildings: *Absolutely nothing.* Nothing at all. How can it mean anything if they don't know about it, if they have never heard about Jesus, if nobody has ever told them?

Then my text itself seemed to bounce off the walls as well, only this time through the words of Paul, who quoted Isaiah 52:7 in the midst of a similar list of questions:

For there is no difference between Jew and Gentile – the same Lord is Lord of all and richly blesses all who call on him, for, "Everyone who calls on the name of the Lord will be saved."

How, then, can they call on the one they have not believed in? And how can they believe in the one of whom they have not heard? And how can they hear without someone preaching to them? And how can anyone preach unless they are sent? As it is written: "How beautiful are the feet of those who bring good news!"

—Romans 10:12–15

Actually, there is nothing beautiful about feet. The only thing that makes feet beautiful is when they are wearing the running shoes of the gospel (Eph. 6:15). Then they are feet that belong to people who are willing to:

"Go, tell it on the mountain" – the mountain of human arrogance, that Jesus Christ is born and is reigning.
"Go, tell it on the mountain" – the mountain of human despair, that Jesus Christ is born and is returning.
"Go tell it on the mountain" – the mountain of human bondage, that Jesus Christ is born and is Redeemer, Saviour, and Lord.

That was how I finished my sermon.

The Resurrection of the Dead

At the return of Christ, the dead will be raised. Belief in the resurrection of the dead was a distinctively and uniquely Jewish conviction. As N. T. Wright has demonstrated with exhaustive research, the concept of resurrection is very different from the idea merely of life after death. The belief that human beings survive after death in some other form and in some other place or realm is common across human cultures, and it was certainly there in the cultures that surrounded the Jews before and after the lifetime of Jesus. But the belief in what Wright calls "life *after* life after death" – that is, resurrection life in a new body on a renewed earth – is not found anywhere else than in the faith of Israel, built upon various scriptural (i.e., Old Testament) foundations.[2]

From the further New Testament teaching on this, we may affirm two things about the resurrection of the dead as an integral part of that great final event: it will be universal for the whole human race, and it will be a decisive act of God.

Universal

All human beings who will have ever lived on planet Earth and died will be raised to life at the last day. Once again, this is an affirmation of faith that goes beyond our ability to understand. All the dead being raised! It is better not even to try to visualize the mechanics of it, let alone the logistics of it. Only God, whose power is beyond our understanding, has the infinite capacity to orchestrate an event of such proportions. Nevertheless, the Bible clearly teaches that he will do so. John's vision of the last day includes the following:

> Then I saw a great white throne and him who was seated on it. The earth and the heavens fled from his presence, and there was no place for them. And I saw the dead, great and small, standing before the throne, and books were opened. Another book was opened, which is the book of life. The dead were judged according to what they had done as recorded in the books. The sea gave up the dead that were in it, and death and Hades gave up the dead that were in them.

> —Revelation 20:11–13

No human person will be lost sight of. All lives are in the hands of God and are remembered by God. "Great and small", says John. Nobody is too great to be spared this resurrection (which is why it is threatening to the powerful of the earth; no wonder the Sadducees who colluded with Roman rule dreaded and denied it). Nobody is too small and insignificant to be forgotten (which is why it is a great comfort to those who have put their faith in God while being trampled underfoot in this life).

There will be resurrection for all—no matter how they died, or where they died, or what happened to their body during or after death. The resurrection is not just a resuscitation of intact corpses of those recently dead. That is the stuff of horror movies, not the Bible's teaching on resurrection. Biblical resurrection means the miraculous action of God restoring to visible bodily life human beings whose mortal remains may have vanished to dust, or flames, or seawater—long centuries or even millennia ago. All human persons made in the image of God will be raised at the return of Christ. Death is the end of a person's presence and participation in the history of the world in this age. It is not the end of the person himself or herself.

An Act of God

Once again, we have questions about this that the Bible simply does not answer, such as: What age will we be at the resurrection—the same as when we physically died? What then about babies who died at or shortly after birth? What about people who died very young without a full earthly life? Or what about those who died after years of utter physical and mental degeneration? We simply cannot say how God will raise everyone to a meaningful new personal existence that in one sense includes all that our earthly aging has meant (such as gaining wisdom), and yet in another sense transcends it (no more sinking into degenerative aging).

What kind of body will the resurrection body be? Paul gave a short answer to that question in one place: "like the risen body of Jesus" (Phil. 3:21); and a much longer one in another place, involving complicated agricultural comparisons (1 Cor. 15:35 – 43). Even Jesus was asked a question by those who thought the whole idea of the resurrection could be made to sound absurd: what happens to somebody who has had several marriage partners as a result of spouses' deaths (Matt. 22:23 – 33)? Part of Jesus' enigmatic answer is to remind the sceptics of "the power of God", and that is all we can appeal to with all such questions. It is a fundamental part of biblical faith from way back in the Old Testament that the living God has the power to raise the dead.

I have already said that for us here and now, living in the physical world in the bodies we now have, it is by definition impossible to conceive what it will be like when we are raised to new dimensions of life and potential, or how all the realities of life now will somehow be both retained and yet transcended. The best I think I can do as I struggle to understand this part of our biblical faith is to believe that the redemptive and restoring power of God is so great that *everything* that has made our lives worthwhile, blessed, and fulfilled in the present will be gloriously real and part of what we will be then; and that *nothing* that has spoiled, shortened, robbed, or broken our lives here will affect what we will enjoy then.

We will return to the resurrection of the body in our final chapter when we think about life in the new creation.

Furthermore, the Bible teaches that all persons will be raised into a form of personal life in which they will face the judgment of God. And because it is resurrection into that presence of God – God on his throne – it is also a decisive moment.

According to Jesus, every person will be raised into one of only two possible destinies.

> Very truly I tell you, a time is coming and has now come when the dead will hear the voice of the Son of God and those who hear will live. For as the Father has life in himself, so he has granted the Son also to have life in himself. And he has given him authority to judge because he is the Son of Man.
>
> Do not be amazed at this, for a time is coming when all who are in their graves will hear his voice and come out – those who have done what is good will rise to live, and those who have done what is evil will rise to be condemned.

—John 5:25 – 29

The dead will be raised either to enter into the full, eternal, resurrection life of Jesus Christ himself, demonstrated at his own resurrection, or to face condemnation and destruction. For that will indeed be the distinction put into operation by the third great item on the programme of this cosmic event – the day of judgment.

The Day of Judgment

All that the Bible has said previously about the day of the Lord or the day of Christ is summed up in that great image in Revelation 20, quoted above: *the great white judgment throne of God*. The God who sits in judgment is the Lord of history and of humanity; that is, the Lord of life, the universe, and everything.

The first thing we need to say about the day of judgment may seem surprising: It is good news! It is actually part of the gospel. Indeed Paul speaks about "the day when God judges everyone's secrets through Jesus Christ, *as my gospel declares*" (Rom. 2:16, my emphasis). The day of judgment is something we should be glad about, even as we tremble at the prospect of it. Why is that?

God Will Put Things Right in the End

First, it assures us that we live in a moral universe in which evil and wickedness will not finally win. This takes us back to chapter 3. All through history God's people have drawn great comfort from the conviction that in the end, God will vindicate his own justice by dealing decisively and irreversibly with all that resists and contradicts his loving purpose for creation. We long for that day. It is *good* to know that evil will not ultimately triumph. The gospel brings us that assurance as good news, along with all the rest that it tells us, of course, about how and why that will be so. We need this good news about a coming day of judgment every time we look at the world around us.

As we saw in chapters 1 and 2, we struggle desperately with the prevalence of injustice. We are rightly angry, along with so many biblical writers in the psalms and prophets, when people who behave abominably appear to get away with it with utterly frustrating impunity. We see those who are brutal, cruel, greedy, heartless, and shameless. We watch them cheating and trampling on the weak and laughing all the way to the bank. Somehow *we* feel cheated if they get away with it right up to death. They *should* have faced justice, we complain. Death alone seems not enough; "they cheated justice", we think.

Now of course, there is often an ungodly kind of anger and a repulsive desire for vengeance buried within such feelings. But there is also, I think, something that deeply reflects the truth that it would be universally wrong if those who do evil never faced up to the consequences of their deeds.

At the same time, our hearts break with grief and despair when people who are poor, vulnerable, defenceless, and voiceless suffer the most terrible oppression, violence, and cruelty. "Is there no justice?" we cry. Will they never have restitution and vindication? We agree with Job's accusing question as he witnessed such things in the world around him: "Why does the Almighty not set times for judgment? Why must those who know him look in vain for such days?" (Job 24:1).

Job goes on in that chapter to list a range of social horrors that are all too familiar in our own day. And at first he concludes, with despairing cynicism:

> The groans of the dying rise from the city,
>   and the souls of the wounded cry out for help.
> But God charges no one with wrongdoing.

—Job 24:12

But then Job goes on (as did the writer of Ps. 73) to draw comfort from the conviction that whatever the appearances may be, in the end God will act justly, and those who perpetrate such enormities will eventually stand (and fall) before the judgment of their Creator:

> But God drags away the mighty by his power;
>   though they become established, they have no assurance of life.
> He may let them rest in a feeling of security,
>   but his eyes are on their ways.
> For a little while they are exalted, and then they are gone;
>   they are brought low and gathered up like all others;
>   they are cut off like heads of grain.

—Job 24:23–24

Of course, such people are human beings like ourselves, and we know that we are only sinners saved by grace. The gospel teaches us that nobody is so wicked as to be beyond the possibility of repentance and forgiveness. Thus, we long and pray for God to bring such people to his feet in humble repentance, to forgiving grace, and to a change of life and the promise of eternal life. The thief on the cross had been (most probably) a brutal murderer in his days as a freedom fighter (from the Jewish point of view) and a terrorist (from Rome's point of view). He admitted he was being justly punished for his crimes, but he turned to Christ in an amazing act of faith and received that gracious promise from the lips of the dying Saviour. That is a supreme moment of gospel truth and saving action for a repentant sinner. We are commanded by Christ to follow his own example, to love and pray for our enemies, as he did, and to pray for their forgiveness and seek their salvation. Saul of Tarsus knew that better than most.

But the same Jesus who told us that there is joy in heaven over one sinner who repents also tells us that a dreadful judgment awaits those who refuse to repent and who go to their graves unreconciled with God, persisting in that refusal and dragging their unrepented and unforgiven wickedness with them.

For on the judgment day of God all wrongs will be exposed. There will no longer be any hiding place. No secret accounts to conceal the fruits of exploitation. No more tight security, bulletproof cars, or safe houses. No more excuses for ourselves or for others. No more skilled lawyers pleading technicalities. No more sentimental allowance for old age and infirmity. No more recourse even to the oblivion of suicide. No more escape at all, by any means, to any place, ever. The day of judgment will reveal everything, assess everything, and deal with everything. All unrepented, persistent wickedness will be met with the verdict of God's perfect justice. And that divine verdict will be public, validated by the evidence, indisputably vindicated, beyond complaint or appeal, irreversible, and inescapable. God will put all things right.

And that is a matter of rejoicing for the whole creation, as Psalm 96 resoundingly celebrates, as we saw above. God is coming to put things right! That is what the Bible means by God "judging". It is not just an act of punishment but an act of rectifying all wrongs, putting right all relationships, and restoring peace and harmony. That is what Christ will return for, says the New Testament, and that is exceedingly good news. It is part of the gospel.

Jesus Is the Judge

Second, the day of judgment is good news because of who the judge will be. The throne that John sees in his great vision in the book of Revelation is, of course, the throne of God. But he also saw that it is occupied by "the Lamb who was slain" – that is, the crucified Christ (Rev. 5:6). Jesus Christ, crucified, risen, and ascended, is the one to whom God has entrusted all judgment on that day, as Jesus himself claimed (John 5:22 – 23).

Peter told Cornelius that Jesus "is the one whom God appointed as judge of the living and the dead", before telling him that the same Jesus was the one through whom he could have forgiveness of sins (Acts 10:42 – 43). Paul told the Athenians the same thing in Acts 17:31 (cf. 2 Tim. 4:1).

"We must all appear before the judgment seat *of Christ*," said Paul (2 Cor. 5:10, my emphasis). So we can be sure that the judgment will combine the love and mercy of God with the perfect justice of God just as much as Jesus Christ did in his own person. The one who will judge all people will be the one who died for all.

It Will Be Completely Just

But if the day of judgment is to be so comprehensive and final, what will be the criteria on which God makes his judgment, and will his judgments be fair? These are important questions because all our experience of human justice, even at its best, is flawed and provisional. In human courts we worry that all the facts may not be available to the judge or jury. We know that lawyers do their best to prove innocence or guilt, and we suspect that evidence can be slanted in one direction or another. We struggle to assess and interpret people's words and actions, and with even greater difficulty, their motives.

With all such limitations, we still do our best to reach verdicts and sentences that have some ring of justice about them, and even then disputes continue through layers of appeal. We know that we must do justice. We applaud those who honestly devote their lives as legislators, police, lawyers, and judges in the service of justice. But we know that in the end all human "just" decisions in this life are partial and provisional.

But not so with God and the final reckoning of the day of judgment. All the evidence will be available, because God in his infinite knowledge knows not only the words and deeds but even the thoughts and motives of every human heart. There will be no possibility of any miscarriage of justice through ignorance of the facts. Nothing will be deliberately suppressed or accidentally forgotten on that day. The God of the Bible is the God who sees all and knows all, and nothing will escape his notice.

> From heaven the LORD looks down
> and sees all humankind;
> from his dwelling place he watches
> all who live on earth –
> he who forms the hearts of all,
> who considers everything they do.

> —Psalm 33:13–15 (cf. Ps. 139:1–6)

In other words, we can be entirely confident that not one human being will depart from the throne of God's judgment with any legitimate complaint of being unfairly treated. God's justice will be infinitely right and true and beyond reproach.

I have a Christian friend who is a circuit judge in England. His daily professional work is trying to see some measure of justice administered in the realm of all kinds of horrendous brokenness–especially in cases involving families. He tells me that this future perspective of the final judgment is one of the things that keeps him going. In the midst of all the ambiguities and provisionality of human justice even at its best, he can rest assured that the final word will be God's. There is a perfect judgment to come, in which we can all have total confidence.

This does not for one moment reduce the enormous responsibility and duty to seek justice with all the skill and wisdom drawn from a lifetime's work in the courts. But it does put all the intricate complexities and difficult decisions into the wider and comforting context of knowing that in the end, it will be "the Judge of all the earth" who will do what is right.

It Will Be according to the Light We Have Received

God knows the circumstances in which everybody will have lived, including the knowledge that was available to them at the time. He knows what they did and did not know, and he will judge accordingly. We will be judged according to the opportunity we have had and by the light we have received.

John put it like this:

> This is the verdict: Light has come into the world, but people loved darkness instead of light because their deeds were evil. All those who do evil hate the light, and will not come into the light for fear that their deeds will be exposed. But those who live by the truth come into the light, so that it may be seen plainly that what they have done has been done in the sight of God.
>
> —John 3:19–21

So the issue is, when the light of God's revelation comes to a person (whether through God's revelation in creation or the fuller knowledge of the gospel of Jesus), has he or she embraced it so far as they have understood it? Or did they shrink from it and reject it, preferring to stay in darkness? God's judgment will take into account what we knew and what we did in the light of what we knew.

Paul had a similar understanding, though he was thinking of the different opportunities available to Jews (who had the light of God's law) and to Gentiles (who did not). Either way, some things were clear to all, and God's judgment will take account of each person's situation:

> ... what may be known about God is plain to them, because God has made it plain to them. For since the creation of the world God's invisible qualities – his eternal power and divine nature – have been clearly seen, being understood from what has been made, so that people are without excuse.
>
> —Romans 1:19–20

> All who sin apart from the law will also perish apart from the law, and all who sin under the law will be judged by the law.... This will take place on the day when God judges everyone's secrets through Jesus Christ, as my gospel declares.
>
> —Romans 2:12–16

So the point is this: nobody will be condemned for what they did *not* know or could *not* do. Rather, we will be judged by how we responded to the light we received – whatever measure of truth and revelation God enabled us to have, by natural or human witness. We will be judged by what we *did or did not do*, in response to what we *did* know.

All human beings have some light, from the creation and from conscience. Some human beings have fuller light through the knowledge of God's revelation in Jesus Christ through the Bible. God knows what we have known and how we responded to the light we have received, to the word we have heard, to the truth we have understood. And God's judgment will be perfectly just and merciful in relation to all these things.

It will be *just*, because the Bible makes it clear that with greater opportunity comes greater responsibility (e.g., Amos 3:2; Matt. 7:1–2; Luke 12:48). So those of us who know that God has blessed us with unbounded opportunities – in our knowledge of the Bible and all the resources available to us – need to remember this sobering fact. What have we done with what we received?

It will be *merciful*, because God is our Creator and is fully and intimately aware of our creaturely limitations. He mercifully remembers our weakness and frailty ("for he knows how we are formed, he remembers that we are dust", Ps. 103:14). And he mercifully knows our ignorance, to which Jesus appealed even as they crucified him (Luke 23:34; cf. 1 Tim. 1:13).

It Will Be according to the Lives We Have Lived

The day of judgment will not be a time for words but for evidence in the form of deeds. Never mind the claims, what does the record actually show? The final description of the day of judgment in the Bible makes this unambiguously clear:

> The dead were judged *according to what they had done* as recorded in the books. The sea gave up the dead that were in it, and death and Hades gave up the dead that were in them, and each person was judged *according to what he had done.*

> —Revelation 20:12–13 (my emphasis)

Paul agrees. "For we must all appear before the judgment seat of Christ, that everyone may receive what is due them for the things done while in the body, whether good or bad" (2 Cor. 5:10).

"But," you may protest, "I thought we are justified by faith, not by works!?"

Yes, of course. We are *justified* by faith. But we will be *judged* by our works. Let me explain.

When I accept what the Bible says about my sin, when I repent of it and put my trust in Jesus, who bore it on the cross, I am indeed put right with God, by his grace, through faith. My sins are forgiven and I can know with full assurance, right here and now, that I will stand in the righteousness of Christ on that final day as part of his redeemed people. So I am saved from God's wrath through faith in Christ. I am justified—declared righteous—by grace through faith.

But as I said, the day of judgment is a day for God's verdict based on evidence, not a day for hearing faith claims. So what will be the *evidence* of my faith? Not just that I *say* I had faith, but that my life has shown it. It is our lives that prove the reality of our faith (or not, as the case may be). I will be judged on the evidence (my works), and they will show publicly and beyond doubt whether or not my life has been built on trust in Christ (my faith).

Jesus was ruthless about this in one of the most sobering things he ever said:

> Not everyone who says to me, "Lord, Lord," will enter the kingdom of heaven, but only those who do the will of my Father who is in heaven.
> Many will say to me on that day, "Lord, Lord, did we not prophesy in your name and in your name drive out demons and in your name perform many miracles?" Then I will tell them plainly, "I never knew you. Away from me, you evildoers!"

> —Matthew 7:21–23

With this saying, Jesus not only makes it clear that it isn't just what we *say* that counts, but also that it isn't just what we've *done*—if it is not doing the will of the Father. Jesus anticipates that there will be many fakes and shams among those who appear to be doing all kinds of exciting ministries and great works in his name. Their false works will not fool him "on that day". Spectacular ministries in themselves are no evidence of true faith.

We might put it like this. The day of judgment will not be a time for courtroom arguments back and forth that will eventually lead to a decision. Still less will it be a time for negotiation and pleading. It will be the time for God to state and declare the decision that will already have been made and to make public the indisputable evidence on which it will have been based. And that evidence will be amply provided by our lives before death.

John Stott summed it up in this way: "The judgment day will be a public occasion. Its purpose will be not so much to *settle* our destinies as to *state* them, and in stating them, to publish the evidence on which they are based, and thereby to vindicate the justice of God."[3]

In fact, the process of judgment has already begun. For our lives here and now are either rejecting the revealed truth of God and the salvation he offers us – *and proving it in the way we live;* or, accepting God's verdict on our sin, trusting in Christ's death for salvation, and thus standing in the righteousness of God through faith – *and proving it in the way we live.* The day of judgment will be a final, public, indisputable, and irreversible confirmation of the choice we have made all our lives, and it will demonstrate and vindicate the perfect justice of God.

Or, as John Stott further summarized it, our eternal destiny is *settled* in life, *sealed* at death, and *stated* on the day of judgment.

The verdict, then, will depend on that choice that is evident in our actions: either for life, to be lived with God through Christ in the new creation for eternity; or for rejecting God, ending up in condemnation, exclusion from God forever, and eternal destruction.

> [God] will punish those who do not know God and do not obey the gospel of our Lord Jesus. They will be punished with everlasting destruction and shut out from the presence of the Lord and from the majesty of his power on the day he comes.
>
> —2 Thessalonians 1:8 – 10

Though Paul does not use the term hell here, this passage is probably the most concise summary of the three terrible realities that hell involves: *punishment, destruction*, and *separation from God.* Such terrifying prospects lie well beyond what we can claim to understand. Yet the Bible presents them to the shielded eyes of our faith so prominently and so frequently that we cannot escape them or fail to see how crucial they are. There is an awful, irreversible consequence of remaining resolutely among the wicked. Giving people urgent warning about it along with the means to avoid it was an integral part of the good news that Jesus and the apostles preached.

So then, the day of the Lord, the day of Christ, will surely come. There will be a "great climax". When it comes, three great moments will form the schedule and agenda of that day: the return of Christ, the resurrection of the dead, and the day of judgment.

But what then? What lies on the other side of this momentous event? We move on, with the Bible itself, past the great ending, to the new beginning.

Notes

1. A hymn sung to the world's most hauntingly beautiful melody (in this Irishman's unbiased estimation), "The Londonderry Air".

2. N. T. Wright, *The Resurrection and the Son of God* (Minneapolis: Fortress, 2003). See especially chaps. 2–4 (pp. 32–206), for Wright's comprehensive survey of the concepts of life after death in ancient paganism, in the Old Testament, and in post-Old Testament Judaism.

3. John Stott, from notes of an unpublished sermon.

chapter

11

THE NEW BEGINNING

I was on a plane journey with John Stott when he was already eighty years old. After we landed, the plane had a lengthy taxi from the runway. As we trundled along the pilot asked us to stay seated since, as he put it, "we have not yet reached our final resting place." I turned to John and said, "Well, that's a relief!" But then, feeling embarrassed in case he was looking forward to heaven more than I could profess to be, I wondered if I should have said, "What a pity!"

Of course, if you have a connecting flight to catch, the crew often say something like, "We wish you a safe and pleasant onward journey *to your final destination*." So, what is our "final destination" according to the Bible? Most Christians tend to answer, "Why, heaven, of course".

There is a question that is often used in evangelistic encounters which goes something like this: "If you were to die tonight, are you sure you will go to heaven?"

I must confess I have not been asked this question for a long time, but if I were, my answer now would be, "Yes. But I don't expect to stay there!"

I suppose this might be rather shocking to any earnest evangelist. Where else do I think I might be going later, or where would I want to go instead? Of course I believe, as the apostle Paul did, that when I die I will go to be with Christ in heaven. For Paul, the thought of being with Christ made it a hard choice as to whether he wanted to die or go on living for the sake of the work he had to do. But here's the point: *The heaven I will go to when I die is not my final destination.*

"Heaven when you die" is only a transit lounge for the new creation. Heaven for those who have died in Christ is a place or a state of rest, of waiting, until the great events we were considering in the last chapter: the return of Christ, the resurrection of the body, and the final judgment. "Heaven when you die" is not where we will be forever. It is where we will be safe until God brings about the transformation of the earth as part of the new creation that is promised in both the Old and New Testament.

When I was a teenager, our church youth group was fond of singing the old Negro spiritual, "This world is not my home, I'm just a-passin' through". I played the piano for them, partly because it was a fun tune, but mainly because it got me out of singing it.

> *This heaven is not my home, I'm just a-passin' through;*
> *My treasures are laid up, somewhere beyond the blue.*
> *The angels beckon me from heaven's open door,*
> *And I can't feel at home in this world any more.*

Even as a young Christian it struck me as an unhealthy attitude to life and the world. Of course I knew (as I would have put it in those days) that I would go to heaven when I died and that we are "pilgrims here below". But I still remember thinking, "This world *is* my home. God put me here on earth for a purpose and I want to live here for him. The angels can go beckon someone else. I'm staying."

Now, with a better understanding of what the Bible actually says, I like to think that when I do go to heaven when I die (assuming that I die before Christ returns), I'm going to be playing the piano (or harp) and heartily joining the singing too, in rousing community renderings of "This *heaven's* not my home, I'm just a-passin' through ..." It will be home only until the new heaven and new earth – God's new creation – become our eternal home.

Christians who keep on talking about "going to heaven" – as if that were their last great hope – seem to have missed the whole point of the way the Bible ends. Look again at the wonderful picture in Revelation 21 – 22. It says nothing about us going off to heaven or to anywhere else at all. Rather, it shows us *God coming down to earth*, transforming the whole creation into the new heaven and new earth that he had promised in Isaiah 65:17, and then living here with us – on earth.

In other words, the Bible's last great vision is not of us going "up" there (to heaven), but of God coming "down" here (to earth). That's why I said, I look forward to going to heaven if I die before Christ returns. But I'm not going to stay there a moment longer than it takes to receive my resurrection body and join the rest of redeemed humanity on earth once Christ does return. That's where Revelation 21–22 clearly locates the bride of Christ and the city of God. Not "up" there but "down" here!

Immanuel means "God with us"–and that's how the Bible ends. God coming to be with us (repeated three times in Rev. 21:3), not us going off to be with God.[1]

But I am jumping ahead. Let's think first about this new creation.

The New Creation

"Behold, I will create new heavens and a new earth" (Isa. 65:17).
"Then I saw a new heaven and a new earth, for the first heaven and the first earth had passed away" (Rev. 21:1).

The use of the double term is a way of expressing universality; "heaven and earth" encompasses the whole of God's original creation, as Genesis 1:1 shows. So the scope of God's redeeming work is as vast as the whole universe he created. It is also a way of telling us clearly that although we are heading for a *new* reality, it is not a fundamentally *different* reality. We are not leaving the created order for some other "spiritual" order. Rather, we will be leaving the old *sinful* order of things and will find ourselves in a renewed, restored, redeemed creation. But it is still "heaven *and* earth," not "heaven *instead of* earth". To repeat, the Bible does not promise us that someday we can *leave* the earth and "go to heaven" instead. Rather, it promises us a whole new creation that includes the earth.

So the theological student who said he didn't understand eschatology but it wasn't the end of the world was right–or at least partly right. It is not the end of the planet, but the end of the old world order of sin and evil and the emergence of a new creation. Or as Captain Kirk might have said, "It's the earth, Jim, but not as we know it."

In chapter 3 we listed some of the things in Revelation 21–22 that will *not* be there in the new creation.

- *There will be no more sea* (21:1). The sea represented chaotic, restless evil in Old Testament symbolism, the place from which the rampaging beasts in Daniel's visions had come to trample the nations. All such unruly rebellious hostility will have gone.
- *There will be no more death, mourning, crying, or pain* (21:4). All suffering and separation will be ended for there will be nothing any longer to cause them.

- *There will be no more sin*, for there will be no more sinners (21:7 – 8); the new creation involves exclusion as well as inclusion – exclusion of the unrepentantly and persistently wicked.
- *There will be no more darkness and night* (21:25; 22:5), in the sense of all that they represented. The light of God's presence will dispel the darkest evils.
- *There will be no more impurity, shame, or deceit* (21:27) – things that are among the original marks of our fallenness.
- *There will be no more international strife* (22:2), for the nations will find healing through the tree of life and the river of life.
- *There will be no more curse* (22:3). With the reproach of Eden lifted at last, earth will be freed from its subjection and its redeemed inhabitants freed from bondage to its curse.

But what *will* be there? Let's turn again to Revelation 21 – 22 as well as to the Old Testament passage that undoubtedly formed the scriptural basis for John's vision: Isaiah 65:17 – 25. You will find it helpful to have them open as you read on. Let's think first about what these passages say about the *place* itself. Then we will go on in the following section to see what they say about the *people* who will live there.

The Garden City

Have you noticed that the Bible begins in a garden and ends in a city? Not everybody likes that thought, since many people hate cities and love their gardens – gardens that give them a tiny microcosm of the natural world. It's true, though. At the beginning of the Bible story, God puts the human beings he has made in a garden in Eden that he had prepared for them. At the end of the story, God comes to live with his whole redeemed humanity in the city of God.

However, it's not quite so simple or so contrasting. For the portrayal of the city in Revelation actually incorporates the essential elements of the garden in Genesis.

- The garden included gold and precious stones (Gen. 2:12). The city likewise shines with precious stones and is paved with gold (Rev. 21:11, 19 – 21).
- The garden was watered by four rivers. The city likewise contains the river of the water of life flowing from God's throne right down the main street (Rev. 22:1 – 2, a picture that John owes to Ezek. 47:1 – 12).

- Most important, the garden had the tree of life at the centre, but human beings had been barred from access to the source of eternal life in their condition of sin and rebellion (Gen. 3:22–24). The tree of life spans the river of life in the city of God (Rev. 22:2), and those once barred from it will have eternal access to it (22:14)–a vivid picture of the wonderful promise that there will be no death at all in the new creation (21:4).

The combination of garden and city has another resonance, I think. The original garden was *planted by God*. But the first cities were the *creation of human beings* (Gen. 4:17; 10:8–12). In one sense, the city is the hub of human longing for security in the midst of restless vulnerability of life as a race of sinners. And the first city is portrayed as having been built by Cain, the first murderer. Cities and sin are so interpenetrating as to be almost synonymous.

Yet the city is also in many ways the pinnacle of human collective achievement. Great cities are monuments to the incredible human capacity for cooperation, coordination, creativity, and culture. Cities require extraordinary feats of organization, problem-solving, imagination, and ingenuity. Ants can produce an ant heap. Bees can produce a hive. And these we know are hugely cooperative enterprises. But only humans can build cities.

I live in London, England. Frequently as I walk or ride around, I find myself astonished at what everybody seems to take for granted. This place works! We all complain when the underground trains get delayed or overcrowded. But really, the times of failure are vastly outweighed by the incredible complexity of what does happen–successfully and unremarkably–every day. I think of all the systems of communication, transport, sewage, lighting, water, electricity, gas, food supplies, waste disposal, street cleaning, emergency and security services; all the facilities for working, shopping, and playing; sport and culture centers; all the schools, factories, and hospitals; all the creativity of architecture, parks and gardens, art and music–it goes on and on, and has been going on for centuries of rich human history as well. What an astonishing monument to human brilliance every city is. Even the most sprawling and chaotic cities on earth somehow manage to work–as I used to similarly marvel while living in India.

Of course, we must agree immediately that cities are monuments to human arrogance and sin as well. The statues and memorials ogled by the tourists often celebrate people and events riddled with sordid greed and oppression. And cities are filled with greed, violence, immorality, exploitation, and the vulnerability of the millions who drift into them in search of something better than agrarian poverty. Cities, like the humans who live in them, stand in crying need of radical redemption.

But that's exactly my point. God's plan *is* to redeem the city – to turn the greatest symbol of human ambiguity into the unambiguous triumph of God's redeeming power.[2]

There is, then, great meaning in the fact that God chose to make an ordinary earthly city the focal point of his "residence" on earth in Old Testament times. Jerusalem was a preexisting city. It was not "holy" because God built it miraculously himself, or even because David built it (he extended it, but did not found it). The Jebusites (a Canaanite tribe) built it. But God chose it and turned it into a microcosm of his plan to redeem this human invention into "the city of God".

Thus, "Jerusalem" becomes not merely the name of an earthly city – with a terribly ambiguous history of appalling wickedness in biblical and modern times – but the name of the eternal city of God, which effectively means the whole new creation. Both Isaiah 65:18 – 19 and Revelation 21:2 use the name in this redemptive way. The "new Jerusalem" is the Bible's way of telling us that God's plan is the redemption of the city.

So, by putting the garden and the city together in its final imagery, the Bible combines the *restoration* of all that God originally made and intended his creation to become, with the *redemption* of all that human beings have achieved in the exercise of their capacity as creatures made in the image of God – however flawed and permeated with sin that achievement has been.

In human history, we build cities for *security*; we try to create enough *space* for everybody; and we try to add some *beauty* to the city – in its architecture and gardens, and so on. In reality, of course, for many urban millions from ancient to modern times, life in the city is far from secure, spacious, and beautiful. For the urban poor, cities are places of vulnerability and violence, unimaginable overcrowding, and soul-destroying ugliness.

So it is wonderful that the picture John gives us of the garden city of the new creation has total *security* (the metaphor of 200-foot thick walls), infinite *spaciousness* (the metaphor of a 1,500-mile cube), and breathtaking *beauty* (the metaphor of precious stones and metals). The new creation will be rich in all the things we long for in our cities, while all the things we so deplore will be eradicated for ever.

The Glory of Civilizations

So what is going to be there, in the garden city of God, in the new creation? According to several of the sharply shocking stories that Jesus told, there will be great surprises in store as regards *who* will be there (and who will not). But I think many Christians are going to be even more surprised as to *what* will be there. For so many of us have absorbed a mental picture of "heaven" that essentially includes nothing of what we know here on earth. This vacuous vision has two main sources – both different from, and destructive of, what the Bible actually teaches.

Misplaced Dualism

From Plato and then through gnostic influences, folk Christianity has often polarized the physical and spiritual realms. In contrast to the Bible, which affirms that the whole material creation is "good", this popular view regards the material world (including our bodies) as inherently evil and only the spiritual world as good. Or, in more evangelical language, only the spiritual world has real permanence because it is "of God" in some way, whereas the material world is temporary, decaying, and of no eternal significance.[3]

So it naturally follows, in this way of thinking, that nothing of the earth or on the earth will survive into the eternal future after "the end of the world". How could it? Only the spiritual world (God, angels, and redeemed souls in heaven) will be eternal. Physical bad; spiritual good. Very platonic. Very *not* biblical.

Scenarios of Obliteration

Another popular belief is that the whole earth is heading for extinction anyway, in a great fiery obliteration that will leave nothing of the present world in existence. Only souls go to heaven, so what's the earth needed for? A cosmic incinerator is its destiny.

This view has been based on a misunderstanding of a passage in 2 Peter about "the day of the Lord." Peter describes it in this way: "But the day of the Lord will come like a thief. The heavens will disappear with a roar; the elements will be destroyed by fire, and the earth and everything in it will be laid bare" (2 Peter 3:10).

At the time of the King James Version, the only available Greek manuscripts had the final verb of that sentence as "will be burnt up", and so this thought entered Christian expectations. Much earlier manuscripts that have since been discovered indicate that the original word was "will be found". What this probably means is that as the purging fires of God's judgment do their work, the earth and all deeds done on it will be fully exposed and "found out" for what they really are. The same Greek word "found" is used in a similar way in 1 Peter 1:7, also in the context of the purging judgment of fire: "... so that your faith – of greater worth than gold, which perishes even though refined by fire – *may be proved* [*found*] genuine and may result in praise, glory and honor when Jesus Christ is revealed" (same word, my emphasis).

Thus, more recent translations handle 2 Peter 3:10 in this sense. For example:

"the earth and every deed done on it will be laid bare"(NET)
"the earth and everything that is done on it will be disclosed"
(NRSV)
"the earth and the works that are done on it will be exposed" (ESV)

So we should understand the destructive fire of this passage as the fire of God's moral judgment, which will destroy all that is wicked. In this sense it is exactly parallel to the destructive water of God's judgment at the time of the flood, which Peter uses in the preceding verses as the great historical prototype for the final judgment to come: "By these waters also the world of that time was deluged and *destroyed* [same word as in vv. 10 and 11]. By the same word the present heavens and earth are reserved for fire, being kept for the day of judgment and *destruction of the ungodly*" (2 Peter 3:6 – 7, my emphasis).

The language is the same: destruction. But what was destroyed in the flood? Not the earth itself, but the wicked people on it at the time. Likewise, what will be destroyed in the fire? Not the earth itself, but all that is sinful upon it. That is why Peter can urge his readers, in view of the coming destruction, not to try to escape out of the world but to live morally godly lives in it (2 Peter 3:11), in preparation for the new creation, "where righteousness dwells" (v. 13). Thus, we should not see in this passage an *obliteration* of the universe, but a moral and redemptive *purging* of the universe, cleansing it of the presence and effects of all sin and evil.

But then what? What survives? What "carries over" into that new creation, purged of sin? Once again both Isaiah and Revelation help us here. Isaiah foresaw a day when the nations would turn to the God of Israel for salvation and, in doing so, would bring all their wealth and resources as offerings to him and for the benefit of his people (e.g., Isa. 23:18, which probably uses Tyre as a prophetic symbol for the fruits of trade in general; Isa. 60:5 – 11).

Now we might be expecting that such "materialistic" prophecies would be recognized in the New Testament as intended only in a spiritual sense, describing the ingathering of people from many nations through evangelism. Certainly such a sense is included in the way Paul saw his own evangelistic ministry as a means of fulfilling such prophecy (Rom. 15:16). But Revelation will not let us simply spiritualize away the great earthiness of the Old

Testament vision. The city of God in the new creation will be filled not just with the rescued souls of people from many nations, but with the accumulated cultural richness of human civilizations:

> The nations will walk by its light, and the kings of the earth will bring their glory into it. Its gates will never be shut by day – and there will be no night there. People will bring into it the glory and the honor of the nations. But nothing unclean will enter it.
>
> —Revelation 21:24–27, NRSV

This is a wonderful promise. But we have to ask carefully: What constitutes "the glory" of kings and the "glory and honor of the nations"? This cannot be imagining some pageant of crowned heads, parading their own pomp and pride in a great procession of the powerful into heaven. I don't think the Bible, after all it has said about God's rejection of the arrogance of the great and after all that Jesus said about "the last being first", means to end with the idea that the great and powerful of the earth get to stay that way "when we all get to heaven".

What makes kings glorious (to the extent that they are at all) is the accumulated work of their subjects – whether in creating the wealth their kingdom is built on, or (in our sinful world) fighting to protect it or to extend it. What brings honour to nations is the accumulation of cultural achievement over many generations. Art, literature, music, architecture, styles of food and dress, the richness of language and culture – and so much else – these are the things that national distinctives are built on, which at their best enrich our humanity and at their most trivial support the tourist industry. And these are things that all human beings participate in and contribute to, however humbly. These, I think, are what is implied by the language of national glory and honour, as represented by "the kings of the earth". These are the things they will be bringing into the city of God, in John's vision.

Now of course, all such national glory and honour is shot through also with human pride, greed, violence, and immorality. Cultural glories go along with cultural horrors. The splendour of all civilizations has been built on shameful foundations. We know that all too well in our fallen world. But if only human civilization could be purged of all such marks of the fall ... How glorious then would it be! Then we would be able to see in all such national cultural achievements not merely the proud posturing of arrogant human beings, but the stupendous product of human creativity through the ages. It would all resound in praise of the God who created us in his own image with such limitless capacity. The glory of humanity and the glory of God would at last be in harmony and not opposed to one another. But what we have in Revelation is not just a longing – if only this could be true. The Bible promises that it *will* be so. It's not a matter of "If only ..." but "When ...!"

All that has enriched and honoured the life of all nations in all of history will be brought in to enrich the new creation. The new creation will not be a blank page, as if God will simply crumple up the whole of human historical life in this creation and toss it in the cosmic bin, and then hand us a new sheet to start all over again. The new creation will *start* with the unimagineable reservoir of all that human civilization has accomplished in the old creation – but purged, cleansed, disinfected, sanctified, and blessed. And we will have eternity to enjoy it and to build on it in ways we cannot dream of now as we will exercise the powers of creativity of our redeemed humanity.

Speaking personally, I find enormous comfort and hope in this thought, precisely because it goes way beyond what I can understand. I don't understand *how* it will be so, but the firm biblical affirmation *that* it will be so fills me with great excitement and anticipation.

As I said, I live in London. The British Library is one of my favourite places to go and write, and not just because it is only a fifteen-minute walk from my home. It has hundreds of miles of shelves, deep underground, housing millions of books, many going back to the days when books were first invented. It houses the accumulated learning, wisdom, wit, and literature of multiple human civilizations and languages – and that's only a fraction of what the whole world's libraries and museums include. I sometimes sit and think: How many lifetimes would I need to ever absorb and enjoy the treasures of this place alone? And what will happen to all this cultural achievement – the labour of the lifetimes of generations of human beings made in God's image – when Christ returns? Will it all simply be obliterated, extinct in an instant, lost and forgotten for all eternity? I cannot believe that is the plan of God.

I don't understand *how* God will enable the wealth of human civilization to be redeemed and to be brought cleansed into the city of God in the new creation, as the Bible says he will. I don't imagine it will be a matter of dusty old books, any more than I will be there in my dusty old body. But I know I will be there in the glory of a resurrection body, as the person I am and have been – but redeemed, rid of all sin, and raring to go. So I believe there will be some comparable resurrection glory for all that humans have accomplished in fulfilment of the creation mandate – redeemed but real.

We lament the "lost civilizations" of past millennia, civilizations we can only partially reconstruct from archaeological remains or in epic movies. But if we take Revelation 21 seriously, they are not "lost" forever. The kings and nations who will bring their glory into the city of God will presumably not be limited only to those who happen to be alive in the generation of Christ's return. Who can tell what nations will have risen or fallen, or what civilizations will have become "lost" by then—like the lost civilizations of previous millennia? No—the promise spans all ages, all continents, and all generations in human history. The prayer of the psalmist will one day be answered—for all history past, present, and future:

> May all the kings of the earth praise you, Lord,
>   when they hear what you have decreed.
> May they sing of the ways of the LORD,
>   for the glory of the Lord is great.
>
> —Psalm 138:4–5

Think of the prospect! All human culture, language, literature, art, music, science, business, sport, technological achievement—actual and potential—all available to us. *All of it with the poison of evil and sin sucked out of it forever.* All of it glorifying God. All of it under his loving and approving smile. All of it for us to enjoy with God and indeed being enjoyed by God. And all eternity for us to explore it, understand it, appreciate it, and expand it.

If this is the new creation that the Bible promises, you can understand why I don't want just to "go to heaven when I die". Who wants just heaven when God promises heaven *and* earth?

The Healing of the Nations

The older I get, the harder it is to resist the temptation to get cynical about the international world we live in. I resist cynicism because of the Bible's affirmation that ultimately all human history is under the sovereign providence of God. So I live by faith in that truth, like Habakkuk, even when events seem to scream otherwise—as they often do. For we live in a world that seems to lurch from one generation into another with repeating cycles of violence, bloodshed, and war. Every year we sing about "Peace on earth" at Christmas, and we welcome the New Year with hopes of some solution to at least some of the running sores of human conflict. But every year we endure the same frustrating crescendo of arrogant aggression, relentless hatreds, and unfathomable suffering.

Conflict is so enmeshed with human life on this planet that it is almost impossible to imagine life without it. Indeed, at a purely human level, an enormous amount of the world's economy is dependent on the continuation of conflicts around the globe.

At over one trillion dollars in annual expenditure – an incomprehensible figure that continues to rise – global military spending and arms trade surpasses all other categories of global spending. The figures are astounding: In 2005 global military expenditure reached over $1,118 billion, fully 2.5 percent of world GDP or an average of $173 per human being. Accounting for 43 percent of global military expenditure, the United States is the principal determinant of world trends. American military spending, at $420 billion, dwarfs that of other high-spending countries, including China, Russia, the United Kingdom, Japan, and France – each ranging from 6 to 4 percent.[4]

All this makes the Bible's promise of ultimate peace between nations in the new age of God's new creation such a counterintuitive vision. It is one thing to long for peace. It is another thing to proclaim peace as the final reality that God himself (and only God) will bring about. But that is what the Bible does.

The prophets of the Old Testament hold out the vision of the era when God's anointed king will rule the world of nations. Among other benefits of his reign will be peace with justice. The destructive implements of war will be turned into productive implements of feeding the hungry. Not only will there be no more war; when God intervenes, there will be no need even to learn war, on the prudential grounds that "if you want peace, prepare for war". Even the pedagogy of violence will be redundant (Isa. 2:4; Mic. 4:3). War and all that goes with it will be forever destroyed by God himself. That is part of what the Bible anticipates when humanity finally knows who God is (Ps. 46:8 – 10).

So when we come to the Bible's closing portrayal of the new creation, this feature is expressed in a beautiful pictorial way. When the kings of the earth bring their wealth into the city of God, they will not fall to fighting over it, as in the old order of things. There will be no more death, so there can be no more war. On the contrary, the tree of life, flourishing by the river of life, will provide abundant fruit and leaves, "and the leaves of the tree are for *the healing of the nations*" (Rev. 22:2, my emphasis).

This beautiful image of healing the nations reminds us that the international world we live in at present is fundamentally *sick*. Relationships between nations are as broken and dysfunctional as those between individuals. War between nations mirrors the disorder and disease that rack the human body, mind, and spirit. We need mending, healing – at every level of our humanity, right up to the world of nations.

Again, what a wonderful prospect it is to imagine those nations that, down through history, have lived and died with intractable hatreds, prejudices, injustices, and bitter feuds, finding healing from the tree of life in the new creation.

Paul speaks of the reconciling power of the cross, breaking down barriers and turning enemies into friends – of God and of one another. This is the rich theological content, amplified to the international scale, that Revelation captures in a single, hauntingly beautiful phrase – "the healing of the nations."

The Harmony of Creation

We have already thought about suffering within the present created order and suffering imposed upon it by our greedy and destructive ways. When Paul says that the whole of creation is "groaning", he was right (Rom. 8:22). Fortunately, he was thinking of a groaning that also has a happy ending, namely, the groaning of a woman in childbirth. The future is bright with the prospect of a new birth, of new life. Similarly, the future of this creation is already bright with the hope of the new creation being brought to birth within the straining womb of the old.

Whatever we think about the fact of animal predation in the present world order (i.e., whether it is the result of the fall of human beings or something fundamentally prior to that), we are unambiguously told that it will not be the final state of creation. Just as there will be no more death among human beings, so there will be no more violence between animals.

This is a picture that we owe primarily to Isaiah, though it is implicit, I believe, in Revelation. Isaiah concludes his wonderful portrait of human life in the new creation with the well-known words:

> "The wolf and the lamb will feed together,
>   and the lion will eat straw like the ox,
>   but dust will be the serpent's food.
> They will neither harm nor destroy
>   on all my holy mountain,"
>
> says the LORD.
>
> — Isaiah 65:25

The pairing of animals is significant – the predatory and the prey (wolf and lamb); the wild and the domestic (lion and ox). No longer will there be such polarization in the new creation. There will be peaceful coexistence among animals as well as between animals and humans. For there will be no more harm or destruction in the new creation. No more death is the promise for animals as much as for humans. Death in all its forms will be nonexistent, not even a memory in the new creation.

Revelation does not speak directly of this dimension of the new creation – that is, the restoration of ecological wholeness and harmony. But at two points it certainly points in that direction. First, in John's mind-boggling vision of the whole universe under the governance of God and the Lamb on the throne, he sees four "living creatures", which would appear to represent the whole animate creation, including human beings – the word "living creatures" being reminiscent of the language of Genesis 1: "The first living creature was like a lion, the second was like an ox, the third had a face like a man, the fourth was like a flying eagle" (Rev. 4:7).

They seem representative of the wild animals, domestic animals, the birds, and humanity. Furthermore, they surround the throne of God himself and are integrally involved in bringing praise and glory to him – as all creation was intended to do. So there may be an implication here, in the highly symbolic language of John's vision, that the population of the new creation is not confined to saints and angels but will include a renewed animal kingdom also, fully involved in its own way in the praise of God.

This impression is strengthened when we reach the climax of John's initial vision. For this comes not merely with the songs of redeemed humanity or the worship of billions of angelic hosts. Rather, the grand finale of the crescendo of praise that John witnesses comes from the whole of creation, as complete as it was when God pronounced it all very good in Genesis 1.

> Then I heard every creature in heaven and on earth and under the earth and on the sea, and all that is in them, saying:
>
> "To him who sits on the throne and to the Lamb
>   be praise and honor and glory and power,
>   for ever and ever!"
>
> The four living creatures said, "Amen," and the elders fell down and worshiped.
>
> —Revelation 5:13–14

The Redeemed Humanity

What a place the new creation will be, then! But what about the people there? Revelation tells us that there will be people from every tribe and nation, language and people – a great salad bowl of humanity in all our profusion of colours, shapes, and textures. Ethnic and cultural diversity will be a mark of the new humanity, but without the strife and confusion that disfigure them in the old humanity. Variety will be the spice of life then as now. Some things, however, we will enjoy in common, according to the Bible's great vision. Let's look at three aspects of life in God's new creation that the Bible clearly teaches us. Redeemed human life in the new creation will be bodily life, life in intimate relationship with God, and life enriched by fulfilling work.

Resurrection Bodies

"I believe in the resurrection of the body", says the Apostles' Creed. It does not say, "I believe in the immortality of the soul", though a great deal of folk Christianity seems to imagine that it does. If the earliest Christians had gone around saying they believed in the immortality of the soul, almost nobody would have taken any notice, for that was and is one of the commonest beliefs in many human cultures. What they actually proclaimed was the resurrection of the body – and that was something surprising and countercultural, and for many even in their day, laughably unbelievable. It was, however, the unambiguous implication of the historically witnessed fact of the resurrection of Jesus of Nazareth.

The bodily resurrection of Jesus is crucial to our understanding of the new creation and our own life within it. The risen Jesus is, in fact, the "firstfruits" of the new creation, that is, the guarantee of all that is yet to come for the rest of creation, including those who are in Christ. When God raised Jesus from the dead, he was saying *Yes* to Jesus, vindicating all that he had taught and claimed in his earthly lifetime as against those who at his trial had rejected him as a false teacher and failed messiah.

When God raised Jesus from the dead, he was also saying *Yes* to creation, affirming the goodness of physical bodily life that he himself had created. God did not just take Jesus' spirit back to heaven, releasing it from the "tomb" of bodily existence (that is the Platonic, dualistic view of reality that the Bible never teaches). The actual tomb was empty. "See the folded grave clothes where thy body lay." The earthly body of Jesus was not left behind to rot but was transformed into the glorious risen body in which he appeared to his disciples.

This was so unprecedented (for it was not just that he had "come back to life" – like Lazarus, for example – only to die later), that the shocked disciples thought he was a ghost – an apparition, some ectoplasmic look-alike of his deceased self. But Jesus quite deliberately and dramatically killed that idea:

> They were startled and frightened, thinking they saw a ghost. He said to them, "Why are you troubled, and why do doubts rise in your minds? Look at my hands and my feet. It is I myself! Touch me and see; a ghost does not have flesh and bones, as you see I have."

—Luke 24:37–39

Seeing them still unconvinced (who would be the first to try touching a ghost?), Jesus stood there calmly chewing and swallowing a piece of fish. John records that the risen body of Jesus was capable of lighting a fire, cooking fish and bread, and eating with his disciples (John 21:4–13). Ghosts don't do early morning picnics in bright daylight on the beach.

For over a month of such appearances, Jesus left his disciples totally certain that he was utterly, really, real–fully and bodily risen to a dimension of life that could interact with and enjoy physical life here on earth, and yet also transcended it and was not limited or constricted by its normal boundaries. It was not that Jesus was *less* real than his earthly body had been–but that he was even *more* real. He had all the properties of bodily life, and then some. There were dimensions of his new reality beyond the three we know and live in.

This was what the disciples went out and proclaimed from the day of Pentecost on. It is so important to see, in the book of Acts, that the apostles affirmed that God had raised Jesus as an objective, physical, historical, publicly witnessed event. For Peter, it was as undeniable as the fact (a few weeks later) that there was a man running and jumping around Jerusalem who had been paralysed all his previous life. The authorities could not deny that fact for they saw the evidence (Acts 4:16), and the apostles could not deny their fact for they had seen the evidence (4:20). "You've seen a man healed; we've seen a man raised!"

Unfortunately, we have tended to turn the massive cosmic shock of the bodily resurrection of Jesus (the earth shook when he rose) into a matter of subjective private piety–*Jesus lives in me*. Please don't misunderstand me. Of course I believe in the personal experience of the indwelling Christ. My childhood memory, from which I date my life as a Christian, is of the day I knelt and "asked Jesus to come into my heart". It's a precious truth that I still hold dear. But it is not what the New Testament means when it proclaims the resurrection of Jesus. The apostles did not mean merely that the spirit of Jesus somehow lived on in their hearts or through their heroic efforts to keep his memory alive.

Recently I visited Graceland in Memphis, Tennessee–the former home of Elvis Presley and the most visited tourist attraction in the United States after the White House. The brochure proudly, if somewhat optimistically, declares: "Graceland–Where Elvis Lives". Even apart from the nutters who fondly believe Elvis is actually still alive somewhere, the whole place is dedicated to keeping him "alive" in some sense, through his musical legacy. But at the end of the tour you confront reality in the Garden of Meditation, for there he is in his grave, as dead as his parents on either side. Elvis may live on in some people's hearts, but Elvis is, sorry folks, actually dead.

The message of the New Testament is not that Jesus simply survived death, or that he lived on in people's memory, or even that he died and merely "came back to life". No, the New Testament proclamation is "God raised him from the dead" (Acts 2:24). "You killed the author of life, but God raised him from the dead" (3:15). "They … laid him in a tomb. But God raised him from the dead" (13:29 – 30). Jesus did not "die and *come back* ". Jesus died and *went on* to a wholly new level of being – resurrection life in his glorious resurrection body.

So although I used to sing it very heartily and meaningfully in my youth and I still love its up-beat tune and sentiments, there is something of a deafening anticlimax (biblically) at the end of the familiar old song:

> *He lives, he lives, Christ Jesus lives today.*
> *He walks with me, and talks with me, along life's narrow way.*
> *He lives, he lives, salvation to impart;*
> *You ask me how I know he lives?*
> *He lives within my heart!*

Wonderful and true – but not how the apostles answered the question in the book of Acts. They were decidedly *not* proclaiming "Jesus lives in our hearts". The religious and political authorities would not have minded that one bit, for it would have been as unthreatening as it was pitifully sentimental, just so long as Jesus was actually still in the tomb. The apostles were proclaiming that this same Jesus of Nazareth, whom the authorities had killed, had been bodily raised up by God and the tomb was empty. This was an objective witnessed fact, not subjective religious devotion to their late leader's memory.

I stress all this at length not only because it is important that we understand what the Bible actually teaches about the resurrection of Jesus, but even more so (in relation to what we are thinking about in this chapter) because the Bible tells us that the resurrection body of Jesus is the prototype and model for our own future lives in the new creation. *We will be like him!* (Phil. 3:20 – 21; 1 John 3:2).

How strange, then, that so many Christians still persist in the idea that we will be like *what he emphatically said he was **not*** – ghosts or spirits or disembodied souls. We talk about our souls going to heaven when we die, as if that were the sum total of our blessed hope. To the extent that it is biblical at all, such language speaks only of the truth that when we die in Christ we are totally safe, that in some sense we are then "with Christ", which means being where he is, currently in heaven. Our souls – in the sense of the persons we truly are – are not extinguished at death but are held safe by God's power. But heaven in that sense is not at all our "final destination", as we said earlier.

We long eagerly, with the whole of creation, for "the redemption of our bodies" (Rom. 8:23). We do so precisely on the foundation of the resurrection of Jesus: "If the Spirit of him who raised Jesus from the dead is living in you, he who raised Christ from the dead will also give life to your mortal bodies because of his Spirit who lives in you" (8:11).

When God ushers in the new creation, we will live in it in resurrection bodies like Christ's. This is what Paul explicitly teaches, at great length in 1 Corinthians 15, and in short simplicity in Philippians 3:

> But our citizenship is in heaven. And we eagerly await a Savior from there, the Lord Jesus Christ, who, by the power that enables him to bring everything under his control, *will transform our lowly bodies so that they will be like his glorious body.*
>
> —Philippians 3:20–21 (my emphasis)

We notice again that Paul does not speak about our "going to heaven", but of Christ's coming *from* there and transforming our earthly bodies into the likeness of his glorious resurrection body–for our life in God's new creation.

"Like his glorious body", says Paul. The stories of the resurrection are the best model we have (in fact they are the only model we have) for thinking about what it will be like for ourselves when we start our new redeemed life in the new creation. What do those stories tell us? We learn (from Jesus himself on the very day he rose) that he had flesh and bones (Luke 24:39); that he could eat and drink; that he could be touched; that he could break bread and bake it; that he could walk and talk. We learn from all the stories that he could be recognized as the real Jesus they remembered. And yet, in some ways he was also different, for he could come and go, appear and disappear, ignore doors and walls, as if the physical world no longer set boundaries for his life in the way it does for us (and had for him too for thirty years or so).

And we will be like him!

Resurrection life will have continuity with this life, inasmuch as we will be recognizably the same persons as we have been in this life (as the risen Jesus was). Yet it will also have discontinuities with this present life. Some of those discontinuities lie way beyond our present ability to understand or even imagine, because they will transform some aspects of life that are such an integral part of what it means to be human in the present creation (such as age and gender). Yet, even where our resurrection life transcends present realities, it will incorporate the best of what those aspects mean for us (especially in terms of our relationships). It was the risen Jesus who asked Peter, "Do you love me?" Indeed, all that is precious will be amplified and clarified, "for now we see only a reflection as in a mirror; then we shall see face to face. Now I know in part; then I shall know fully, even as I am fully known" (1 Cor. 13:12).

Whatever it may be like, we can rest assured that, for those who are in Christ, anything that has blessed and enriched us in this life will not be lost but rather be infinitely enhanced in the resurrection, and anything that we have not been able to enjoy in this life (because of disability, disease, or premature death – or simply through the natural limitations of time and space) will be amply restored or compensated for in resurrection life.

The Presence of God

Our life in the new creation will be not only bodily life, modelled on the risen Jesus. We will also be living with the intimate, unthreatening, and unthreatened presence of God. Or, to put it rather more biblically, God himself will be living with us. This is a prominent theme in Revelation 21–22, expressed in several ways – of which the first is from the mouth of God himself: "I heard a loud voice from the throne saying, 'Look! God's dwelling place is now among the people, and he will dwell with them. They will be his people, and God himself will be with them and be their God'" (Rev. 21:3).

This is the language of the Old Testament projected into the new creation. "Dwelling place" is literally "tent", and it calls to mind the way God lived in the midst of his people symbolically in the tabernacle and then the temple. The combination of being the people of God and having God be with them as their God was the greatest of the covenant privileges of Old Testament Israel. Now, says God, that limited national privilege of Old Testament times will be the universal reality for people of all nations (the word "people" is actually plural in Greek; the best manuscripts read, "they will be his peoples").

We already noted that the description of the city of God calls to mind the garden of Eden. The imagery of the river and water of life in 22:1–2 points to this. And we remember that prior to the fall, God walked and talked with Adam and Eve in the intimacy of that garden. But in the vision of Revelation, that life-giving presence will fill the whole creation and bring healing to all nations.

We live now in an earth that has been cursed by God since the day of our sin in Adam. So although human beings can indeed know God's presence in this fallen world, as the Bible so abundantly shows, it is always a presence that is clouded by our sin and simply by the sin-fraught realities of living in a world under God's curse. Revelation rolls back the curse to welcome the unhindered presence of God with the simple, world-changing words, "no longer will there be any curse" (Rev. 22:3).

Most precious of all, there will be no need for a temple in the new creation, because the whole creation itself will be the dwelling place of God so that, rather than being hidden in a separate Holy Place, the Lord will be as visible to all as the light itself. The one thing that even Moses was not allowed, for all his intimacy with God – namely, to see God's face (Ex. 33:20 – 23; Num. 12:8 is literally "mouth to mouth"), will be the joyful experience of all God's servants, for "they will see his face" (Rev. 22:4).

I love the way the book of Revelation shifts its perspective from "up there" to "down here". It moves from the earliest visions of John, in which, like the prophets of old, he is ushered "up" into the throne room of God (in ch. 4 – 5) and witnesses all that is going on in heaven, as it were. Like Isaiah, it is as if he, a human being, is allowed for a while to sit in on all that God is doing in his heavenly government of earthly affairs, like a spectator watching from the edges and asking occasional questions. But at the end of the book, when he contemplates the transformed, redeemed new creation, his picture is not of our going "up" to watch what God is doing, but God's coming "down" to live among us and make his presence intrinsic to all that we are doing. Not us with God in heaven, but God with us on earth.

Kings are bringing the glory of civilization into the city of God. Nations are being healed. There is serving and reigning to be done. The new creation, the new Jerusalem, the city of God – whatever picture we choose – is a busy place filled with all the potential of a transformed humanity, empowered by the same Spirit that raised Jesus from the dead, getting on with the task we were created and redeemed for, without tears, death, pain, or curse, but with the unmediated presence of God among us, living in the light of his face.

The Blessing of Work

Yes, we will be busy! But what about the biblical picture of heaven as "rest", you may wonder. Aren't some of the biblical characters said to "rest with their ancestors" when they died? What about all those funeral phrases about going to our "eternal rest", not to mention the ubiquitous R.I.P. on tombstones – "Rest in Peace"?

We need to remember that the biblical concept of rest does not simply mean the cessation of all activity. The original creation Sabbath was the beginning of human history, in which we were to enjoy creation along with our Creator through exercising our mandate of rule and care within it. When God gave the Israelites "rest" in the land, it meant freedom from their enemies, so that they could get on with the job of farming the land. "Rest" meant the enjoyment of working in peace and seeing the fulfilment of one's labours.

So, as we noted, even in Revelation 21 and 22 there are hints of the work that will occupy the redeemed in the city of God. But the Old Testament picture of the new creation on which Revelation builds is far more explicit about this, in delightfully earthy ways.

You really ought to pause and read Isaiah 65:17–25 right now–slowly and imaginatively. It draws, of course, on the realities of family life in ancient Israel and uses the everyday experience of a farming people to contemplate what God's "new heavens and a new earth" will be like. Behind the imagery, there are important truths being taught and a richly rounded vision being shared.

And in the middle of it, there is the clear assumption that there will be work for us in the new creation. In contrast to the myths of paradise found in some cultures and religions, we will not lounge about in shady groves, with fruit and wine dropping miraculously into our mouths, surrounded by luxuries and sensuous delights suited to our tastes and gender. The myth of eternal ease is tantalizing, but not biblical. So when I hear a most enjoyable Australian gospel group, Steve Messer's Strange Country, singing a song called, "When I Take My Vacation in Heaven",[5] I enjoy the rhythmic optimism but decline the concept. I enjoy my vacations enormously, but the thought of eternity as a never-ending idle vacation is mind-numbing.

No, the point that Isaiah makes is not that we will be freed from all work, but that the work we do will be freed from all frustration. The curse of weariness, loss, defeat, injustice, futility, and misfortune will be gone. Our work in the new creation will be productive, enjoyable, satisfying, of lasting value, blessed by God–and environmentally safe (see Isa. 65: 25)! We were created in the image of God, who is himself a worker. In the new creation we will have unlimited scope to exercise all the capacities and potential of that image, to the glory of God and our own satisfaction, forever.

> They will build houses and dwell in them;
>   they will plant vineyards and eat their fruit.
> No longer will they build houses and others live in them,
>   or plant and others eat.
> For as the days of a tree,
>   so will be the days of my people;
> my chosen ones will long enjoy
>   the work of their hands.
> They will not labor in vain,
>   nor will they bear children doomed to misfortune;
> for they will be a people blessed by the Lord,
>   they and their descendants with them.

—Isaiah 65:21–23

Conclusion

I have just read through this chapter again, and I cannot suppress the rising emotional tide of excitement and anticipation that I always feel when thinking (or singing) about these great biblical truths about the new creation. Who can understand them? None of us, of course, with any kind of comprehensive grasp. The God I don't understand has more things in his new heaven and earth than we can even dream of, let alone build into our puny theologies. But just working through the things that we *can* understand to some extent – on the grounds that the Bible teaches them so emphatically – is enough to set the pulse racing and the imagination soaring.

And frankly, I am inspired to even greater gratitude for these massive biblical certainties, unfathomable biblical depths, and mind-stretching biblical vistas when I weigh up the alternatives. For of course, there are many alternative worldviews about death and beyond.

While writing this part of the book, I read through all three volumes of Philip Pullman's trilogy, *His Dark Materials*.[6] I enjoyed them immensely, such is Pullman's extraordinary power of imagination and brilliant storytelling skill. But of course, Pullman's worldview is aggressively atheist. The prime source of evil in his narrative is the church and all its representatives. The chief cause of the problems of the world (or rather of all the worlds Pullman calls into imaginary existence) is "the Authority" – the alleged creator and supreme power in all universes. By the end of the tale, the latter is exposed as a tired old fraud who disintegrates the moment he is taken out of his glass box, and the former is curtailed and shorn of power.

The ironic thing, in my view, is that the kind of church Pullman attacks is indeed worthy of attack – the self-serving, dogmatically authoritarian, violent, torturing, corrupt institution that Christendom has been at times. No Christian could defend what Pullman rightly pillories. But a further irony is that the kind of worldview he wants to attribute to Christianity is the very dualistic version we have argued here is far from biblical – with its otherworldly obsession with souls and heaven. Instead, Pullman revels in descriptions of the goodness of the material world, the wonders of nature, the joys of living as sensate creatures in a world of colour, sound, taste, smell, touch, and texture, and the thrill of exploring them all. But this is entirely biblical! And not only does the Bible extol all these wonders of creation as we know it now, but tells us we will enjoy them in even more abundant measure than we can imagine in the new creation.

As against the biblical vision of gloriously rich life in resurrection bodies in a renewed creation, what can Pullman offer? At one point in the story, inspired no doubt by Virgil, Dante, and Milton, Pullman's two heroes, Will and Lyra, find themselves in the world of the dead – a world of sad and shadowy ghosts, including friends and family of their own. Now Will and Lyra are the redemptive figures in the whole trilogy, who accomplish at terrible cost the measure of "salvation" that the story eventually reaches.

But what can they do for the souls of the dead? Will has a "subtle knife", capable of cutting anything in the universe, including holes between one world and another. With it he cuts a hole out of the world of the dead, to let all the innumerable hosts of all the dead of countless generations flood out to freedom. The grateful ghosts surge through that opening. To what? Real life back on earth? Any kind of real personal existence? Not at all. The greatest thing they are all longing for and which happens as they joyfully and gratefully escape from the ghostly life of souls (to which one presumes the Authority and the church had condemned them) – is extinction! They simply dissolve back into the elements of the universe.

> Will enlarged the window as wide as he could … making it big enough for six, seven, eight to walk through abreast, out of the land of the dead.
>
> The first ghosts trembled with hope, and their excitement passed back like a ripple over the long line behind them, young children and aged parents alike looking up and ahead with delight and wonder as the first stars they had seen for centuries shone through into their poor starved eyes.
>
> The first ghost to leave the world of the dead was Roger. He took a step forward, and turned to look back at Lyra, and laughed in surprise as he found himself turning into the night, the starlight, the air … and then he was gone, leaving behind such a vivid little burst of happiness that Will was reminded of the bubbles in a glass of champagne.[7]

I read that and I think, *Is that it? Is that the best that the atheist imagination can offer? Death as the popping cork of a champagne bottle, a little bursting bubble of happiness, and then … nothing. Nothing personal. Nothing gloriously human. Just dissolution into the "everything" of the rest of the universe.* And then I read 1 Corinthians 15 and the gospel narratives that provide the historical evidence for the resurrection of Jesus of Nazareth, and my heart leaps to say, "Thank you, Lord, that you have given me 'new birth into a living hope through the resurrection of Jesus Christ from the dead' (1 Peter 1:3)."

There were those in the world of the apostles who believed in a future beyond death much as Pullman describes. Either you lived on in shadowy nonlife as a miserable vapid soul in the underworld, or you dissolved back into the atoms you came from in a never-ending recycling of life. No wonder the message of bodily resurrection and of real personal life in the new creation – as a witnessed fact about Jesus, and as a wonderful hope for all who trust in him – was such indescribably good news.

It still is.

Notes

1. See the excellent study of this theme in Michael E. Wittmer, *Heaven Is a Place on Earth: Why Everything You Do Matters to God* (Grand Rapids: Zondervan, 2004), esp. 205 – 6.

2. One of the most thorough and stimulating surveys of the biblical theme of the city, its human origins, redemptive future, and rich biblical symbolism, is Jacques Ellul, *The Meaning of the City* (Grand Rapids: Eerdmans, 1970).

3. Wittmer, *Heaven is a Place on Earth*, provides a good critique of this dualistic way of thinking. See also, Darrell Cosden, *The Heavenly Good of Earthly Work* (Peabody, MA: Hendrikson; Milton Keynes: Paternoster, 2006).

4. Jonathan Bonk, "Following Jesus in Contexts of Power and Violence", *Evangelical Review of Theology* 31 (2007): 342 – 57.

5. On Steve Messer's Strange Country album, *It's Real!*

6. Philip Pullman, *The Golden Compass* (New York: Knopf, 1966); idem, *The Subtle Knife* (New York: Knopf, 1997); idem, *The Amber Spyglass* (New York: Knopf, 2000).

7. Pullman, *The Amber Spyglass*, 382.

CONCLUSION

As I come to the end of this rather meandering series of reflections on a few of the tough questions of faith, I am aware that there are many more questions than answers – both in what I have written and probably still in your mind as my conversation partner in the process. I am keen to find out if Gordon, whose conversational question conceived this book, thinks that the baby now born comes anywhere near offering an answer that is satisfying – at least as far as it goes.

But the more practical question is, How should we respond in the light of the things we have considered together? Each part of the book seems to suggest its own response.

In Part 1 we wrestled with the original question: "What about evil and suffering?" I suggest that the Bible calls us to accept that there is a mystery about evil that we neither can nor should ever rationally understand. But the Bible also allows us to bring our lament and protest into the presence of God and join the chorus of biblical characters who cry out to God with the "Why?" and the "How Long?" of suffering faith. Most of all, the Bible lifts up our eyes and our hearts to rejoice in anticipation that since suffering and evil were not the first word about creation, they will not have the last word either. God will finally defeat and banish them altogether from his new creation through the work of Christ.

Our response must surely stand alongside the writer of Psalm 73, pained and frustrated by the apparent success of the wicked in the present, but bringing that pain and frustration into the presence of God along with the worshiping company of God's people, to find there an anchor for faith and a fresh and eternal perspective that brings hope.

Part 2 faced up to the embarrassment that many people feel about "the God of the Old Testament", especially the violence that was there sanctioned in his name. The first thing we did was to refuse to accept that this is simply an Old Testament problem. So our response needs to be a greater determination to read the Bible as a whole and clear our heads of those shallow popular clichés that are nothing but caricatures of the Old and New Testaments and do so much damage to our biblical understanding. But "reading the Bible as a whole" means reading it in the light of the centrality of Christ and in recognition that it is, as a whole, the story of God's salvation.

From that perspective we can see, on the one hand, that the conquest narrative stands as one episode of God's historical judgment within the long story of God's ultimate salvation – and thus is never reproached or questioned on the lips of Jesus. But on the other hand, we also see that it was indeed a limited historical act of God, which Jesus decisively did not accept as a model for how his followers should behave either toward those who rejected him or toward their own future enemies. So, for ourselves, to accept (even with grief and emotional recoil) that God acted justly in that biblical narrative is *not* to accept that Christians have *ever* been justified in using it as a rationale for violence or genocide. Nor should we allow our rejection of all such tragedies that disfigure the history of the church to spill over into a rejection of the biblical story within the explicit moral and theological framework that the Bible provides for it.

Part 3 can probably claim to be the heartbeat of the book, for all the other problems we considered come back eventually to the cross – or rather, need to be seen in the light of the cross. If only we could understand the full mystery of the cross, the other things we do not now understand would shrivel to insignificance. But of course, as the supreme act of God in Christ for the redemption of the universe, the cross presents unfathomable mysteries that lie beyond our comprehension, though not beyond our humble gratitude and worship.

In the chapters of Part 3 I tried to untangle some of the more confusing false opposites that hinder our understanding of the cross, so that we can at least rejoice in what God in Christ accomplished for us there with as much clarity of understanding as the biblical revelation opens up for us. And for those depths that lie beneath the level of our probing minds, we can cheerfully allow ourselves, with Charles Wesley, to be "lost in wonder, love and praise".

Part 4 seems to me to call for the most practical response. That might seem paradoxical, since it is concerned with something that hasn't happened yet – the so-called end of the world. As we saw, that is really a rather inappropriate phrase. For the Bible does not end (as a book) with "the end", but with a new beginning and a glorious promise for the whole creation. What does it mean to live our lives now in the light of that future? This is what so much of the practical teaching of the New Testament is about that I am sorely tempted to write another chapter just on that! But, in summary, there must be consequences for our faith and for our lives.

The Bible teaches us these great certainties about the Great Climax (chap. 10) and the New Beginning (chap. 11), not merely to stimulate our curiosity but to strengthen our faith. We are called to live in this great hope. We are those who already know how the present story of the world will end and what lies beyond that ending. By that, I don't mean we have a timetable all mapped out and then spend our time obsessing over what symbolic details of the Bible can be implausibly matched to current events. Rather, we hold fast to the great unequivocal affirmations of the New Testament: Christ will return, the dead will be raised, there will be final judgment, God's justice and mercy will be fully displayed and vindicated, and God's victory over evil, God's salvation of his people, and God's restoration of creation will be complete. This is the climax of the great story we are part of. We have a hope. We have a future. We have a gospel. And so we live with courage and faith, bearing witness to these great truths.

And there are consequences for our lives. What does this great throbbing biblical hope mean when we go back to daily life and work tomorrow? Two things at least, I think.

(1) *All our work **now** contributes to the content of the new creation.* This is the implication of what I argued in chapter 11 about the purging and redemption, rather than the obliteration, of all that humanity as the image of God will have accomplished in history. However infinitesimally small we may think that the little slice of space and time occupied by our own lives on earth is, it really does count. God builds with exceedingly small building blocks (human lives), but he builds on an ultimately vast scale, and his redeeming power is infinite, cosmic, and eternal.

So work matters. Society matters. Our contribution to human life and well-being matters. Our use of created resources matters. Our care of the earth matters. Our relationships with one another – socially, politically, economically, internationally – all matter. And they matter not just for here and now, but for eternity, for the new creation. In other words, what we accomplish with our lives on earth is not just some meaningless charade destined for a cosmic incinerator. The new creation will somehow – in ways only God can imagine and plan for – include all that we have accomplished by our work in this creation. Purged and redeemed, yes. Freed from all accretions of greed and guilt, of violence and covetousness, of deceit and pride, yes. But not obliterated and forgotten forever.

In my view, this gives great value and significance to the ordinary world of everyday life and work. It is not merely a temporary and disposable arena for evangelizing souls. Please do not misunderstand me. The workplace is every Christian's mission field, and our witness to the lordship of Christ and the truth and ethic of the gospel must govern the way we function there. But when some Christian preachers say that the only reason Christians have for going to work during the week is to evangelize and that nothing else they do counts for anything, I long to challenge their unbiblical dualism and their woefully inadequate doctrines of creation, humanity, and eschatology!

(2) *All our behaviour **now** must be governed by the standards of the new creation.* The thrust of New Testament ethics is that we are called to live now in the light of the future, by the standards of the kingdom of God, which has already invaded this world through the life, death, and resurrection of Christ, but will eventually be established fully in the age to come. This produces the familiar tension that all Christians experience between the standards of the kingdom of God and the realities of the present age. But it is a tension we cannot and should not try to escape.

It is of the essence of biblical prophecy that revelation regarding the future is intended to bring about change in the present – change of action, or attitude, or both. So what the Bible clearly reveals to us about the new creation should govern how we strive to live now.

Negatively, it will be a world free from sin, deception, cruelty, hatred, greed, lust, pride, exploitation, oppression, and the like. If that is the case in God's new creation, such things should have no place in the way we live now. To put it bluntly, as we consider any course of behaviour or any attitude, posture, or mood, if it won't do *then* (in the new creation), it won't do *now*.

Positively, it will be a place of peace, justice, love, wholesome relationships, unadulterated goodness, fulfilment of human life, and harmony with all creation. If that is what we look forward to, we should be striving after such things here and now.

We are to live, then, as people who not only have a future, but who know the future we have and who go out and live in the light of that future, in preparation for it, and characterized by its values.

The Day of the Lord is certainly coming, as surely as the Lord Jesus Christ promised, "I am coming soon." Are you prepared for that Day, by trusting in the same Jesus as Saviour before you stand before him as Judge?

The new creation is already being brought to birth within the womb of this old creation. Are you investing your life and work in it and living now by its standards as a citizen of the city of God?

FOR FURTHER READING

This is merely a very short selection of some books I have found helpful out of the very many that have been written on all four of the big issues we have been wrestling with.

What about Evil and Suffering?

Blocher, Henri. *Evil and the Cross: Christian Thought and the Problem of Evil*. Leicester: Apollos, 1994.

Carson, D. A. *How Long, O Lord? Reflections on Suffering and Evil*. Grand Rapids: Baker; Leicester: Intervarsity Press, 1990.

Wenham, John. *The Goodness of God*. London: Intervarsity Press, 1974. Republished as, *The Enigma of Evil: Can We Believe in the Goodness of God?* Grand Rapids: Zondervan, 1985.

Wright, Nigel G. *A Theology of the Dark Side: Putting the Power of Evil in Its Place*. Carlisle: Paternoster, 2003.

Wright, N.T. *Evil and the Justice of God*. Downers Grove, IL: InterVarsity Press, 2006.

What about the Canaanites?

Gundry, Stanley N. ed. *Show Them No Mercy: 4 Views on God and Canaanite Genocide*. Grand Rapids: Zondervan, 2003.

Peels, Eric. *Shadow Sides: God in the Old Testament*, Carlisle: Paternoster, 2003.

Thompson, Alden. *Who's Afraid of the Old Testament God?* Grand Rapids: Zondervan, 1988.

Wright, Christopher J. H. *Old Testament Ethics for the People of God.* Leicester: Intervarsity Press; Downers Grove, IL: InterVarsity Press, 2004.

What about the Cross?

Holmes, Stephen R. *The Wondrous Cross: Atonement and Penal Substitution in the Bible and History.* London; Hyderabad, India; Colorado Springs: Paternoster, 2007.

Jeffery, Steve et.al., ed. *Pierced for Our Transgressions: Rediscovering the Glory of Penal Substitution.* Wheaton: Crossway, 2007.

Marshall, I. Howard. *Aspects of the Atonement: Cross and Resurrection in the Reconciling of God and Humanity.* London; Hyderabad, India; Colorado Springs: Paternoster, 2007.

Meynell, Mark. *Cross-Examined: The Life-Changing Power of the Death of Jesus.* Leicester: Intervarsity Press, 2001.

Stott, John R. W. *The Cross of Christ.* Leicester: Intervarsity Press; Downers Grove, IL: InterVarsity Press, 1986.

Tidball, Derek. *The Message of the Cross.* Leicester: Intervarsity Press; Downers Grove, IL: InterVarsity Press, 2001.

Tidball, Derek, et.al., ed. *The Atonement Debate: Papers from the London Symposium on the Theology of Atonement.* Grand Rapids: Zondervan, 2008.

What about the End of the World?

Bock, Darrel L. *Three Views on the Millennium and Beyond.* Grand Rapids: Zondervan, 1999.

Cosden, Darrell. *The Heavenly Good of Earthly Work.* Peabody, MA: Hendrikson; Milton Keynes: Paternoster, 2006.

Holwerda, David E. *Jesus and Israel: One Covenant or Two?* Grand Rapids: Eerdmans; Leicester: Apollos, 1995.

Johnston, Philip, and Peter Walker. *The Land of Promise: Biblical Theological and Contemporary Perspectives.* Leicester: Apollos; Downers Grove, IL: InterVarsity Press, 2000.

Milne, Bruce. *The End of the World: The Doctrine of the Last Things.* Eastbourne: Kingsway, 1979.

Riddlesbarger, Kim. *A Case for Amillennialism: Understanding the End Times.* Grand Rapids: Baker; Leicester: Intervarsity Press, 2003.

Walker, P. W. L., ed. *Jerusalem, Past and Present in the Purposes of God.* Second ed. Grand Rapids: Baker; Carlisle: Paternoster, 1994.

Wittmer, Michael E. *Heaven Is a Place on Earth: Why Everything You Do Matters to God.* Grand Rapids: Zondervan, 2004.

Wright, N.T. *Surprised by Hope: Rethinking Heaven, the Resurrection, and the Mission of the Church.* London: SPCK, 2005; San Francisco: Harper-One, 2008.